APPROACHING PUBLIC POLICY ANALYSIS

APPROACHING PUBLIC POLICY ANALYSIS

An Introduction to Policy and Program Research

Kent E. Portney
Tufts University

Prentice-Hall
Englewood Cliffs
New Jersey 07632

Library of Congress Cataloging-in-Publication Data

Portney, Kent E.
  Approaching public policy analysis.

  Includes index.
  1. Policy sciences. 2. United States—Politics and
government—1945–   . I. Title.
H97.P67 1986   361.6'1'0973   85-25649
ISBN 0-13-043811-1

Cover design: Ben Santora
Manufacturing buyer: Barbara Kelly Kittle

Printed in the United States of America

10 9 8 7 6 5 4 3 2 1

ISBN 0-13-043811-1   01

Prentice-Hall International (UK) Limited, *London*
Prentice-Hall of Australia Pty. Limited, *Sydney*
Prentice-Hall of Canada Inc., *Toronto*
Prentice-Hall Hispanoamericana, S.A., *Mexico*
Prentice-Hall of India Private Limited, *New Delhi*
Prentice-Hall of Japan, Inc., *Tokyo*
Prentice-Hall of Southeast Asia Pte. Ltd., *Singapore*
Editora Prentice-Hall do Brasil, Ltda., *Rio de Janeiro*
Whitehall Books Limited, *Wellington, New Zealand*

To Marilyn

Contents

List of Tables and Figures

Preface

This book is about public policy analysis. It is an attempt to provide students with an understanding of contemporary policy analysis by describing many existing policy studies. I have selected a title, *Approaching Public Policy Analysis,* that contains a *double entendre* conveying two major themes. The first is that we can approach conducting public policy analysis from several different perspectives. The second is that the current state of public policy analysis has not yet evolved into a unified field of study. Rather, public policy analysis today consists of pieces of many other fields of study that, when aggregated, seem to approach a field of public policy analysis.

I have presented descriptions of contemporary public policy analysis within a framework I hope will help students understand the diversity of opinion and results it contains. Perhaps more important, I have tried to provide a sense of the relationship between the approach, or methodology, of public policy analysis and the substance of such analysis. It is my view that these issues are closely related, yet few texts on public policy analysis offer much insight into this relationship.

At the same time, I argue that public policy analysis, as defined by three specific approaches and their respective studies, is at a stage in its development when it must focus on integration. I suggest in Chapter 1 that there is very little communication among researchers who take one or another of the three approaches to public policy analysis. In some instances, the relationships among researchers adhering to the various approaches are not just uncommunicative, they are often downright hostile. Obviously, the root causes of such hostility and lack of communication are subtle and deep and cannot be overcome easily. But implicit in my argument is the idea that it must be overcome. One of the tasks in the development of public policy as a maturing discipline is the pursuit of a more integrated approach. Until the hostility is subordinated to other pursuits, progress toward a more unified discipline will be slow at best.

Regarding the materials I have incorporated herein: There is much that I have *not* included, despite consequent disadvantages, and my decisions about what to include occasionally created a dilemma. Some of the more interesting contemporary policy debates have not been discussed. My intent is to focus on primary policy research rather than on policy position papers, secondary inter-pretations of primary research, or policy opinions. In other words, if a work does not consist of primary research, I probably did not discuss it here in much depth.

This type of omission provides a pedagogical opportunity. If there are studies not included that the course instructor thinks important, it will be easy to incorporate them into the course within the framework of this text, and with discussion and debate. Indeed, particular position papers can be contrasted with the weight of empirical analyses to form the basis of such discussions.

This text is the product of much labor, not just on my part but on the part of many others. In thanking as many as possible, I wish to accept the blame for any errors of commission or omission. First, I express my gratitude to my colleague Jeff Berry for encouragement and feedback. I also thank Sheldon Danziger of the Institute for Research on Poverty, who repeatedly refreshed my memory about antipoverty policies. Also, thanks to my colleague Graham Wootton, who helped me clarify some details about energy policy. Rich Eichenberg read, reviewed, and made helpful comments about several chapters. Vance Dickson did much of the library work for Chapter 4. All the students who have suffered through the evolution of this framework, especially the graduate students in my Public Policy Analysis courses over the past five years, are too numerous to mention by name, but they provided me with invaluable feedback, often causing me to re-think and refine my ideas. The editorial staffs, especially Stan Wakefield, Audrey Marshall, Barbara Bernstein, and Maria Chiarino, deserve my gratitude for the grace and speed with which they got this book into production. Finally, I would like to thank Tom Dye who provided me with a level of understanding about the approaches to public policy analysis and the field of political science; without his influence, this book could never have been written.

K.E.P.

CHAPTER ONE

What Are the Approaches to Public Policy Analysis?

Over the past few years, there has been an almost unprecedented growth in the application of social research to problems of public policy. At the same time, the number and variety of people who call themselves public policy analysts have mushroomed. Despite these facts, or more likely because of them, it has become increasingly difficult to explain what public policy analysis is.

This problem was driven home to me not long ago when one of my students innocently asked me what public policy analysts do. My immediate response, of course, was to say that public policy analysts analyze public policies. But when my student stared back at me with the all-too-familiar glazed look, I knew I had failed to provide an adequate answer. My next answer was that public policy analysts do a lot of very different things, and what they do depends on their training, where they work, for whom the analyses are being conducted, and so on. Again, this did not seem to strike a chord of understanding in my student, since it really was not a specific answer. So I embarked on a more lengthy explanation that I hoped would ultimately provide some level of understanding about what public policy analysts do and what public policy analysis is.

As pedestrian as my attempt to answer the student's question was, I eventually provided what I believe to be an honest reflection of how varied the field of public policy analysis is. With this in mind, I set out in search of a more succinct way of describing what public policy analysis is about. I discovered that no existing book really presented public policy analysis in as much breadth as I envisioned it. In this search, I settled on the idea that there are three major approaches to public policy analysis. I hope that my introduction to these three approaches to public policy analysis will provide a breadth of understanding that heretofore has been possible only with much experience in doing policy research. Before describing these approaches, I will explain what I mean by an *approach.*

THE IDEA OF AN APPROACH

When we speak of *approaches* to public policy analysis, we are really suggesting that there are many different ways of doing public policy research. Very different sets of *methods* can be brought to bear on practically any public policy problem. Yet my use of the term intends to capture more than just differences in methods. In some sense, when I refer to approaches, I am actually trying to capture the ideas associated with the term *paradigm.* How does this term apply to public policy analysis?

Paradigm is often used to refer to a predominant set of beliefs in an academic discipline or area of study. At any given time, nearly any particular area of study is dominated by a set (or several sets) of knowledge or beliefs almost universally accepted as being true. For example, Einstein's theory of relativity is a set of beliefs or expectations that has dominated the field of physics for many years. Such a body of knowledge or beliefs can be said to characterize a paradigm of thought.

The concept of paradigm has been applied in many important ways. Thomas Kuhn used it to trace the evolution of scientific disciplines, where each discrete stage in their development was characterized as a paradigm.[1] Kuhn was interested in understanding what stages a discipline must go through in the process of becoming mature or scientific. In a similar way, the idea that a discipline moves through a number of different paradigms has been applied to a field related to public policy analysis called public administration. For example, Robert Golembiewski traced the development of public administration through at least five successive paradigms, with each having its own predominant set of beliefs.[2]

At the same time, however, Golembiewski notes that since about the mid-1950s, public administration cannot be characterized as having a single paradigm, but rather it has had several competing predominant modes of thought. Indeed, this may be an important step in the evolution of some social scientific disciplines. The idea that an area of study can possess several different (often competing) paradigms at the same time, and that this constitutes an important step in the evolution of public policy analysis as a discipline, underlies my description of public policy analysis.

Perhaps more important, there is a strong implication that at some point in the evolution of a discipline, a synthesis must occur among the competing approaches. Although this synthesis may occur in many different ways, it almost always begins with a full understanding of the contributions of each approach. The result of this synthesis is, presumably, the production of a body of knowledge that is perceived to be somehow better than its predecessors. Based on this assumption, which is obviously open to debate, it is my hope that we can at least begin to understand the different approaches to public policy analysis currently in use. And in the process, we can begin to understand the proper role of each of these approaches, especially some of the conditions under which each is appropriate.

The area of study we refer to as public policy analysis can really be thought of as currently having three major paradigms, or approaches. In other words, contemporary public policy analysis can be said to be composed of three major modes of thought about what public policy analysis is. We will refer to these approaches as the *policy making process* approach, the *policy cause and consequence* approach, and the *policy prescription* approach. What makes these modes of thought paradigms is that practitioners in each adhere strongly to the belief that what they do is public policy analysis and what other people do is

---

[1] Thomas Kuhn, *The Structure of Scientific Revolutions,* 2nd ed. (Chicago: University of Chicago Press, 1970).

[2] Robert Golembiewski, *Public Administration As a Developing Discipline,* Vol. I (New York: Marcel Dekker, 1978).

something else. The argument underlying this book is that each approach constitutes one slice of the public policy analysis pie.

There are, of course, more than three approaches described in this book, but these three represent the *dominant* frameworks for studying. Whenever possible, we will allude to types of studies which do not strictly follow these three approaches. In Chapter 8, there is a more complete discussion of analyses which span more than one of the three approaches.

Some may argue that new developments in public policy analysis have not necessarily led to greater understanding of public policies.[3] Yet it is my contention that the similarities and differences between these approaches provide the foundation for understanding contemporary public policy analysis. With this in mind, we are ready to look at some general descriptions of these approaches.

GENERAL CHARACTERISTICS OF THE THREE APPROACHES

Now that we are clear about what we mean by the term *approach* and we have characterized the three approaches to public policy analysis, we can examine some general characteristics of each one. Each approach carries its own implicit definition of public policy and develops its own research methodology (the basic steps a researcher goes through to do the research), its own terminology, or jargon, and its own underlying assumptions. So we will try to begin to build a picture of the similarities and differences among these approaches. If you have difficulty visualizing policy research in one or another of the approaches, you might find some solace in knowing that all the subsequent chapters discuss specific research in each of the areas. But we will begin by examining each of the approaches in detail.

Analysis Approach Number One:
The Policy Making Process

The policy making process approach has its roots in the field of political science. It should not be surprising, then, that this approach defines public policy not as a product of government action but as a political process. To understand this approach, often called the study of public policy making, we will first look at what the policy making process is, and then we will look at why it is considered political.

THE STEPS IN THE POLICY MAKING PROCESS   In most general discussions describing this conception of public policy research, the policy making process

[3] Susan B. Hansen, "Public Policy Analysis: Some Recent Developments and Current Problems," *Policy Studies Journal,* Vol. 12, No. 1, Sept. 1983, pp. 14–42.

consists of about five major "steps in the process."[4] For a proposal to become public policy, it must first move through stages of problem formation, policy formation, policy adoption, policy implementation, and sometimes policy evaluation. Figure 1.1 provides a graphic illustration of this sequence of policy making stages. Each of these stages itself constitutes a smaller process. In other words, we might speak of the process of policy implementation, or the process of policy adoption.

Taken as a whole, these stages represent the process whereby some important problem emerges (such as a gasoline shortage or a rapidly increasing rate of inflation) to which policy makers must, and eventually do, respond. *Problem formation* refers to the process whereby some problem (often a crisis or near-crisis situation) emerges and becomes recognized. *Policy formulation* reflects the process in which various political actors, such as interest groups, legislative leaders, executive branch officials, the electorate, the courts, and others, interact to develop a specific proposal or series of alternative proposals in response to the emerging social problem. This step in the process may also be referred to as policy agenda-setting or policy initiation.

Policy adoption refers to the process in which legislators, courts, executive officials, and others actually enact a specific policy response, usually in the form of legislation, executive orders, administrative regulations, or court decisions. *Policy implementation* focuses on the events that occur when some policy adoption is turned over to an administrative unit to be put into effect. *Policy evaluation* refers to the process whereby governments go about reviewing what has occurred previously, often attempting to determine whether programs or policies have worked and should be continued. When we encounter such terms as *policy adoption* or *policy implementation,* we get a hint of the policy making process approach to public policy analysis.

Analysis of these various stages of the policy making process often focuses on the institutions in and out of government. The underlying idea is that understanding the institutional participants' values, positions, resources, and so on, is important in understanding how policy decisions get made. For example, if an analyst were interested in understanding why the Environmental Protection Agency (EPA) decided to implement its "Superfund" hazardous-waste cleanup as it did, that analyst must understand the EPA as a political institution.

FIG. 1.1. Stages in the Public Policy Making Process

Stage 1	Stage 2	Stage 3	Stage 4	Stage 5
Problem Formation →	Policy Formulation →	Policy Adoption →	Policy Implementation →	Policy Evaluation

[4] See James E. Anderson, *Public Policy-Making,* 2nd ed. (New York: Holt, Rinehart & Winston, 1979), p. 25.

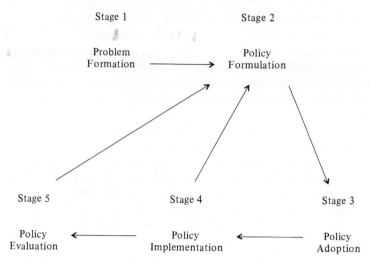

FIG. 1.2. Stages in the Circular Policy Making Process

SOME VARIATIONS ON THE POLICY MAKING PROCESS THEME   There are a number of variations or elaborations on the policy making process theme. Sometimes the stages in the policy making process are studied as a time-ordered sequence of events, but some scholars, such as Charles Lindblom, argue that the events do not necessarily take place in such a time-ordered fashion.[5] He suggests that policy formulations can be ongoing, taking place even when some aspects of the policy are being implemented. The implication is that development of public policy in any given area is a never-ending circular process, as illustrated in Figure 1.2. Governments spend much of their time reformulating responses to problems they have already acted on.

THE TYPOLOGIES OF THE POLICY MAKING PROCESS   The policy making process has been further elaborated in works by Theodore Lowi and by Randall Ripley and Grace Franklin. In these works, the authors argue that there are "typologies" of public policy making processes. They suggest that the policy making processes differ from public policy to policy depending on whether the policies are "distributive," "regulatory," "redistributive," or "structural."[6] They argue that all policies that are distributive have very similar policy making pro-

[5] Charles Lindblom, *The Policy-Making Process*, 2nd ed. (Englewood Cliffs, N.J.: Prentice-Hall, 1980), pp. 5-7.

[6] Theodore Lowi, "American Business, Public Policy, Case-Studies, and Political Theory," *World Politics*, Vol. 16, July 1964, pp. 677-715; and Randall Ripley and Grace Franklin, *Congress, the Bureaucracy, and Public Policy*, rev. ed. (Homewood, Ill: Dorsey, 1980).

cesses associated with them and that these processes are very different from those associated with regulatory, distributive, or structural policies.

Distributive policies, according to Ripley and Franklin, are programs aimed at promoting, usually through subsidies, private activities deemed desirable to society. The distributive policy making process tends to be of low visibility with a high degree of cooperation and logrolling ("If you vote for my bill, I'll vote for yours") among the legislators involved. Such policies include mass-transit grants and grants for public facilities construction. The idea behind distributive policies is that in order for one group to gain, other groups do not necessarily have to lose. In other words, everyone gains with distributive policies. It has been argued that because there are no groups trying to prevent other groups from benefiting at their expense, the political system finds it very easy to intervene in ways that often provide "too much" public policy.

Regulatory policies attempt to limit the number of specific service providers (competitive), as in airline regulation, or to protect the public by setting conditions under which private activities can occur (protective), as in environmental regulation. The regulatory policy making process tends to be very unstable over time and usually involves major legislative bargaining and compromise. Competitive regulatory policy carries a substantial vulnerability to capture of regulatory agencies by the industries being regulated.

Redistributive policies, such as the war on poverty, are efforts to manipulate intentionally the distribution of wealth or other valued goods in society. Redistributive policy making processes tend to be very ideological and often involve substantial class conflict.

Finally, structural policies, such as defense budgeting, include efforts at procuring, developing, and organizing national defense activities. Structural policy making processes tend to be characterized by subgovernments (small groups of legislators, bureaucrats, and interest group representatives) that make nonconflictual and often decentralized decisions.

How do we know whether a specific public policy proposal is distributive, regulatory, redistributive, or structural? This is not an easy question to answer. According to the works of Ripley and Franklin, the "intention," or "aim," of the policy gives the key.[7] Lowi, however, suggests that the perceptions of the policy actors involved is what determines whether a policy can be said to be of one type or another.[8] This creates a bit of a problem for research, since we usually do not have information about how policy makers and administrative officials perceive different public policies. In the conduct of policy making process research, we are often forced to infer the policy makers' perceptions from their behavior. But since their behavior is itself part of the policy making process, we end up classifying policies on the basis of some process character-

---

[7] Ripley and Franklin (see Note 6), pp. 20–28.
[8] Lowi, pp. 690–91.

istics. This means, to some degree, that we have used the policy making process characteristics to help define whether a policy is distributive, regulatory, redistributive, or structural. We will see this problem emerge in research on several different public policies' processes.

This policy making process typology is by no means universally accepted as valid or useful. Although Lowi suggests that we must look at the intent in order to categorize policies, researchers have sometimes mistakenly focused on the impacts policies produce. In other words, some have argued that because any given policy may have the impact of both redistributing and protecting through regulation, such a policy cannot be placed into a single category.[9] This, as suggested above, probably represents a misunderstanding of Lowi's concepts.

SOME ASSUMPTIONS OF THE POLICY MAKING PROCESS APPROACH

The policy making process approach makes certain implicit assumptions. Perhaps the two most important assumptions relate to its definition of public policy and to the role of politics in public policy making.

In discussions of the policy making process, there has been some disagreement about exactly what the definition of public policy is. Is it synonymous with legislation? Does it have to be the result of government action? Many recent discussions have come to the conclusion that there really is a general definition available. Thus, in the policy making process approach, public policy is unambiguously defined as a goal-directed course of action followed by an actor or set of actors in an attempt to deal with a public problem.[10] Public policy, in this conception, is not the impact that governmental decisions have on people or problems; rather, it is the direct reflection of what happens in the policy making process.

A second, related, assumption of the policy making process approach is that politics is the key factor in understanding (determining) what does and what does not get done in government. This preeminence of politics, according to Lindblom, assumes that pure analysis will never tell us what the best public policy is; only politics can determine that. This assumption has led Garson to describe the policy making process approach as "anti-synoptic" (or anti-scientific) in contrast to pure analysis, which is synoptic.[11] Indeed, as we will see shortly, this is one point over which the approaches fundamentally disagree.

[9] For an introduction to some of the literature on this subject, see G. D. Greenberg et al., "Developing Public Policy Theory," *American Political Science Review,* Vol. 71, No. 4, Dec. 1977, pp. 1534–43; E. Ostrom, "Is It B or Not–B? That Is the Question," *Social Science Quarterly,* Vol. 61, No. 2, Sept. 1980, pp. 198–202; and P. J. Steinberger, "Typologies and Public Policy: Meaning Construction and the Policy Process," *Social Science Quarterly,* Vol. 61, No. 2, Sept. 1980, pp. 185–97.

[10] James E. Anderson, David W. Brady, and Charles Bullock, *Public Policy and Politics in America* (North Scituate, Mass.: Duxbury, 1978), p. 5.

[11] G. David Garson, "From Policy Science to Policy Analysis: A Quarter Century of Progress?" *Policy Studies Journal,* Special Issue No. 2, 1980–81, pp. 535–44.

Recently the tension between politics and analysis—sometimes referred to as a distinction between facts and values—has prompted some analysts to propose a policy making process which explicitly incorporates the results of analysis. This process often is referred to as the *policy advocacy* process. Foster, for example, suggests that analysis must be placed squarely within a process in which analysts provide best possible cases for their competing positions.[12] This policy making process resembles the legal process.

CONDUCTING POLICY MAKING PROCESS RESEARCH With all of this in mind, one might wonder what a researcher does when conducting public policy analysis according to this approach. As later chapters will demonstrate, public policy making process analysts attempt to identify and describe all the important interactions among political actors that surround a specific public policy. Sometimes such analysts focus only on one stage of the public policy making process; sometimes they try to relate what happens in one stage to what happens in other stages. For example, George Edwards suggests that the way some policies are implemented depends in part on how the policies were adopted.[13] Usually such analysts conduct in-depth case studies. In any event, it is probably safe to say that such analysts find the policy making process a useful framework for understanding the role of politics in public policy development and for anticipating what kinds of public policies might be successfully developed in the future.

Analysis Approach Number Two: The Causes and Consequences of Public Policies

Another approach to public policy analysis is what we will refer to as the *cause and consequence* approach, in which the focus is on either intended or unintended impacts of governmental decisions or nondecisions. In this approach, as exemplified in the works of Thomas R. Dye, the explicit definition of public policy relies on terminology from systems analysis, such as inputs, outputs, and outcomes.[14] Public policy decisions are usually considered outputs, and the impacts of those decisions on people or problems are considered outcomes.[15] Here the definition of public policy clearly focuses on the *results* of government ac-

---

[12] John L. Foster, "An Advocate Role Model for Policy Analysis," *Policy Studies Journal,* Vol. 8, No. 6, Summer 1980, pp. 958–64. Also see M. Kourilsky, "An Adversary Model for Educational Evaluations," *Evaluation Comment,* Vol. 4, 1973, pp. 3–8; and M. Levine, "Scientific Method and the Adversary Model: Some Preliminary Suggestions," *Evaluation Comment,* Vol. 4, 1973, pp. 1–3.

[13] George C. Edwards, *Implementing Public Policy* (Washington, D.C.: Congressional Quarterly Press, 1980), Ch. 2.

[14] Thomas R. Dye, *Understanding Public Policy,* 4th ed. (Englewood Cliffs, N.J.: Prentice-Hall, 1981), pp. 41–45.

[15] Thomas R. Dye, *Policy Analysis: What Governments Do, Why They Do It, and What Difference It Makes* (University, Ala.: University of Alabama Press, 1976), Ch. 1.

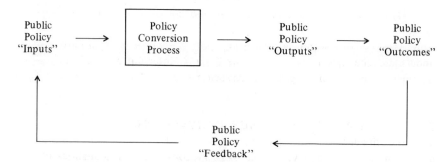

FIG. 1.3. Causes and Consequences Conception of Public Policy

tion or inaction. Public policy in this approach is not a process, as was the case in the policy making process approach, but a result. As illustrated in Figure 1.3, outputs are usually considered the direct result of governmental actions, such as the passage of legislation. Outcomes are usually considered the intended or unintended effects that those outputs have on people or problems. An example of an outcome would be when governmental action actually reduces hunger in the United States. In some instances, outcomes also include the effects of the *failure* of government to take action, since some researchers believe that "nondecisions" as well as decisions constitute public policy outputs.[16]

In any case, according to the cause and consequence approach, it is of the utmost importance to understand what kinds of factors (input variables) seem to be *causally* related to public policy outputs or outcomes. In this view, public policies constitute key dependent variables to be explained by analysis. Such analyses usually do not delve into the policy conversion processes themselves, although process characteristics have at times been conceptualized as one of a number of input factors.[17] For example, some researchers have attempted to study whether making public policy decisions through democratic procedures actually has the effect of ensuring different (even better) decisions than using nondemocratic procedures.

What we often refer to as policy or program evaluation research and policy impact analysis are really subsets of research falling into this category. In most evaluation studies, the important question is whether governmental programs or policies "caused" the impact that they were supposed to. For example, when we instituted a system of preschool education for disadvantaged youth called Head Start, it was important to know whether the program had the intended effect of improving the later educational performance of the participating youngsters, whether it "caused" an improvement in performance.

[16] Peter Bachrach and Morton Baratz, "The Two Faces of Power," *American Political Science Review*, Vol. 56, 1962, 947–52.

[17] Dye, *Policy Analysis*, Ch. 1.

Occasionally, research in the cause and consequence approach seeks to examine the effects, or consequences, of policy decisions on people or problems. This type of research, sometimes called *policy impact analysis,* attempts to understand the extent to which governmental interventions have improved, worsened, or created new problems for society.

SOME CAUSE AND CONSEQUENCE APPROACH ASSUMPTIONS While the key to distinguishing cause and consequence public policy research lies in the definition of public policy, we can examine some additional qualities of this kind of research. As is the case with the policy making process approach, the cause and consequence approach makes some important assumptions. First, it explicitly uses a causal conception of social events: It assumes that it is possible to develop a clear idea of the cause-and-effect relationships that exist.[18] Second, it assumes that social science research techniques applied to important public policy problems can uncover these causal relationships in a value-neutral way. In other words, it assumes that researchers can work toward finding results that are unambiguous and not dependent on political or value biases. It also seeks to conduct the best and most rigorous research possible, usually accepting the belief that totally value-free and apolitical policy research is probably not possible. As we will see shortly, the assumption that rigorous research or analysis can provide answers to important public policy questions distinguishes the first approach from the other two.

This assumption does not mean that policy cause and consequence researchers claim to be totally value-free. Indeed, some see that their task consists of developing a systematic understanding of the way values determine and relate to public policies. A policy cause and consequence study might seek out the effects of decisions to pursue a particular course of action. For example, such a study might conclude that attempting to control air pollution by regulating automobile emissions has not really improved air quality. Such a study does not make a judgment about the value of improving air quality. Rather, it suggests that if that is what we wish to do, regulating auto emissions does not seem to help very much. This study is value-neutral because it makes no judgment about the normative desirability of improving air quality.

The value-neutrality assumption of most cause and consequence analysis at times has led researchers to examine values as explicit causes of public policies, with the aim of converting values into independent variables and examining their empirical relation to policy-dependent variables. For example, research has attempted to ascertain whether greater political participation, a highly valued goal

---

[18] Frank Scioli and Thomas Cook, eds., *The Methodology of Policy Studies* (Lexington, Mass.: Lexington Books, 1973). See also Thomas R. Dye, "Politics Versus Economics: The Development of the Literature on Policy Determination," *Policy Studies Journal,* Vol. 7, No. 4, Summer 1979, pp. 652–62.

in American culture, produces more desirable public policy outputs. After reading such studies, one might be less than fully satisfied that the research has been done well, but policy cause and consequence research assumes that this kind of analysis is possible.[19]

CONDUCTING CAUSE AND CONSEQUENCE RESEARCH   Again, you might wonder what public policy cause and consequence analysts do. In the broadest sense, such researchers might do any or all of the things that are considered empirical social science research. The only thing that distinguishes cause and consequence analysis from other kinds of empirical social science research is the choice of variables. Cause and consequence analysts choose variables that attempt to measure public policy inputs, outputs, or outcomes rather than other social phenomena. A study may try to determine what caused government to pursue a specific policy result. Thus, public policy may be treated as the dependent, or output, variable being caused by events or other input variables. Alternatively, a study may wish to understand what impact has been created by a public policy. For example, a researcher may wish to determine whether a government employment program caused participants' incomes to be higher than they otherwise would have been. Thus, public policy may be treated as the independent variable causing some output.

Such analysts usually start by formulating some basic testable hypotheses, collecting data about relevant variables, and subjecting the data to some sort of systematic statistical analysis, often using a computer. In some of the more rigorous program evaluations, the researchers get involved in the actual design of the public policies and try to collect their data based on an experimental design.[20] In other cause and consequence analyses, a researcher will collect data after a policy or program has been operating for a while, sometimes for many years. Usually such researchers believe that public policy cause and consequence analysis will help policy makers understand where and when government action might be able to remedy social or political problems in the future. But the main focus is on understanding what happened in the past, often the fairly recent past.

Analysis Approach Number Three:
Public Policy Prescription

The final approach, which we will refer to as the *public policy prescription* approach, attempts to use a variety of economic, mathematical, computer science, and operations research techniques to systematically help us answer the ques-

---

[19] For example, see Thomas R. Dye, *Politics, Economics, and the Public* (Chicago: Rand McNally, 1966). For a more thorough examination of the encroachment of values into policy cause and consequence research, see William Dunn, ed., *Values, Ethics, and the Practice of Policy Analysis* (Lexington, Mass.: Lexington Books, 1983) and Frank Fischer, *Politics, Values, and Public Policy* (Boulder, Colo.: Westview Press, 1980).

[20] In this usage, I mean any sort of experimental or quasi-experimental design. Such distinctions will be evident in later usages. See Donald T. Campbell and Julian C. Stanley, *Experimental and Quasi-Experimental Designs for Research* (Chicago, Ill.: Rand McNally, 1963).

tion, What policy should we pursue in the future? [21] We should note that all three approaches try to provide some useful information about what government policies should be pursued in the future. But only the public policy prescription approach explicitly defines public policy as what our governments should do in the future.

Public policy analysis rooted in this approach often appears to be extremely technical. It often uses techniques with fancy names, such as microsimulation modeling, linear programming, queuing modeling, time-series forecasting, and estimating future costs and benefits to prescribe the best course of future action. Some of these techniques go a step further than those used in the cause and consequence approach in that they take information derived from cause or consequence studies and systematically project it into the future. In other words, policy prescription research may make an implicit assumption about specific causes or consequences, but because it attempts to systematically extend this information into the future, it is qualitatively different from research in the cause and consequence approach. Some public policy prescription analyses make no causal assumptions whatsoever.

Prescriptive analyses might try to answer questions concerning which of several alternative policies should be adopted. For example, such a study might try to determine whether our government should attempt to reduce poverty by increasing welfare payments or by investing in jobs programs; whether we should stabilize the price of gasoline by deregulating petroleum or by subsidizing research and development for large oil companies; whether we should raise revenues from an increase in personal income taxes or from an increase in general sales taxes; or whether we can cut specific government programs without hurting the poor. Questions like these are obviously not easy to answer, yet they are very important ones for public policy makers. Public policy prescription analyses assume that answers to these questions must be rooted in systematic analysis rather than someone's intuition.

PUBLIC POLICY PRESCRIPTION ASSUMPTIONS The public policy prescription approach actually makes two different types of assumptions. First, each technique, when applied to a specific public policy problem, requires that the analyst make certain analytic assumptions. These assumptions differ markedly depending on the technique, the problem, and the researcher involved. The results derived from such analyses often are sensitive to the assumptions made by the researcher. Yet most of these studies make some effort to check how sensitive the results are to any particular assumption by altering it. For example, if we were using a technique to project the size of the federal budget deficit for each of the next three years, we would have to make an assumption about what the rate of inflation will be in each year. Of course, we cannot know what the

---

[21] Edith Stokey and Richard Zeckhauser, *A Primer for Policy Analysis* (New York: W. W. Norton, 1978).

rate of inflation will be next year, let alone the year after, but our technique requires that information. So we might assume that the rate of inflation will be eight percent each year and make our projections accordingly. Then we could go back and change our assumption to reflect a ten-percent rate of inflation and see how much our budget deficit projections differ.

The second type of assumption made by public policy prescription analysis relates to how these studies do and should affect public policy decisions. As is the case with the cause and consequence approach, public policy prescription analyses tend to assume that a single best course of action can be found through analysis and that this course of action should be followed as a matter of rational public policy making. In many instances, the public policy prescription approach assumes that the politics of public policy making can and should be subordinated to analysis. Many researchers who adhere to this approach believe that politics get in the way of rational and efficient public policy decision making, and would like to get the politics out of policy making. Since analysis is rational and politics often seem not to be rational, politics (irrationality) should be subordinated to analysis (rationality). This is a major point of difference between the public policy prescription approach and the other two. In fact, this is such an important point that—after we take a brief look at what policy prescription approach analysts do—we should take a few minutes to examine it and several other points of comparison more closely.

CONDUCTING POLICY PRESCRIPTION RESEARCH As before, you might wonder what public policy prescription analysts do. In some ways, it is very difficult to be specific about what these analysts do because it depends on which technique is being used. Public policy prescription research is probably the most technical and least intuitive of all public policy research. And because public policy prescription researchers rely on a variety of techniques, such as benefit-cost analysis, linear programming, etc., they actually end up doing lots of different things. In short, they start by examining the details of the policy problem at hand and deciding which, if any, of the prescriptive techniques is potentially capable of providing an answer to the problem. Once the researcher decides which technique is appropriate, the actual analysis requires that some analytical assumptions of the sort we just discussed be made. Then the researcher does a series of calculations (typically with the assistance of a computer) to derive a numerical answer (or a series of answers). Based on the numerical answer(s), the researcher makes a judgment about what seems to be the most appropriate course of public policy action.

HOW DO THE THREE APPROACHES COMPARE?

While each of the three approaches to public policy analysis contributes something unique to our understanding of any particular public policy issue, each approach also has something to say about the other approaches. These points of comparison and contrast offer important sources of debate among policy analysts.

As already discussed briefly, the public policy making process approach argues that public policy making is, always has been, and always will be, political in a democratic society. Because of this view, the approach suggests that public policy analysis that fails to account for politics will ultimately always be subordinated to politics. This view also tends to mean that policy making process analysts will view other kinds of analysis as suspect, perhaps even as having been co-opted by one side or another in the political process. It is this view that, in part, leads Garson to characterize this approach as *anti*synoptic rather than just *non*synoptic.[22]

Public policy making process conceptions of analysis deal with this by placing the policy evaluation stage squarely within the larger policy making process. This permits analysts to conceive of evaluation, or analysis, within the broader political context of public policy making. In this view, research conducted within both the cause and consequence approach and the public policy prescription approach constitute analysis. In short, public policy making process analysts often believe that getting the politics out of public policy making is, and should be, impossible.

The public policy cause and consequence approach questions the assumption that politics is the key determinant (cause) of public policy decisions, as implied by the policy making process approach. Instead, as noted by Thomas R. Dye, the extent to which politics affects decisions should be treated as purely hypothetical, a question that should itself be answered through empirical public policy consequence research.[23] The result of much of this research suggests that economic and fiscal factors are the important causes of what governments do, that politics and political systems are only of secondary importance. Even so, the debate concerning the extent to which politics determines public policy decisions continues. One way of looking at this debate is that it is really a struggle between competing approaches to public policy analysis.

Finally, the public policy prescription approach often attempts to find ways of making politics a more rational process. While the vast majority of prescriptive policy analyses never deal with this issue directly, some attempt to prescribe ways of improving the policy making process. For example, what has become known as public choice research attempts, among other things, to find efficient voting rules for elections. Overall, the public policy prescription approach does not deny the role of politics in public policy making, as the cause and consequence approach often does. But because prescriptive approaches conceive of politics as essentially irrational, it often seeks to improve or overcome politics. With all of this in mind, we can now begin to look at some of the public policy research that has been done.

[22] Garson, pp. 535–44.

[23] Thomas R. Dye, "Politics Versus Economics: The Development of the Literature on Policy Determination," *Policy Studies Journal,* Vol. 7, No. 4, Summer 1979, pp. 652–62.

WHERE DO WE GO FROM HERE?

At this point, you might ask where we go from here in our study of public policy analysis. We could spend much more time investigating the techniques of research associated with each of the approaches. However, it is probably more important and useful to begin examining a wide range of public policy analytic studies from the various approaches. In order to do this, we have chosen six broad public policy areas. Each of the following chapters will examine contributions made by studies from the three approaches to our understanding of each of these six policy areas. As we will see, the research in each of these approaches makes an important contribution to our understanding of every policy area.

We have selected six major policy areas to discuss. In Chapter 2, we focus our attention on public environmental policy analyses. In subsequent chapters, we address energy policy, national defense and foreign policy, welfare and anti-poverty policy, physical and mental health policy, and tax and revenue policy. In each of these broad policy areas, we review some of the major policy analysis studies that emerge from each of the three policy analysis approaches.

As you read these chapters, you will discover several important things. First, in each policy area there is an abundance of research from all three of our policy analysis approaches. Second, while the studies using each approach are very important, the studies from any one approach are not sufficient to provide us with a full understanding of the specific policy area.

We obviously could not hope to cover all of the policy research that has been conducted in the policy areas we have chosen. Whenever possible, important studies or topics that could not be discussed because of space constraints are identified, and citations are provided in the event that you would like to pursue them on your own.

One final note: We consider the purpose of this book is to introduce students to systematic public policy research. The policy studies reviewed in this book should be consistent with this purpose. As a result, a decision was made to exclude materials that do not constitute primary research, for example, position or opinion papers and the like. Rather, we focus on studies that attempt to provide some systematic test of policy-relevant hypotheses or rigorous analysis.

The decision to focus on this type of policy analysis has important implications. While it serves the purpose of this book well, the trade-off is that we may end up being unable to discuss some of the more recently debated issues of public policy, because there is an inevitable lag between the time when our governments take actions and the time when researchers are able to study these actions. However, most of the issues raised in this book are probably controversial enough to provide stimulus for interest and discussion.

A secondary purpose of this book is to suggest ways that the three approaches to public policy analysis can be integrated. Once we understand some aspects of existing policy analyses, we can begin to entertain some specific methods of accomplishing this. So in the last chapter, we suggest how these three approaches can ultimately lead to the synthesis of a more comprehensive, and perhaps even more mature, field of public policy analysis. With all of the preliminaries out of the way, we can now turn our attention to the area of public environmental policies.

FURTHER READING

The Policy Making Process Approach

General

ANDERSON, JAMES E. *Public Policy-Making,* 2nd ed. New York: Holt, Rinehart, & Winston, 1979.

ANDERSON, JAMES E., DAVID W. BRADY, and CHARLES BULLOCK. *Public Policy and Politics in America.* North Scituate, Mass.: Duxbury, 1978.

CHELF, CARL P. *Public Policymaking in America.* Santa Monica, Calif.: Goodyear, 1981.

JONES, C. O. *An Introduction to the Study of Public Policy.* Belmont, Calif.: Wadsworth, 1970.

LINDBLOM, CHARLES. *The Policy-Making Process,* 2nd ed. Englewood Cliffs, N.J.: Prentice-Hall, 1980.

RIPLEY, RANDALL, and GRACE FRANKLIN. *Congress, the Bureaucracy, and Public Policy,* rev. ed. Homewood, Ill.: Dorsey, 1980.

Specific Stages in the Process

BARDACH, E. *The Implementation Game.* Cambridge, Mass.: MIT Press, 1978.

EDWARDS, GEORGE C. *Implementing Public Policy.* Washington, D.C.: Congressional Quarterly Press, 1980.

KINGDON, J. W. *Agendas, Alternatives, and Public Policies.* Boston: Little, Brown, 1984.

NACHMIAS, R. *Public Policy Evaluation.* New York: St. Martin's, 1981.

NAKAMURA, R., and F. SMALLWOOD. *The Politics of Policy Implementation.* New York: St. Martin's, 1980.

POLSBY, N. W. *Political Innovation in America: The Politics of Policy Initiations.* New Haven, Conn.: Yale University Press, 1984.

RIPLEY, R. *Congress: Process and Policy.* New York: W. W. Norton, 1975.

RIPLEY, RANDALL, and GRACE FRANKLIN. *Bureaucracy and Policy Implementation.* Homewood, Ill.: Dorsey, 1982.

WILLIAMS, W., ed. *Studying Implementation.* New York: Chatham House, 1982.

The Policy Cause and Consequence Approach

DYE, THOMAS R. *Policy Analysis: What Governments Do, Why They Do It, and What Difference It Makes.* University, Ala.: University of Alabama Press, 1976.

NACHMIAS, R. *Public Policy Evaluation.* New York: St. Martin's, 1981.

POISTER, T. *Public Program Analysis.* University Park, Md.: University of Maryland Press, 1976.

TUFTE, E. R. *Data Analysis for Politics and Policy.* Englewood Cliffs, N.J.: Prentice-Hall, 1974.

The Policy Prescription Approach

GRAMLICH, G. *Benefit-Cost Analysis of Government Programs.* Englewood Cliffs, N.J.: Prentice-Hall, 1981.

HAVEMAN, R., and K. HOLLENBECK, eds. *Microeconomic Simulation Models for Public Policy Analysis.* New York: Academic Press, 1980.

ORCUTT, G., S. CALDWELL, and R. WERTHEIMER. *Policy Exploration through Microanalytic Simulation.* Washington, D.C.: Urban Institute, 1976.

STOKEY, EDITH, and RICHARD ZECKHAUSER. *A Primer for Policy Analysis.* New York: W. W. Norton, 1978.

CHAPTER TWO

Analyses of Public Environmental Policies

When we speak of public policies toward the environment, we are really speaking about one or another of a group of public policies all of which attempt to regulate or improve the quality of our physical surroundings. These policies span a wide variety of specific environmental problems, including water and air pollution, solid waste treatment, toxic and hazardous waste disposal, wetlands protection, and so forth. Governmental policies toward our environment usually attempt to reverse damage already caused and to prevent damage from occurring in the future. To many people, protecting the environment is the same as protecting our health. To other people, the link between environmental policies and our health is less convincing. In any case, by applying the three approaches to public policy analysis to research on environmental policies, we can see that there are three distinctly different specific definitions of public environmental policy. We can apply the three general definitions of public policy we discussed in Chapter 1 to do the following:

> To identify what environmental legislation and administrative actions have been pursued;
> To establish what factors seem to influence or cause our governments to pursue or not pursue various actions;
> To examine what effect our efforts have had on the quality of our environment; and
> To learn what seem to be the best ways to clean up the environment in the future.

As we do this, we will begin to see how different public policy analysts can differ in their views about environmental policies. Initially, we will examine the policy making process surrounding various legislative and administrative activities.

THE ENVIRONMENTAL POLICY MAKING PROCESS

As we discussed in Chapter 1, the policy making process approach focuses on goal-directed courses of action followed by an actor or set of actors in an attempt to deal with a public problem. As we apply this conception of public policy to the issue of the environment, we start by examining each of the stages in the process. We will begin with a brief look at what kinds of events have raised our consciousness about threats to our environment (problem formation). Then we will examine some studies that describe the courses of action formulated, adopted, and implemented by our governments to improve and protect the quality of the environment.

Some of the studies we will discuss use an explicit policy making process framework. For example, Rosenbaum's *Environmental Politics and Policy* develops the idea of "policy cycles," which are identical to the general policy making stages we referred to in Chapter 1.[1] In looking at these studies, we will examine some of the main actors involved. This will lead us directly to a look at federal and state environmental legislation and administrative regulations. We will see that in many areas administrative actions are every bit as important as legislation in determining what gets accomplished.

The Formation of Environmental Problems

The analysis of public policy making processes begins with an examination of how the policy issue became a social and/or political problem in the first place. This, as you will recall, constitutes an analysis of the problem formation process. So initially, we should examine what happened to make at least some of us believe that serious environmental problems exist.

A variety of events have helped to trigger and shape our awareness of actual and potential environmental problems. The vast majority of these events have occurred since 1960. For example, according to Peters, the 1962 publication and widespread publicity surrounding Rachel Carson's book *Silent Spring* helped to identify environmental pollution as a serious problem and to launch the "environmental movement." Carson's book described the kinds of damage lethal pesticides routinely used by farmers and others were causing to bird and other wildlife populations. Carson warned that this damage would eventually lead to the horror of springtime without chirping birds.[2]

Air pollution has been a widely recognized problem since the mid-1950s,[3] but it was not until the mid-1960s, when large numbers of people were made ill by blankets of air pollution in southern California and in Pittsburgh, that air pollution emerged as a serious problem of national importance. In the late 1960s, according to Liroff, the Santa Barbara oil spill and the occasion of the Cuyahoga River in Cleveland actually catching fire because of massive concentrations of flammable industrial pollutants went a long way toward convincing our leaders that major environmental problems existed.[4]

It was not until perhaps as late as 1978, when the residents of a small subdivision of Niagara Falls, New York, began to link the high incidence of various illnesses to toxic chemical wastes dumped in nearby Love Canal, that the issue of toxic waste disposal began to receive widespread attention.[5] And in the

---

[1] Walter A. Rosenbaum, *Environmental Politics and Policy* (Washington, D.C.: Congressional Quarterly Press, 1984).

[2] Rachel Carson, *Silent Spring* (Boston: Houghton Mifflin, 1962), p. 274.

[3] Clarke E. Cochran et al., *American Public Policy: An Introduction* (New York: St. Martin's, 1982), pp. 94, 106.

[4] Richard A. Liroff, *A National Policy for the Environment: NEPA and Its Aftermath* (Bloomington, Ind.: Indiana University Press, 1976), p. 3.

[5] Congressional Quarterly, *Health and the Environment* (Washington, D.C.: Congressional Quarterly, Inc., 1981), pp. 1–2. See also Adeline Gordon Levine, *Love Canal: Science, Politics, and People* (Lexington, Mass.: Lexington Books, 1982).

face of growth in the nuclear power industry during the 1970s, the closing of the only two radioactive waste disposal areas in the country, combined with the accident at Three Mile Island in Pennsylvania in 1978, began to raise fears about nuclear pollution.[6] These and other events have combined over the past two decades to increase people's awareness of major environmental problems.[7] Let's take a look at what our governments have done to deal with these problems.

The Formulation of Environmental Policies

Once there is fairly widespread recognition that a problem exists, the policy making process begins. As a starting point for our examination of environmental policies as courses of action, we can look at how the various proposals to solve these problems have been formulated. In order to do this, we will identify the main actors involved in formulating legislative responses to some of these rather major problems. The formulation of legislative responses is usually the result of interactions between major interest groups and members of Congress, especially members of key legislative committees. In some ways, when our administrative agencies decide how to enforce environmental legislation, they formulate specific regulations. Although this represents a type of policy formulation, we will examine it within the broader context of environmental policy implementation.

In recent years, a number of large and influential environmental interest groups have begun to play important roles in the environmental policy making process.[8] These groups, many of which are listed in Table 2.1, began exerting increased pressure on legislators in order to help formulate and adopt major proenvironment legislation. To some observers, the evolution of these interest groups worked to help counterbalance the historical pattern of influence by interest groups from major industries, many of which were at least partly responsible for creating environmental problems in the first place. In terms of political conflict, the emergence of environmental interest groups sets the stage for confrontation between the "long-term public interests of protecting the environment" and the "short-term economic (profit) interests of major sectors of the economy."[9]

So the question remains, how does environmental policy get formulated in the United States? The answer is, it gets formulated through a process of interaction between various legislators and many of these environmental and industry interest groups. To understand a little more about how this happens,

[6] Congressional Quarterly, pp. 71–73.

[7] Walter A. Rosenbaum, *The Politics of Environmental Concern* (New York: Praeger, 1973), p. 3.

[8] Carl P. Chelf, *Public Policymaking in America: Difficult Choices, Limted Solutions* (Santa Monica, Cal.: Goodyear, 1981), p. 322.

[9] Harold Sprout and Margaret Sprout, "Environmental Politics: What Role for Political Scientists?" in Stuart Nagel, ed., *Environmental Politics* (New York: Praeger, 1974), p. 8.

TABLE 2.1. Major Environmental Interest Groups

American Nature Association
Citizens Committee on Natural Resources
Citizens for Clean Air
Coalition for Water Project Review
Common Cause
Council of Conservationists
Defenders of Wildlife
Environmental Action
Environmental Policy Center
Friends of the Earth
Izaak Walton League
League of Conservation Voters
National Audubon Society
National Clean Air Coalition
National Wildlife Foundation
Natural Resources Defense Council
Sierra Club
Trustees for Conservation
Wildlife Management Institute

we must take a look at how Congress itself divides the labor with regard to environmental problems and legislation. Consequently, we must look at some aspects of the "environmental committees" of Congress.

Until very recently, a number of different congressional committees shared or divided jurisdiction over environmental issues. These committees—the House and Senate Interior and Insular Affairs committees, the House Agriculture and the Senate Agriculture and Forestry committees, and the House Science and Astronautics and the Senate Aeronautical and Space Sciences committees—each had some responsibility and jurisdiction for dealing with environmental problems.

Surprisingly, there was no single House or Senate committee focusing its attention on such issues, although one or another of the committees may have had subcommittees focusing on environmental legislation. It was not until 1977 that the Senate reorganized to include the Committee on Environment and Public Works, even though jurisdiction for some important environmental areas remained with the Commerce Committee.[10] In fact, Kenski and Kenski point out that even with the reorganization, environmental legislation might involve any number of congressional committees or subcommittees.[11]

The significance of this fact is twofold: first, no single committee exer-

[10] Congressional Quarterly, *Congressional Quarterly Almanac, 1981* (Washington, D.C.: Congressional Quarterly, Inc., 1981), p. 503.

[11] Henry C. Kenski and Margaret Corgan Kenski, "Congress Against the President: The Struggle Over the Environment," in Norman J. Vig and Michael E. Kraft, eds., *Environmental Policy in the 1980's: Reagan's New Agenda* (Washington, D.C.: Congressional Quarterly Press, 1984), pp. 104–12.

cised sole responsibility or jurisdiction over environmental problems; and second, each committee having partial jurisdiction had to deal with environmental problems at the same time it had to deal with other, sometimes conflicting, problems. It was here that the conflict between protecting the environment and permitting unrestricted economic growth and development of natural resources often emerged. Perhaps the single most in-depth, although clearly proenvironment, study of the workings of these committees is the Ralph Nader Congress Project Report *The Environmental Committees.*[12]

This Nader report presents an uncomplimentary picture of how Congress has traditionally treated issues of land management, water resource development, air-quality control, and others. The report provides case study analyses of each of these environmental committees. What emerges is a view of the committees as staffed and operating to the benefit of "entrenched economic interests." For example, the study of the House and Senate Interior and Insular Affairs committees, which maintain jurisdiction over all federally owned public lands (about one-third of the country's land area) clearly links the committee's operations to economic interests. Much of this federal land has been leased to oil and natural gas companies for current and future production, mined for a variety of minerals, cultivated for timber, and leased for cattle grazing.

The report asserts that private interests obtained much more benefit from these arrangements than did the general public. These committees have included many representatives from Western states who have shared the interests of the industries wishing to develop these resources. In the words of the Nader Report itself, "the flow of campaign funds, the impact of voting blocs, and, not infrequently, the economic interests of the legislators themselves, feed a business–congressional fraternity that attains the unity of a common ideological fervor."[13]

The Agriculture committees exercised partial jurisdiction over environmental policies as a result of their concern about farmers' abilities to use various fertilizers and pesticides to aid farm production. Over the years, there has been much concern that pesticides such as DDT and fertilizers such as organic phosphates would seriously contaminate the soil and ground water and threaten the health of humans and wildlife. In the view of the Congress Project Report, the Agriculture committees have been captured by the agribusiness sector of the economy. These committees, so it claimed, were more interested in preserving price supports than in protecting the environment.

While the exact motivations of particular members of Congress can always be questioned, it is clear that developing anything like a comprehensive set of environmental policies would be difficult at best. Indeed, in their case study

---

[12] Nader Congress Project, *The Environmental Committees: A Study of the House and Senate Interior, Agriculture, and Science Committees* (New York: Grossman, 1975). See also J. Clarence Davies and Barbara S. Davies, *The Politics of Pollution,* 2nd ed. (Indianapolis: Bobbs-Merrill, 1975).

[13] Nader Congress Project, p. xiii.

The Politics of Pollution, Davies and Davies describe how the fragmented nature of Congress's jurisdiction over pollution issues has delayed or prevented the formulation of solutions to pesticide contamination, noise control, environmental finance, and other important issues.[14] Generally, the fragmented jurisdiction over such issues has served to ensure that all affected interests must receive some benefit out of the proposed solution before it becomes public policy.[15] In other words, the policy formulation process has been designed to try to ensure that no single established interest will suffer at the hands of another interest.

The Decade of the Environmental Movement

By the late 1960s and early 1970s, this pattern of fragmentation began to change. The evolution of the environmental movement in the United States began to increase and reflect public and policy makers' awareness of environmental problems. Many scholars have attempted to explain why concern about the environment was able to become transformed into an effective social movement. Certainly, media attention paid to events such as air pollution emergencies in California and Pennsylvania, the 1969 Santa Barbara oil spill, and other environmental destruction attributed to the carelessness of private industry played a role. But there had been such events years, even decades, before, and they did not have the same social impact. Another explanation is that near the end of the Vietnam War era, Americans began to change their beliefs in conjunction with a larger consciousness-raising experience about the importance of the environment.

Whatever the cause of this change, by the early 1970s, a number of major national environmental interest groups had emerged as a potent force in American politics. They began to establish Washington lobbying offices, hire experienced lobbyists, and effectively involve themselves in the policy making process in which representatives of major sectors of the private economy had been involved for years.[16] The immediate effect of this was to help change the way environmental policies were formulated in Congress. The proposals emerging from congressional committees became much more proenvironment.[17] As we will see in our examination of environmental policy adoptions, this had a significant effect on the nature of the legislation enacted by Congress.

The increased role of environmental interest groups in national politics continued until the election of Ronald Reagan in 1980 and the subsequent appointments of James Watt as secretary of the interior and Anne Gorsuch Burford

[14] Davies and Davies (see Note 12), pp. 61–67.

[15] Davies and Davies, pp. 61–67.

[16] Jeffrey M. Berry, *Lobbying for the People* (Princeton, N.J.: Princeton University Press, 1977), pp. 212–85.

[17] Berry, pp. 212–85.

as administrator of the Environmental Protection Agency (EPA). These events, along with the elections of more conservative members of Congress, have gone a long way toward reasserting the role of economic and resource development in shaping national environmental policy.[18]

Environmental Policy Adoptions

When we speak of policy adoptions, we usually refer to legislative enactments, but as we saw in Chapter 1, there are other types of adoptions. In fact, part of what administrative agencies do when they implement public policies can also be considered policy adoptions. And when the courts are asked to decide cases involving interpretation of legislation, they are in some ways adopting public policies. But we will deal with these actions as part of the implementation process. So leaving a discussion of these court-based environmental policy actions for later, we can begin by looking at what policies Congress has adopted over the past 30 years or so. The major policy legislation enacted by Congress in this period is summarized in Table 2.2.

Perhaps partly because of the environmental policy formulation framework we just examined, environmental policy adoptions have traditionally been the result of piecemeal legislation. Most of the enacted legislation dealt with

TABLE 2.2. Major Environmental Policy Adoptions, 1954–1983

Multiple Surface Use Act of 1955 strengthened restrictions on strip-mining.

Air Pollution Act of 1955 made money available for air pollution studies.

Clean Air Act of 1963 created a matching-grant program for states to control air pollution.

National Wilderness Act of 1964 established the National Wilderness Preservation System to protect certain government lands from being developed.

Motor Vehicle Air Pollution Control Act of 1965 authorized setting of standards for automobile pollution.

Solid Waste Disposal Act of 1965 provided funds for research into better ways of disposing of solid wastes.

Water Quality Act of 1965 required the states to establish water quality standards and authorized the secretary of HEW to establish minimum standards for states that failed to do so on their own.

Clean Waters Restoration Act of 1966 helped state and local governments pay the costs of complying with the Water Quality Act standards.

---

[18] Edwin H. Clark II, "Reaganomics and the Environment: An Evaluation," in Vig and Kraft (see Note 11), pp. 341–58.

TABLE 2.2. (cont.)

Air Quality Act of 1967 provided additional funds for states to establish air quality standards and authorized the secretary of HEW to establish minimum standards for states that failed to do so on their own; also created the Air Quality Advisory Board.

National Wild and Scenic Rivers Act of 1968 authorized the protection of some rivers and streams within wilderness areas.

National Environmental Policy Act of 1969 established the Council on Environmental Quality and required environmental impact statements.

Water Quality Improvement Act of 1970 established that oil companies can be held liable for spills and costs of clean-ups and established the Office of Environmental Quality.

Clean Air Amendments of 1970 established the goal of reducing auto air pollution by 90 percent within specified deadlines.

Resource Recovery Act of 1970 provided additional assistance in the disposal and recycling of solid wastes.

Federal Water Pollution Control Act of 1972 provided federal grants for water clean-up, set goals and timetables for clean waters, and set effluent discharge standards.

Endangered Species Act of 1973 created the list of endangered species to be earmarked for special protection.

Safe Drinking Water Act of 1974 authorized EPA to set minimum standards for certain chemicals and bacteria in drinking water.

Toxic Substances Control Act of 1976 authorized screening of chemicals for safety before marketing.

Federal Land Policy and Management Act of 1976 rewrote the laws dealing with public lands.

Resource Conservation and Recovery Act of 1976 authorized a federal program for hazardous waste management and tracking waste from "cradle to grave."

Surface Mining Control and Reclamation Act of 1977 strengthened control over strip-mining.

Clean Water Act of 1977 authorized EPA to establish "best available technologies" and "best conventional technologies" standards for pollutants specified in the 1972 Act.

Clean Air Act Amendments of 1977 addressed problems of "nonattainment" and prevention of significant deterioration of the quality of air.

Comprehensive Environmental Response, Compensation, and Liability Act of 1980 established the Superfund to finance clean-up of hazardous waste sites and chemical spills and permitted recovery of clean-up costs from responsible parties.

small pieces of the environment, and no real attempt was made at any sort of co-ordination. According to Harold and Margaret Sprout, legislative policy makers would usually "opt for publicly acceptable short-run solutions" to environmental problems, "without regard for possibly long-run damaging, even catastrophic, consequences."[19] Traditionally, if you wanted to understand what our environmental policy was, you would have had to examine a large number of individual, sometimes disparate and conflicting, pieces of legislation.

As an example, between 1955 and 1967, Congress enacted no fewer than four major pieces of air pollution legislation: the Air Pollution Act of 1955; the Clean Air Act of 1963; the Motor Vehicle Air Pollution Control Act of 1965; and the Air Quality Act of 1967. The same pattern tended to be true for other types of environmental issues as well, such as toxic and hazardous waste disposal, water quality control, land use and resource development, and coastal zone management, to name a few.

At the same time, however, all of this legislation, taken together, did represent a sort of national policy on the environment. By the late 1960s, especially with the enactment of the National Environmental Policy Act (NEPA) in 1969, the federal government began trying to adopt a national, more comprehensive and less fragmented, environmental policy. This act was the first major piece of legislation that addressed pollution and environmental problems of all types. Included in this act were provisions for:

> The establishment of the Council on Environmental Quality (CEQ), a federal agency within the Executive Office of the President, to advise on environmental policy issues and to assess the impact of federal actions;
>
> The requirement of "Environmental Impact Statements" to be filed by any federal agency whenever it makes a recommendation, a report, or a proposal for legislation or major federal actions potentially affecting the quality of the human environment;
>
> Making environmental impact statements available to the public for inspection;
>
> Specifying that the President submit an environmental quality report to Congress each year.

This act, by itself, did little to directly improve the quality of the environment. Indeed, Wenner suggests that NEPA was more symbolic than substantive.[20] But in 1970, President Nixon created the Environmental Protection Agency (EPA) by executive order. This agency was designed as an independent regulatory agency; it was the cornerstone of President Nixon's attempt to consolidate the federal government's fragmented environmental improvement administration into a single agency. The job of implementing national environmental policies became the explicit task of the EPA and the CEQ. This, along

[19] Sprout and Sprout, p. 8.

[20] Lettie M. Wenner, *One Environment under Law: A Public Policy Dilemma* (Santa Monica, Cal.: Goodyear, 1976).

with NEPA, helped to establish the first national environmental policy. We will take a look at how the EPA and CEQ have worked when we examine environmental policy implementation.

After the EPA was created by executive order, Congress continued to enact legislation directed toward improving specific environmental conditions. This legislation included the Water Quality Act of 1970, the Clean Air Amendments of 1970, the Federal Water Pollution Control Act of 1972, the Toxic Substances Control Act of 1976, and others. The major difference between these and their predecessors is that a single agency, the EPA, was given principal responsibility for implementing, coordinating, and enforcing these policies.

There have been several important analyses of the processes involving NEPA (which created the CEQ) and the creation of the EPA. Perhaps the study that most explicitly uses a policy making process approach is Liroff's *A National Policy for the Environment*.[21] According to Liroff's analysis, NEPA was not really the result of a policy making process very different from the processes associated with the earlier piecemeal legislation.

Describing the policy formulation and adoption stages of NEPA, Liroff suggests that although the expected array of lobbying groups was not very active over NEPA, the bill was subjected to considerable bargaining and conflict between key legislators in both the House and the Senate. In the Senate, the conflict occurred between the chairman of the Interior Committee and the chairman of the Air and Water Pollution Subcommittee of the Public Works Committee. In the House, the NEPA bill was cosponsored by all but one of the members of the Fisheries and Wildlife Conservation Subcommittee of the Merchant Marines and Fisheries Committee. But the bill ran into a roadblock in the Rules Committee of the House because of objections raised by the chairman of the House Interior Committee.[22] Liroff's analysis suggests that much of the conflict and bargaining took place over "turf" issues within Congress, and that despite the sometimes protracted debate, Congress never really considered in any way the consequences NEPA would have on the agencies, on the courts, or really on the environment.

The 1980 presidential and congressional elections changed the nature of environmental policy. Conservative candidates argued persuasively that excessive regulation of the economy, including environmental regulation, was at the heart of our national economic woes. The election of many of these candidates, and the subsequent appointments of James Watt and Anne Gorsuch Burford, helped to fashion an era with diminished emphasis on government intervention in environmental quality. Most of the change has been the result of changes in the implementation rather than changes in legislation. We will see how this has happened in our discussion of policy implementation.

[21] Liroff, p. 3.
[22] Liroff, p. 11.

Environmental Policy Implementation

There is perhaps no better example of the importance of the policy implementation stage of the policy making process than is found in the case of environmental affairs. From the fragmented implementation of the earlier piecemeal legislation in the 1950s and 1960s to the operation of the CEQ and EPA in the 1970s and to the conservative changes during the early 1980s, the role of implementation turns out to be central in determining what actually gets accomplished in environmental protection. As Liroff notes with regard to the single most important environmental policy adoption:

> Congress did not really enact a national policy when it passed NEPA. Rather, it enacted only a statement of national environmental policy. The policy that actually followed NEPA's passage was the sum of all federal agency actions that had an environmental impact.[23]

As we suggested in Chapter 1, when we examine implementation, we usually focus our attention on how government agencies administer and how courts interpret legislative adoptions. Therefore, we will first concentrate on several studies of the agencies responsible for the environment. We will also take a brief look at some analyses of how the courts have entered the realm of environmental implementation process.

The most important aspects of environmental policy implementation focus on the operation of the Council on Environmental Quality and the Environmental Protection Agency. The EPA has developed responsibility for administering most of what we would consider to be environmental legislation enacted at the federal level of government. From 1970 to 1980, the EPA grew to become the single largest federal regulatory agency.[24] In making its decisions about how to implement environmental policies, it has unavoidably made decisions that affect a variety of established and emerging political interests. This, as we will see, has made EPA's existence at times a politically turbulent experience.

ENVIRONMENTAL POLICY IMPLEMENTATION AND THE EPA   The implementation of environmental policies by EPA (as with nearly all regulatory and administrative agencies) relies heavily on the issuance of federal rules and regulations. The regulations are written and issued by the agencies and carry the force of law even though they are rarely ever enacted or ratified by Congress. These regulations are the things that give specific meaning to the vague language our legislators often put into statutes. So even after a piece of legislation becomes law, there is often the opportunity for affected interests to influence the

---

[23] Liroff, p. 6.
[24] Congressional Quarterly, *Health and the Environment*, p. 4.

specifics of these regulations. This fact often makes the public policy implementation stage a point of continuous political conflict.

With its establishment in 1970, the EPA was faced with improving the quality of the environment based on the various adopted policies discussed earlier. For example, EPA gained the authority under NEPA to review and comment upon "environmentally impacting" actions of other agencies as a result of the 1970 Clean Air Act.[25] To perform this function, EPA had to decide what the words in the legislation really meant as applied to specific cases. It had to translate the words into action. For example, in the 1972 Amendments to the Water Pollution Control Act, Congress stated that the EPA should ensure that by 1977 private concerns use the "best practicable technology" to end pollution of lakes, rivers, and streams. It also stated that by 1983, it should use the "best available technology."

The terminology in the Act had to be broad and nonspecific because Congress could not possibly know what the best practicable or available technologies would be years in the future. But this had the effect of dumping an immense amount of decision-making responsibility into the hands of the EPA. As you might expect, different interests disagree about what constitutes the best practicable or best available technologies. This is an example of how important environmental implementation is, and there are dozens of others.

ENVIRONMENTAL POLICY IMPLEMENTATION AND THE COURTS The political struggles over how to implement the various pieces of environmental legislation have involved nearly every institution of government in the nation. Perhaps the most important institution outside of the administrative branch itself is the court system. The courts have become an integral part of the environmental policy implementation process, and they have done so for many different reasons.

Without question, the courts have become part of the policy making process for political reasons. Often, when one major political interest fails to obtain its desired result from the legislature (in the form of legislation) or from an administrative agency (in the form of rules or regulations), it may file a lawsuit to "appeal" the previous decisions or actions. Whatever else the courts are, they clearly serve an appellate function in the implementation stage of the policy making process.

In recent times, especially since the decade of the Seventies, federal government prosecutions in the courts have increased. In the early 1970s, there was a tendency for federal government suits to involve prosecutions of industry for violations of the law. Since about 1980, about half of the cases involving the

[25] Frederick R. Anderson, *NEPA in the Courts: A Legal Analysis of the National Environmental Policy Act* (Baltimore: Johns Hopkins University Press, 1973), pp. 259–64; and Liroff, pp. 165–76.

federal government represent intergovernmental disputes, many of which have been initiated by the states.[26]

Over the years, literally thousands of civil lawsuits have been filed involving environmental issues. Many of these suits are the result of the NEPA we discussed earlier. In other words, when EPA tries to implement aspects of NEPA, there will inevitably be some group of people who feel aggrieved by EPA's decisions. Such aggrieved parties are likely to sue EPA in order to change or reverse the decision. Liroff suggests that environmentalists were the principal users of lawsuits, and for good reason. In his words, "environmentalists tried to mobilize judicial resources in achieving their goals because their own resources were scarce."[27]

In addition, environmentalists used litigation for a number of political purposes: for its symbolic value; as a catalyst to stimulate intervention by other agencies; as a bargaining weapon with federal agencies; and to call legislative attention to matters that had been left to administrative discretion when they felt it should not have been.[28] After experiencing remarkable early success in winning such lawsuits, proenvironment interest groups found by the 1980s that business interest groups had taken the offensive in court.[29]

Typically, the environmental policy implementation process consists of a large number of agency decisions (or nondecisions) and subsequent court rulings challenging those decisions. Over time, a specific environmental policy evolves. And as the agencies and courts alter and clarify their decisions over time, the exact details of the implemented policies change. Decisions concerning how and when NEPA's environmental impact statements must be done, what constitutes federal action under NEPA, what happens when one or another party (federal, state, or local agencies, private businesses, etc.) fails to comply with NEPA mandates, and many other decisions have evolved through this type of process.[30]

THE REAGAN STRATEGY FOR ENVIRONMENTAL IMPLEMENTATION

Much recent attention has been focused on how the Reagan administration's Secretary of the Interior, James Watt, and EPA Administrator, Anne Gorsuch Burford, directed the implementation of existing legislation until their departure from federal service. Both Watt and Burford had built reputations opposing regulation of the environment as members of the Mountain States Legal Foundation,

[26] Lettie M. Wenner, "Judicial Oversight of Environmental Deregulation," in Vig and Kraft (see Note 11), pp. 182–84.

[27] Liroff, p. 150.

[28] Liroff, p. 151.

[29] Lettie M. Wenner, "Interest Group Litigation and Environmental Policy," *Policy Studies Journal*, Vol. 11, No. 4, June 1983, pp. 671–83.

[30] Anderson, passim.

a conservative Denver public interest law firm specializing in suing the government on behalf of pro-development interests.

Although few systematic studies of the changes in implementation under the Reagan administration are available, the media have begun to document some of the ways these changes have been brought about. For example, Montgomery suggests that implementation of programs to reduce environmental lead levels, air pollution, and hazardous waste have been seriously altered partly for philosophical reasons, although he suggests that this is partly the result of ineptitude. In his words, "the effect of the new administration" on environmental policy implementation "has been less to alter existing regulations than to delay the institution of new rules."[31] A study by Andrews discusses the development of the Reagan administration strategy of delay, suggesting that this has been part of the reemphasis on stimulating rather than impeding economic growth.[32]

The changes in environmental policy brought about by James Watt through the Department of Interior have apparently been substantial. For example, through the Bureau of Land Management, federal Wilderness Areas have been leased in record amounts for oil and gas exploration, coal mining, and other resource development. To at least one analyst, the way Watt operated the Interior Department reflected a capture of the department by industry, establishing an iron triangle that worked to industry's benefit.[33]

IMPLEMENTATION OF "SUPERFUND" Implementation of environmental policies has also provided a source of tension between Congress and the executive branch. During 1983, for example, much controversy erupted over the EPA's implementation of the Comprehensive Environmental Response, Compensation, and Liability Act of 1980 (CERCLA). This act established what has become known as the Superfund, a specific pool of money intended to help pay some of the enormous costs of cleaning up many of the worst hazardous waste sites in the country. Such sites include Woburn, Massachusetts, Price's Pit, New Jersey, and the Stringfellow Acid Pits in California, to name a few. When Congress began to suspect that the EPA was not vigorously acting to force the responsible parties to pay the clean-up costs, it requested that EPA turn over agency records of actions taken. After the EPA administrator Burford refused

[31] M. R. Montgomery, "The Politics of Pollution," *The Boston Globe Magazine,* July 25, 1982, p. 10. See also Anthony Z. Roisman, "What Have They Done to Environmental Rules?" *The Nation's Health,* May 1982, pp. 7–8; and Paul Goldberg, "Muzzling the Watchdog," *Washington Monthly,* Dec. 1981, pp. 34–39.

[32] Richard N. L. Andrews, "Deregulation: The Failure at EPA," in Vig and Kraft (see Note 11), pp. 161–80.

[33] Paul J. Culhane, "Sagebrush Rebels in Office: Jim Watt's Land and Water Policies," in Vig and Kraft (see Note 11), pp. 293–317.

to comply, Congress cited her for contempt of Congress.[34] This, of course, is an extreme case of what may happen in the implementation process.

Even with changes in leadership at EPA, including the return of William Ruckelshaus as its chief administrator, and with reauthorization of Superfund by Congress, little action has been taken to actually clean up hazardous waste sites.[35] Ruckelshaus argues that progress has been substantial given the state of the technology available to perform clean-up operations and public misconceptions about the risks of hazardous-waste treatment.[36] Others have suggested that the federal government, acting largely through EPA, must take the lead in resolving conflicts over hazardous waste issues.[37]

This represents an example of the classic confrontation between analysis and politics we discussed in Chapter 1. On the one hand, we have federal administrators and industry who believe that scientific analysis directed toward developing new technologies for chemical-waste treatment will help us resolve the hazardous waste problem in the United States. On the other hand, we have many state administrators and policy advocates who seek to resolve these problems politically, perhaps recognizing that scientific analysis will never provide complete and satisfactory answers for everyone.

Federalism and the Environmental Policy Making Process in the States

Just as the policy making process approach has been applied to federal environmental policies, so too has this approach been applied to state and local governments. In many instances, the states are faced with implementing aspects of federal policies, and the states and their local governments often formulate, adopt, and implement a wide variety of their own environmental policies. There are very few comprehensive studies of the environmental policy making processes in the states. There are, however, several studies focusing on the state experiences with federal water pollution policies and on state environmental management.

Perhaps the single best study of the state environmental policy making processes, especially the processes of implementing federal policies, is *Federalism and Clean Waters* by Harvey Lieber. Lieber examined the process that Congress went through to formulate and adopt the 1972 Water Pollution Control Act and then compared congressional intent to the process that EPA and five

[34] Ward Sinclair, "House Subcommittee Votes to Cite EPA Administrator for Contempt," *Washington Post*, Dec. 1982, p. A6. See also Walter A. Rosenbaum, pp. 51–56.

[35] Steven Cohen, "Defusing the Toxic Time Bomb: Federal Hazardous Waste Programs," in Vig and Kraft (see Note 11), pp. 273–91.

[36] William D. Ruckelshaus, "The Role of the Affected Community in Superfund Cleanup Activities," *Hazardous Waste*, Vol. 1, No. 3, 1984, pp. 283–88.

[37] See Anthony D. Cortese and Ann E. Rappaport, "Improving the Federal–State Partnership in Hazardous Waste Control," *Hazardous Waste*, Vol. 1, No. 3, 1984, pp. 289–99.

states went through to implement the act. Lieber's study turns out to be very critical of federal government attempts to impose uniform national standards on all the states regardless of how well they apply in those places or how much they are needed. In short, he found that this federal legislation actually altered the policy making process in Mississippi to result in cleaner water, a result that probably would not have occurred in the absence of the federal policy. He concluded that Texas' policy making processes were fully capable of achieving the goal of clean water without federal intervention, while the federal policy was completely inappropriate for Wyoming. And only parts of the federal policy influenced New York's and Washington State's policy making process to the benefit of cleaner water.[38]

In a somewhat more detailed examination of the implementation or administrative apparatus of some states, Haskell and Price looked at the executive branch environmental management agencies in Illinois, Maine, Maryland, Michigan, Minnesota, New York, Vermont, Washington, and Wisconsin.[39] Although their state-by-state analysis is much too lengthy to summarize here, it is an important attempt to examine all of the "environmental" agencies in these states to ascertain whether there seem to be specific organizational frameworks that are able to produce more effective environmental policy implementation. They suggest that the kinds of organizational structures states choose largely reflect their commitment to environmental problems, with the most committed having a more unified administrative arrangement. In other words, states that take seriously the challenge of cleaning up the environment are likely to have one or two major agencies with full responsibility for the environment rather than a larger number of agencies. Haskell and Price do argue that creating what they call super departments—combining pollution controls with conservation, land use, and resource management programs—leads to more political conflict at the implementation stage than creating a regular department responsible for pollution policy implementation separate from the other functions.[40]

Environmental Policy as Protective Regulatory Policy

As we noted in Chapter 1, some policy making process researchers have begun to use Lowi's policy typology (distributive, regulatory, redistributive, and structural policies) in their attempts to discern different policy making process

[38] Harvey Lieber, *Federalism and Clean Waters: The 1972 Water Pollution Control Act* (Lexington, Mass.: Heath, 1975), p. 192.

[39] Elizabeth Haskell and Victoria Price, *State Environmental Management* (New York: Praeger, 1973).

[40] Haskell and Price. See also Paul A. Sabatier, "State and Local Environmental Policy: A Modest Review of Past Efforts and Future Topics," in Stuart Nagel, ed., *Environmental Politics* (New York: Praeger, 1974), pp. 160–73.

patterns. Ripley and Franklin have used this typology extensively, and they distinguish between competitive regulatory and protective regulatory policies.

According to Ripley and Franklin, the definition of a protective regulatory policy is one that attempts to regulate private activities for the presumed protection of the general public or major segments of it. In their view, much of what we call environmental policy is protective regulatory policy. For example, our federal government attempts to limit the amount of air pollution being emitted (effluent emissions) by private-sector industrial plants in order to protect the quality of the air that all people breathe; most states attempt to limit the kinds of wastes and chemicals that businesses can dump into rivers and streams in order to protect the quality of everyone's water supply.

But what does knowing that environmental policy is protective regulatory policy tell us? According to Ripley and Franklin, there is a strong tendency for these policies to exhibit a somewhat different set of policy making and political processes than other types of policies. We will first take a brief look at what Ripley and Franklin suggest are some of the important characteristics of protective regulatory policy making processes, and then we will look at a specific example of environmental policy.

Ripley and Franklin tell us that protective regulatory policies tend to have political processes that are very visible and volatile. In their words:

> as policies are debated, those entities targeted for regulation are very conscious of what they think is at stake for them. Most [targets of regulation] would prefer to avoid government regulation altogether. But where regulation seems inevitable, they pursue options designed to make the regulation as light as possible or to acquire governmentally conferred benefits [in other areas] as a form of compensation.[41]

Other characteristics of protective regulatory policies include:

> Coalitions of groups involved in decisions are unstable and change over time;
> Groups tend to relate to Congress at the level of the full House or the full Senate rather than at the level of the committees or subcommittees;
> Conflict often arises when some members of Congress try to get exceptions to regulations for special clients and some bureaucrats oppose those exceptions.

Ripley and Franklin provide a particularly illustrative example of these processes in the operation of the EPA during 1974. Due to the 1973 energy crisis, the EPA had to try to resolve the apparent conflict between preserving

---

[41] Randall Ripley and Grace Franklin, *Congress, the Bureaucracy, and Public Policy* (Homewood, Ill.: Dorsey Press, 1979), p. 123.

the environment and increasing domestic sources of energy. (We will examine federal energy policy in more detail in Chapter 3.) The White House and the Federal Energy Office, supported by regulated industries, wanted major exceptions to meeting clean air standards. So the EPA set out to draft amendments to the 1970 Clean Air Act that would delay the strict air quality standards so that domestic coal (which burns dirty) could be substituted for relatively cleaner foreign oil. The EPA did not want to sacrifice clean air, but it was opposed in its efforts first by the White House and the Federal Energy Office and then by members of the House of Representatives. The final compromise was in favor of maintaining the tougher controls supported by the EPA and many members of the Senate.[42] In short, the EPA was successful in fending off the attempt to force it to grant major exceptions to the original legislation.

Although our discussion of the policy making process approach has not covered all of the relevant studies in the field, it has provided a glimpse of this approach to public policy analysis. We can now turn our attention to the causes and consequences approach of public policy analysis.

SOME CAUSES AND CONSEQUENCES
OF ENVIRONMENTAL POLICIES

Although it is probably true that there has been much less environmental policy causes and consequences research conducted than policy making process or policy prescription research, even so there are several important studies that we should discuss. But first, we should refresh our memory about what policy causes and consequences research is.

When we discussed the public policy causes and consequences approach in Chapter 1, we talked in terms of policy outputs and policy outcomes. Although it may have been difficult to explain exactly what these outputs and outcomes are, we can now be more specific by applying the terms to environmental issues. In our general discussion, we noted that policy outputs are usually public policy decisions themselves or characteristics of those decisions. The effects of those policy outputs, whether intended or unintended, are considered policy outcomes. The factors (usually called variables) that are causally related to outputs and outcomes are usually referred to as policy inputs. With these terms in mind, we can take a look at a few studies that use this approach to environmental policy analysis. Along the way, we will see what kinds of specific environmental policy outputs and outcomes have been used.

[42] Ripley and Franklin, pp. 145–46. See also Matthew Holden, *Pollution Control As a Bargaining Process* (Ithaca, N.Y.: Cornell University Press, 1966).

Environmental Policy Outputs
and Outcomes in Water Quality Control

One of the more important areas of environmental policy deals with efforts to protect and improve the quality of our various water supplies. Several studies have examined the factors that seem to be related to decisions (outputs) and to actual improvements in water quality (outcomes).

In one study, Caldwell with Roos looked at pollution control efforts in lower Lake Michigan between 1965 and 1969.[43] They were most interested in determining whether there was a causal link between the decision (output) negotiated with several major industrial corporations to make significant reductions in their effluent discharges (contamination being dumped into the lake) and actual improvements in the quality of the water thereafter.[44] They found that there was no general reduction in the amount of pollution being discharged and no pattern of improvement in the quality of water. Their findings, therefore, called into question the efficacy of depending on voluntary compliance schedules.

Perhaps the most explicit cause and consequence study dealing with water quality is that by Lettie Wenner.[45] Wenner's analysis focused on the enforcement efforts of water pollution control laws in the states, and the effect of these efforts on the quality of water. Her public policy variables included:

ENVIRONMENTAL POLICY OUTPUTS

Extent of water pollution enforcement effort in the states;
Strictness of water pollution quality standards set by the state environmental agencies;
Amount of resources devoted by the states to control water pollution;
Strictness of the law passed by state legislatures.

ENVIRONMENTAL POLICY OUTCOME

Improvement in water quality.

[43] Ted W. Caldwell with Leslie L. Roos, Jr., "Voluntary Compliance and Pollution Abatement," in Leslie L. Roos, Jr., ed., *The Politics of Ecosuicide* (New York: Holt, Rinehart & Winston, 1971). See also Leslie L. Roos, Jr., and Hal J. Bohner, "Compliance, Pollution, and Evaluation," in James A. Caporaso and Leslie L. Roos, Jr., eds., *Quasi-Experimental Approaches: Testing Theory and Evaluating Policy* (Evanston, Ill: Northwestern University Press, 1973), pp. 271–80.

[44] Roos and Bohner, p. 275.

[45] Lettie M. Wenner, "Enforcement of Water Pollution Control Laws," *Law and Society Review*, Vol. 6, May 1972, pp. 481–507. For another cause and consequence study, see J. C. Jones et al., "The Relative Importance of Variables in Water Resources Planning," *Water Resources Research*, Vol. 5, No. 6, Dec. 1969, pp. 1165–73.

Her analysis uncovered some interesting patterns,[46] summarized in Table 2.3 as an implied causal diagram. The arrows show which factors are related to environmental policy outcomes and outputs. Wenner found that the most important influences on the extent of the enforcement effort were the amount of resources expended and the strictness of the law under which administrative agencies operated. The strongest influences on the strictness of the administrative standards developed by the agencies were the strictness of the law and having antipollution interest groups represented on the governing advisory board.

Perhaps most important, the strongest influences on improvements in the quality of water were the extent of the enforcement effort and the specificity of the water quality standards. She also found that the presence of major polluting interests in the states influenced the states to enact stricter laws and to make greater enforcement efforts. In looking at the effects of the seriousness of the original water pollution problem, she found that the more serious the problem, the greater was the enforcement effort, although it had no effect on the strictness of the law, the amount of resources expended, or the strictness

TABLE 2.3. Causal Diagram Implied by Wenner's Analysis*

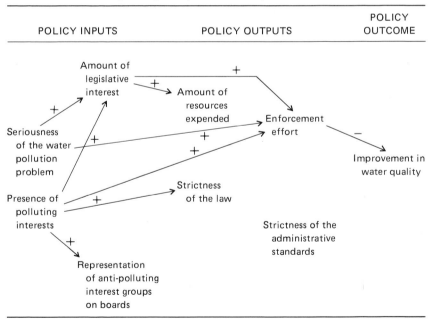

*Derived from the results presented in Lettie M. Wenner, "Enforcement of Water Pollution Control Laws," *Law and Society Review,* May 1972, pp. 481–507.

[46] Wenner's methodology was really not well suited to causal modeling because the analysis consisted entirely of bivariate correlations.

of the standards. These results begin to help us build a picture of how the various factors fit together. We can also examine similar research in the area of air pollution.

**Public Air Pollution Policy
Outputs and Outcomes**

A similar analysis of policy outputs in the area of air pollution was conducted by Kingsley Game.[47] In Game's study, the focus was on identifying factors that were related to three policy outputs as a result of the 1970 Clean Air Act Amendments. The specific outputs he examined were:

> Amount of effort the states made in controlling air pollution;
> Amount of assistance the states managed to get from the EPA for air pollution control;
> Extent to which the states responded to the assistance provided by the EPA.

Using fiscal measures of these factors, Game found some basic patterns. He found that the states that made greater efforts in air pollution control were the states that had developed some type of sub-state agencies for delegation of air pollution control. They were also the states that tended to be more bureaucratized, those with accessible energy resources and more dense populations. The states that received more assistance from the EPA were more bureaucratized. And the states that effectively responded to the EPA assistance tended to be those with sub-state agencies for pollution control, with more people and more mobile residents, and the ones that stayed away from statewide environmental super-agencies.[48]

In an evaluation of auto emissions as a source of air pollution, Paul Mac-Avoy argued that decreases in such emissions over the last decade were caused more by changes in automobile design as a result of responses to economic conditions than as a result of changes mandated by federal regulation.[49] As a public policy question, it is important to know whether federally mandated pollution control equipment in cars is really responsible for causing the reductions in pollution. Reductions in pollution are obviously important policy outcomes. MacAvoy's argument is that changes in cars, such as lighter weight, improved fuel efficiency, and so on, brought about by the rising price of fuel, were largely responsible for causing reductions in auto pollution emissions. In order to examine this, Lawrence White analyzed the amount of hydrocarbon, carbon monoxide, and nitrogen oxide emitted from cars of all types. These chemical

---

[47] Kingsley W. Game, "Controlling Air Pollution: Why Some States Try Harder," *Policy Studies Journal,* Vol. 7, No. 4, Summer 1979, pp. 728–47.

[48] Game, p. 736.

[49] Paul W. MacAvoy, *The Regulated Industries and the Economy* (New York: W. W. Norton, 1979), Ch. 3.

pollutants were all supposed to be monitored and reduced as a result of the 1970 Clean Air Act and the EPA's subsequent National Ambient Air Quality Standards. White's analysis found that "almost all of the actual reductions in emissions should be credited to the regulations themselves" rather than to changes in car design made purely for gas economy.[50]

What Do These Studies Tell Us About Environmental Policy?

From the studies we have looked at, we can draw some basic conclusions about air pollution policy. Yet, perhaps because of the relatively limited number of environmental policy cause and consequence studies, it is just as important to note what we might learn from future studies.

The overriding question in these studies would seem to be whether environmental regulation actually has improved the quality of our water and air, and if so, why. Caldwell with Roos told us that negotiated settlements made between government and industry really made little improvement in water pollution, while Wenner concluded that the quality of water could be improved with strict laws and strict enforcement standards. Game told us that if states organized their enforcement operations properly and developed an administrative bureaucracy other than the super-agency variety, they would be more likely able to make greater effort in the control of air pollution. Finally, White concluded that federal regulation of auto emissions really did reduce the amount of air pollution from that source.

Future cause and consequence research could provide us with some ideas about whether other environmental pollution control policies have worked as designed. It could also lead us to a better understanding of what factors account for the fact that some states do a better job than others in actual environmental improvement. Such studies could also help us understand how public policies might intervene in the complex interactions that create pollution, such as acid rain and contaminated drinking water supplies. Finally, research could suggest more clearly what types of operating pollution control programs seem to be able to improve most the quality of our land, water, and air at the least possible cost.

SOLUTIONS TO POLLUTION: POLICY PRESCRIPTION ANALYSES

Over the past 25 years or so, policy prescription research has been the most prevalent type of environmental policy analysis. Many of these analyses focus on the projected effects of various kinds of policy alternatives. Some studies

---

[50] Lawrence J. White, "U.S. Mobile Source Emission Regulations: The Problems of Implementation," *Policy Studies Journal,* Vol. 11, No. 1, Sept, 1982, pp. 77–87.

look at what would be the predicted result of setting minimum standards for effluent emissions; others examine the anticipated effects of using economic incentives for polluters to reduce their emissions, such as imposing user charges; still others look at what is sometimes called the optimum level of pollution, that is, the amount of pollution that can reasonably be tolerated without doing drastic harm to the economy. Although space does not permit us to delve into any particular study in detail, we can discuss some of these studies to see what methods they use and what conclusions they draw.

Some Alternative Policy Prescriptions

The results of the various environmental policy prescription analyses attempt to tell us what seem to be the most effective economic instruments to get industries or people to clean up or stop polluting the environment. An economic instrument is a fancy name for any policy that would potentially create economic incentives for industries to stop polluting or to reduce the amount of pollution they emit. In general, such policy prescription analyses argue that having the government force industries to comply with minimum standards through regulation is inefficient and wasteful to the economy. So the economic instruments analyzed often are designed to let the costs incurred by any company or industry be set by that company's own actions. In this way, each company can decide for itself whether and at what level it can afford to pollute. For example, some have argued in favor of effluent charges, where a company can pollute, but the more it pollutes, the more it has to pay the government. If a company can afford to pollute, it can. The idea is that eventually the polluting company, in its never-ending search for ways to cut the costs of production, will eventually find a way to reduce or eliminate its effluent emissions.[51] Some of the proposed economic instruments include:

> Direct charges to polluting companies for cleaning up pollution they produce;
> Effluent charges, as discussed above;
> Marketable ambient pollution permits (where a company can buy and sell permits allowing total ambient quality to be polluted only by a specified amount);
> Marketable pollution emission permits.

In general, most of analyses find that these policies are more efficient, or at least have lower costs, than direct government regulation.

---

[51] A. Myrick Freeman III, Robert H. Haveman, and Allen V. Kneese, *The Economics of Environmental Policy* (New York: John Wiley, 1973), pp. 113–22.

Benefit-Cost, Cost-Effectiveness, and Benefit-Risk Analyses

In the world of environmental economics, benefit-cost research has been a mainstay method of analysis. Benefit-cost analysis is simply a method used to compare at least two alternative policies to achieve a particular end result, such as decreased pollution. The basic idea behind benefit-cost analysis is that if two policies are being considered, the policy that produces the greatest benefit relative to its costs should be pursued. As you might imagine, such studies require quantification of benefits and costs, and this is usually done by assessing the dollar values of all benefits and costs.

If we had to state a general pattern in such studies, it would be that such studies find the costs of environmental regulation to be too high relative to its benefits. In the words of Graves and Krumm, "benefit-cost analyses increasingly conclude that the marginal costs of pollution controls are orders of magnitude greater than the demonstrated marginal benefits."[52] Therefore, such studies often suggest that environmental regulation should be kept at a minimum unless we are willing to bear the costs as a society. Clearly, such studies argue that initial improvements in environmental quality can be achieved at much lower costs than improvements after these initial ones. Because the way such studies identify and quantify the costs and benefits of environmental regulation is of supreme importance to their conclusions, we can take a brief look at some of those.

Most benefit-cost studies have a great deal of difficulty quantifying the benefits of pollution controls, although they have less difficulty measuring their costs. In water quality improvement studies, some benefits that have been quantified include:

Availability of water-recreation services;
Better commercial fishing;
Improved drinking water.

These benefits are usually converted into dollar values. For example, improved drinking water has been measured as the dollar savings in the reduced need for water treatment and purification.[53] Such studies rarely look at improved health, which may be the most important benefit from environmental policies. They also have difficulty placing a dollar value on having better-*tasting* water. For the most part, when benefit-cost studies do take these into consideration, they look at the amount of money people are now spending as a result

---

[52] Philip E. Graves and Ronald J. Krumm, *Health and Air Quality: Evaluating the Effects of Policy* (Washington, D.C.: American Enterprise Institute, 1981), p. 1.

[53] Graves and Krumm, p. 1.

of water pollution (for example, to improve the taste of their water) and let the benefit be equal to the amount that they would not have to spend if they had unpolluted water to begin with.

Similar benefits have been identified for air pollution control. These include, for example:

Avoidance of human (health) damage;
Avoidance of property damage;
Increased land values in central cities.

Much more has been done to estimate the health benefits of air-quality improvement, although the ways such analyses assign dollar values to these benefits is often highly debatable. For example, in their study of air pollution control benefits, Freeman, Haveman, and Kneese tell us that

if a premature death because of air pollution is prevented, the value of the additional life is the amount of money that person will earn during his remaining life.[54]

As they point out, if we predict that a nonworking person's life is extended because of improved air quality, the dollar value of that benefit would be zero, for there is no benefit to this consequence according to this definition. Perhaps equally important, the economic value of a human life may be quite different from its social value. It may not be unreasonable to argue that one life is worth an infinite number of dollars, in which case benefit–cost analysis would not be necessary to tell us what policy we should pursue.

We can also list some of the types of costs that have been attached to various environmental improvements. The costs of water and air pollution control include the value of labor, capital, and materials that go into building and operating plants, recycling plants, and so on. These include:

New required capital expenditures by the public and private sectors for constructing facilities;
Increased operating expenses from running the facilities;
The inflationary impact of increased expenditures.

As an example of the kinds of estimates of benefits and costs resulting from these analyses, the President's Council on Environmental Quality estimated that the annual benefits of improved health, vegetation, materials, and property values from air pollution control would be over $16 billion in 1971. The estimated annual costs of meeting the then established air quality standards would be almost $24 billion.[55] Even so, the council never recommended that envi-

[54] Freeman, Haveman, and Kneese, p. 126.
[55] President's Council on Environmental Quality, *Environmental Quality, 1971* (Washington, D.C.: U.S. Government Printing Office, 1971).

ronmental regulation not be pursued because the costs were higher than the benefits.

By about 1977, the focus of environmental regulation began to rely on two variations of benefit–cost analysis called cost-effectiveness and benefit–risk analyses. Cost-effectiveness analysis is usually easier to conduct and often less debatable since it does not deal directly with quantifying benefits. Instead, cost-effectiveness analysis is directed toward answering the question, How can we achieve given environmental quality goals for the lowest possible cost? For example, such an analysis might try to tell us whether it is less costly to achieve a given level of clean air by regulating the pollutants from each of a manufacturing company's smokestacks or by just requiring that the total pollutants being emitted from the entire factory must meet a certain standard. In other words, we could regulate either emissions from each stack or the total emissions from the entire plant, letting the company decide which stacks to clean up. The latter, it has been argued, is able to achieve the same result, cleaner air, at a lower cost.[56]

A good example of cost-effectiveness analysis is presented in Weinstein's study of toxic substances control.[57] Weinstein attempts to systematically identify some situations where fairly expensive policy decisions should be made in favor of regulating possible cancer-causing pollutants. He suggests that decision makers, especially agency officials, should focus their resources on three major situations:

Where no tests have been conducted to examine for the presence of carcinogenic substances and no regulations are in effect;

Where tests have been conducted and carcinogens have been found and where no regulations exist;

Where tests have been conducted and carcinogens have not been found and where no regulations exist.

According to Weinstein's analysis, these are the situations where resources can be used most cost-effectively.

Benefit–risk analysis attempts to tell us whether the environmental risks associated with particular policies (such as licensing nuclear power plants) seem to be outweighed by the benefits provided by these policies. It focuses on benefits and risks as consequences that can be traded off against each other. In other

[56] Winston Harrington and Alan J. Krupnick, "Stationary Source Pollution Policy and Choices for Reform," in Henry M. Peskin, Paul R. Portney, and Allen V. Kneese, eds., *Environmental Regulation and the U.S. Economy* (Baltimore: Johns Hopkins University Press, 1981), pp. 105–30. See also Robert E. Kohn, "A Cost-Effectiveness Model for Air Pollution Control with a Single Stochastic Variable," *Journal of the American Statistical Association,* Vol. 67, No. 337, March 1972, pp. 19–22.

[57] Milton C. Weinstein, "Decision Making for Toxic Substances Control: Cost-Effective Information Development for the Control of Environmental Carcinogens," *Public Policy,* Vol. 27, No. 3, Summer 1979, 333–83.

words, we might be able to obtain increased benefits by pursuing fairly dangerous policies, but we might be able to reduce the risks only by living with fewer benefits. As an example of this kind of research, Haefele looked at whether the benefits from nuclear electricity generation seem to outweigh the risks of nuclear accident.[58] His analysis suggests that the benefits might well be worth the risks.

The Optimum Level of Pollution

Another way environmental pollution policies have been prescribed is through systematic analyses of the optimum level of pollution, that level of pollution (and pollution control) that can produce the best environment with the least harm to the economy. This type of analysis suggests that to have a perfectly clean environment would probably bring the nation's (even the world's) economy to a standstill, and with an unchecked economy, pollution would be a more serious problem than it is.

One technique often used to attempt to identify the optimum level of pollution is called linear programming.[59] The results of such analyses could ostensibly provide an answer to the question of how much environmental regulation there should be. While it is impossible to go into the specific details of this very technical type of analysis, it is probably safe to say that the results have turned out to be ambiguous. Some analyses have demonstrated that less regulation is better;[60] others have argued that it is really impossible to make such optimum prescriptions.[61]

A SUMMARY AND SOME POINTS OF COMPARISON

The implications of these policy prescription studies for future public policies are about as clear as those from any set of studies. Since the studies and their methods are specifically directed toward determining what our environmental

---

[58] Wolf Haefele, "Benefit–Risk Trade-offs in Nuclear Power Generation," in Holt Ashley, Richard L. Rudman, and Christopher Whipple, eds., *Energy and the Environment: A Risk-Benefit Approach* (New York: Pergamon, 1976), 141–84.

[59] Robert E. Kohn, "Linear Programming Model for Air Pollution Control: A Pilot Study of the St. Louis Airshed," *Journal of the Air Pollution Control Association,* Vol. 20, No. 2, Feb. 1970, pp. 78–82. See also Robert E. Kohn, "Application of Linear Programming to a Controversy on Air Pollution Control," *Management Science,* Vol. 17, No. 10, June 1971, pp. 609–21.

[60] Kohn, "Linear Programming Model."

[61] J. M. Marquand, "An Economists' View of Pollution Charges As Regulatory Instruments," in J. A. Butlin, ed., *Economics of Environmental and Natural Resources Policy* (Boulder, Colo.: Westview, 1981), pp. 153–61.

policy should be in the future, their results do not have to be extended by inference. The results of these prescriptive studies, however, do have some important lessons in them when compared to those of studies from the other two approaches. So we should take a few minutes to summarize and compare what all these policy studies have to tell us.

The environmental policy making process research told us how fragmented are the processes of environmental policy formulation, adoption, and implementation. The processes must account for the existence of many diverse interests and involve numerous political and administrative institutions. It also told us that many aspects of the processes, such as the nature of group coalitions, are unstable and change a great deal over time. The policy causes and consequences research told us that despite all this political fragmentation, federal and state environmental regulations really have had an impact on improving the quality of our air and water. And the policy prescription research told us that in the future we should use economic incentives rather than uniform standards and enforcement to try to control pollution.

As we focused our attention on the policy making process research, there was an implicit argument that politics (that is, the way coalitions are formed, which groups and interests are formed, etc.) is the key determinant of what kind of environmental policy we have and whether the environment improves. The policy causes and consequences research we examined tended to suggest that there is some support for that argument. Especially in the analyses by Wenner and Game, there seemed to be a direct link between political system characteristics and environmental policy outputs and outcomes. Politics does seem to be a major factor in determining how much effort we make and how much result we get in improving our environment. Clearly, the policy making process research proceeded under the assumption that there is no single best set of environmental policies, but rather there are only policies that emerge and change over time, that are the consensuses that result from political conflict. Yet the policy prescription analyses did not concern themselves with the issue of whether the prescribed alternatives are politically feasible. Instead, they only investigated what seemed to be the most economically efficient, least costly, or optimum policies to pursue.

FURTHER READING

The Environmental Policy Making Process

LIROFF, RICHARD A. *A National Policy for the Environment: NEPA and Its Aftermath.* Bloomington: Indiana University Press, 1976.
ROSENBAUM, WALTER A. *Environmental Politics and Policy.* Washington, D.C.: Congressional Quarterly Press, 1984.

Environmental Policy Causes and Consequences

MacAVOY, PAUL W. *The Regulated Industries and the Economy.* New York: W. W. Norton, 1979, Ch. 3.

GAME, KINGSLEY W. "Controlling Air Pollution: Why Some States Try Harder." *Policy Studies Journal,* Vol. 7, No. 4, Summer 1979, pp. 728–38.

GRAVES, PHILIP E., and RONALD J. KRUMM. *Health and Air Quality: Evaluating the Effects of Policy.* Washington, D.C.: American Enterprise Institute, 1981.

Environmental Policy Prescription

PESKIN, HENRY M., PAUL R. PORTNEY, and ALLEN V. KNEESE, eds. *Environmental Regulation and the U.S. Economy.* Baltimore: Johns Hopkins University Press, 1981.

ASHLEY, HOLT, RICHARD L. RUDMAN, and CHRISTOPHER WHIPPLE, eds. *Energy and the Environment: A Risk-Benefit Approach.* New York: Pergamon, 1976.

HALVORSEN, ROBERT, and MICHAEL G. RUBY. *Benefit-Cost Analysis of Air Pollution Control.* Lexington, Mass.: Lexington Books, 1981.

CHAPTER THREE

Analyses of Public Energy Policies

The idea that there is an area of public policy called energy policy is a relatively new one. This is not to say that we have never had energy policies in the United States, rather that until fairly recently, we didn't think of energy as a separate area of public policy emphasis. Instead, energy problems were often addressed within the context of different natural resources sectors. For example, we have traditionally focused on the mining of coal, the search for and refining of oil and natural gas, the building of hydroelectric dams, and so forth, as resources that also happen to be sources of energy. It probably wasn't until the 1973 Arab oil embargo that energy began to emerge as a widely recognized, bona fide area of policy concern.

Despite the events of the 1970s, we still have a tendency to look at energy issues only as they relate to (or sometimes conflict with) other policy areas. To some people, energy policy is an extension of environmental policy. To others, it is inseparable from foreign and defense policy (we will look at this in Chapter 4). And to still others, energy policy is really just part of economic development, natural resources, and conservation policy. Even though we often speak today of energy policies, we will see that regardless of the policy analysis approach employed, energy policy analysis focuses on policies toward specific energy sources or sectors, e.g., coal, petroleum, natural gas, nuclear and hydroelectric generation of electricity, geothermal energy, solar energy, and so on. Elements from all of these areas will necessarily enter into our discussion of the research on energy policy.

With this in mind, we can apply each of our three policy analysis approaches to various aspects of energy policy. Again, we can use these approaches:

> To describe what energy legislation has been enacted and what administrative actions have been taken;
> To try to understand what factors seem to cause or influence our governments to choose certain specific courses of action rather than others;
> To decide how much effect these efforts have had on the prices and availability of various energy sources;
> To learn what seem to be the best ways to improve the energy situation in the future.

As we begin this analysis, we will again see that different public policy analysts often come to disparate conclusions, at least in part because their approaches differ. But we will also see that analysts can differ depending on whether they see energy policy as most closely related to natural resources policy, environmental policy, foreign policy, and so on. Initially, we will look at research from the energy policy making process approach.

THE ENERGY POLICY MAKING PROCESS

You will recall from Chapter 1 that policy making process researchers define public policies as goal-directed courses of action followed by an actor or set of actors in an attempt to deal with a public problem. The courses of action can be said to have a number of stages of development, and these stages compose the policy making process. The stages are problem formation, policy formulation, adoption, implementation, and evaluation. We can take a look at research examining each of these energy policy making stages.

The Formation of Energy Problems

The emergence of energy problems on the public agenda provides perhaps the clearest example of a crisis-driven problem formation process. It was probably not until the energy crisis that we began to consider energy a problem worthy of action in public policy.

THE EMERGENCE OF THE ENERGY CRISIS As we noted earlier, we have not always thought of energy as a real area of public policy emphasis. In contrast, it is probably safe to say that today policy makers and analysts are much more likely to speak of energy policy than ever before. So perhaps the first question we have to address is, What happened to make energy issues emerge as important public policy problems, worthy of major governmental attention? As we look at research addressing this question, we will be examining the process of energy problem formation.

Researchers seem to agree that perhaps the single most important event leading to the belief that energy is and should be a separate area of public policy analysis was the 1973 Arab oil embargo and attendant price increases. Arab nations were at war with Israel, which received substantial military aid from the United States. Consequently, the Arab nations boycotted exports of oil to the United States, and decided in their Organization of Petroleum Exporting Countries (OPEC) to more than double the price of oil exported to the United States.[1] In the words of David Davis:

> Being unable to secure victory in real war, the Arabs turned to economic war. If American aid gave Israel an advantage on the Sinai and Golan battlefields, the U.S. would have to pay a penalty for its intervention. If, in the Arabs' views, the U.S. denied them victory, the Arabs would deny the U.S. energy.[2]

Because of the dependence of the United States on oil imported from the Mideast, this OPEC decision eventually had a stunning effect. For the first time, the American people began facing shortages and skyrocketing energy prices. Numerous gasoline stations closed for the lack of gasoline to sell. Motorists waited in lines for hours to buy what little gasoline was available. Long-distance

[1] OPEC, which was founded in 1960, includes as member nations Algeria, Ecuador, Gabon, Indonesia, Iran, Iraq, Kuwait, Libya, Nigeria, Qatar, Saudi Arabia, United Arab Emirates, and Venezuela.

[2] David H. Davis, *Energy Politics,* 3rd ed. (New York: St. Martin's, 1982), pp. 2-3.

automobile travel became nearly impossible. Natural gas stoves stopped working because suppliers had nothing to deliver. Some schools closed because of a lack of heat, and some major cities suffered through blackouts or brownouts (where lights dim because of reduced electric power). In short, the life-style of nearly every American was altered suddenly and drastically. In a relatively short period of time, the era of low-cost energy had come to an end.

These events could not help but create the foundation for an energy crisis. President Nixon stated in a nationwide television address that "no single legislative area is more critical . . . than the energy crisis"; President Ford said, "we must not let last winter's energy crisis happen again"; and President Carter called the energy problem "the moral equivalent of war."[3] Clearly, energy policy constituted an area of paramount public concern.

Although the Arab oil embargo is certainly not the only event that aided the emergence of an energy crisis, its enormous effects on energy prices continued for years to create the perception that a public policy response was needed. After the embargo, public and private responses helped to begin the great search for domestic alternative energy sources. And along with this search came new conflicts between developing these alternatives and damaging our environment, depleting our natural resources, and risking the ostensible dangers of nuclear power plants.

With these sources of the energy problem in mind, we can turn our attention to what specific responses our policy makers have developed and why. But first, we will examine how the United States found itself in a position to be so drastically affected by the OPEC actions by briefly reviewing the history of U.S. energy policy before the energy crisis, even if we didn't think of it then as energy policy.

THE HISTORICAL ROOTS OF U.S. ENERGY POLICY: COAL AND OIL   As we noted earlier, one of the ways researchers have analyzed energy policy is by looking at each source of energy separately. For example, the development of coal as an energy source has a much different history than does the development of oil, or nuclear energy, or other sources. Not only do the physical characteristics of these energy sources differ, but so, too, do their economics and politics. As a result, most policy analysts look at the different fuel sources separately.

One of the earliest U.S. sources of energy was coal. At least partly because of the economics of coal, it was heavily relied on most by 19th century America. Coal mining is a very labor-intensive activity. This fact, along with its physical proximity to the major industrial cities of the Northeast and the laissez-faire environment, made coal an almost ideal fuel source for the 19th century. The

[3] James E. Carter, Television Address to the Nation, April 18, 1977. Text reprinted in Congressional Quarterly, *Energy Policy,* 2nd ed. (Washington, D.C.: Congressional Quarterly Press, 1981), pp. 251–53.

fact that major coal fields existed in Pennsylvania, Ohio. and West Virginia, and that coal companies were able to mine coal without much regard for human welfare or environmental damage, helped to give coal a substantial economic advantage over other possible sources of fuel.

There really was no government intervention in the coal industry until about the time of World War I. Due partly to the economic decline of coal, the war effort, and increasing labor problems, the federal government began to intervene in the coal industry's operations early in the 20th century. For example, beginning with the 1917 Lever Act, the U.S. Fuel Administration was authorized to set prices for coal (and oil) and to decide where coal shipments would go. From then until well into the Depression, the coal industry suffered from the consequences of being unable to adjust to very volatile economic conditions, going from periods of shortage and governmentally fixed prices to oversupply and low prices. And numerous studies have argued that in times of major economic hardship, the miners had to bear much of the burden of the industry's woes. This had the inevitable effect of fueling the emergence of very active labor organizations.[4]

For the most part, government intervention in the coal industry occurred because the major producers wanted it.[5] They wanted to be protected from many of the market forces that kept them in constant turmoil. It was in this environment that the next major governmental intervention occurred in 1933: the establishment of the Bituminous Coal Code, based on the National Industrial Recovery Act (NIRA). This code permitted the federal government to work out a labor–industry agreement regulating "fair competition," minimum prices, and labor concessions. But new dissension emerged between large and small producers, as well as between Northern and Southern producers. When the U.S. Supreme Court declared the NIRA unconstitutional in 1935, Congress responded by enacting the Guffey Act, which established the National Bituminous Coal Commission, a board with the authority to regulate the coal industry.

Oil, which has had the most direct relevance to the energy crisis, began to emerge as an energy source in the early 20th century. As the technology of oil drilling and extraction developed, oil fairly quickly began to displace coal as the preferred source. This change was largely the result of economic market forces. Being a less labor-intensive industry than coal, technological advances decreased the cost of oil production compared to that of coal. World War I also marked the time of government intervention in the oil industry. In this rapidly growing field, federal and state governments began trying to break up the cartel

---

[4] See, for example, Merle Fainsod, Lincoln Gordon, and Joseph Palamountain, *Government and the American Economy* (New York: W. W. Norton, 1959); Morton Baratz, *The Union and the Coal Industry* (New Haven: Yale University Press, 1955); and George S. McGovern and Leonard Cuthridge, *The Great Coalfield War* (New York: Houghton Mifflin, 1972).

[5] See Fainsod, Gordon, and Palamountain, esp. Ch. 20.

arrangements that oil companies had developed to protect themselves from competition. But with World War I and the establishment of the U.S. Fuel Administration, federal policy had, in Davis's words, "laid the groundwork for cozy cooperation between the producers and the government," where the government agency pooled production of all companies, promoted conservation, and allocated supplies in ways that benefited the oil industry.[6]

Congress also put its stamp of approval on this cooperative arrangement between the oil industry and government. Perhaps the most notorious example of this is the 1926 oil depletion allowance, which remained essentially the same until 1975. The oil depletion allowance permitted a petroleum company to deduct 27.5 percent of its gross revenue from its taxable income, provided that the deduction did not exceed half of its taxable income. This led to enormous financial savings for oil companies, based on the rationale that oil wells, like industrial machinery, wear out. Although the depletion allowance gave oil companies considerable short-term savings, in the long run it acted as an incentive for them to pump their wells dry as fast as possible. This created basic instability in the supply of oil and set the foundation for the boom-or-bust cycles that characterized the industry. When major new oil fields were discovered between 1929 and 1931, the excess supply of oil caused the price of oil to fall dramatically.[7]

Subsequent governmental policy toward oil often attempted to protect the oil industry from itself. For example, under the National Industrial Recovery Act, an industry board was established with members appointed by the American Petroleum Institute (a major oil industry organization) to set mandatory quotas on production. And the Connolly Hot Oil Act of 1935 banned the interstate shipping of oil produced illegally above the set quotas. This was a clear attempt to have government protect some large producers against the price-slashing effects of this illegally extracted (hot) oil sold by ruthless small producers.

One additional piece of the history of U.S. oil policy needs to be mentioned: the development of the world oil market, especially in the Mideast, the role of large Western-based multinational petroleum companies, and the American responses to these developments. In some ways, it is this piece that lies at the heart of the energy crisis of the 1970s.

Before the creation of OPEC in 1960, and for some years after, the non-U.S. oil-producing nations did not control the petroleum under their ground. They had oil, but they did not have the technology or the skilled labor to extract it. Instead, beginning in the 1930s, several multinational oil companies—Standard Oil of California, Standard Oil of New Jersey, Socony-Vacuum, Gulf, Royal Dutch Shell, British Petroleum, and the Texas Company—entered into various cooperative arrangements with each other to "manage" Mideastern oil.

[6] Davis, p. 274.

[7] Davis, p. 70. For an in-depth discussion of the politics and economics of the oil depletion allowance, as well as its repeal, see John M. Blair, *The Control of Oil* (New York: Pantheon, 1976), Ch. 5.

For example, in 1947, several companies formed the Arabian American Oil Company (ARAMCO) for the purposes of exploring and developing Saudi Arabian oil. By the early 1950s, the seven multinational companies listed above controlled about 90 percent of the oil produced outside of the Western and communist nations. These cooperative arrangements exercised such tight control that attempts by some nations to nationalize the oil industries within their borders (as Iran did in 1951, Iraq in 1961) were thwarted.[8] These nations often felt that their resources were being exploited by outside interests, and they were powerless to stop it. The large oil companies were able to exercise such tight control that they prevented nationalized oil from being sold until cooperative agreements on profit sharing and control could be arranged, believing that the oil would be worthless without their technology.

Although the United States had traditionally been an oil-exporting nation, by 1947 it had become a net oil importer. By the mid 1950s, there was a tendency for foreign oil to be a threat to the U.S. oil market in the sense that cheaper oil from South America and the Mideast began to displace domestic oil and keep prices down. Eventually, the Reciprocal Trade Agreement Act of 1955 imposed mandatory limits on imported oil under the rationale that limits were good for the U.S. oil companies and that national security required them.

From 1959 to 1973, the importation of oil was heavily influenced by the petroleum industry itself. Under import quotas that the industry had a major part in setting, the Interior Department sold import licenses to specific oil companies. Because foreign oil was cheaper than domestic oil, the companies competed to obtain licenses that would permit them to import as much oil as they could. This advantage was often sought by companies through various forms of financial contributions to particular congressional and presidential candidates.[9] It has been suggested that it was this dynamic that led to the relatively important role for Mideast oil in the United States and that ultimately gave OPEC its leverage in the world oil market.[10]

THE ROOTS OF NUCLEAR ENERGY Analysts tell us that the more recent technology of nuclear energy has followed a very different path of development. It began in the mid 1940s with the development of atomic energy for military purposes. Unlike most other energy sources, nuclear energy's roots are not in the private sector: rather than private companies developing the technology and eventually creating some sort of competitive market for their product, atomic energy was developed with the direct assistance of and coordination by

[8] Raymond Vernon, ed., *The Oil Crisis* (New York: W. W. Norton, 1976). See also Blair (Note 7), esp. Ch. 4.

[9] Davis, pp. 81–82.

[10] Davis, pp. 99–100.

the federal government. Hence, there has been essentially no time during which government has not been involved in nuclear technology.[11]

The beginning of the nonmilitary role of nuclear energy is usually cited as being 1946, when Congress created the Atomic Energy Commission (AEC) as part of the Atomic Energy Act. The AEC was an independent agency, not part of the military or any other existing department, and it was given a fairly direct line of authority to the President. The five commissioners who composed the AEC were civilians appointed by the President.

By 1951, the AEC's role and operation began to change. With the request from Monsanto Chemical Company and a consortium of Dow Chemical and Detroit Edison to be permitted to develop nuclear reactors, the AEC entered a new stage in its history. This was the first time that the AEC had to take on the role of involvement in the commercial electricity field rather than control of military-related research and development. Later, we will examine the importance of the AEC's dual role of licensing commercial facilities and overseeing the military uses of atomic energy.

Disagreements about how safe nuclear electric generation is became an increasingly important aspect of energy politics and policy throughout the 1960s and 1970s. Perhaps the single most important event in this disagreement occurred in March of 1979, when a major accident at the Three Mile Island nuclear plant near Harrisburg, Pennsylvania, caught the nation's attention. Since that event, the growth of the nuclear power industry has slowed almost to a standstill. Many plant projects planned or under construction have been abandoned, although it is not clear whether this is the result of growing public opposition or high interest rates on the capital needed to finance the projects.

Recent Energy Policy Formulations and Adoptions

With the historical outlines of U.S. energy policies in mind, we can look at some analyses of energy policies formulated and adopted since about 1973. Although we will not be able to look at all of the major legislation, we can focus on several of the more important ones. (A list of all the major federal energy legislation adopted since 1973 is presented in Table 3.1.) But before we examine the research on energy policy formulation and adoption processes, we should take a minute to refresh our memories about the general policy making process approach.

As you might expect, the Arab oil embargo and the subsequent energy crisis began to alter the energy policy formulation and adoption processes. The changes brought about by this crisis were largely the result of changes in the

[11] Walter A. Rosenbaum, *Energy, Politics, and Public Policy* (Washington, D.C.: Congressional Quarterly Books, 1981), pp. 107–8.

actors involved in the energy policy arena. The decade of the 1970s witnessed the growth of a different politics of energy than had existed before. To give you some idea of the vast array of interest-group actors, Chubb has identified 73 interest groups (listed in Table 3.2) representing a variety of energy interests. Many of these interest groups became active in energy policy making for the first time during this period. We can take a look at some examples of the resultant energy policy actions.

TABLE 3.1. Major Federal Energy Policy Adoptions, 1973–1983

Emergency Petroleum Allocation Act of 1973 permitted the President to issue allocation and pricing regulations for oil and oil products.

Trans-Alaska Pipeline Authorization Act of 1973 approved the construction of the 789-mile pipeline from Alaska's north slopes.

Highway Speed Limit Act of 1973 lowered the speed limit on interstate highways to 55 miles per hour to foster fuel conservation.

Federal Energy Administration Act of 1974 created the Federal Energy Administration to replace the Federal Energy Office, which had been created by executive order in 1973.

Energy Research and Development Administration Act of 1974 established the Energy Research and Development Administration to take over many research functions of the Atomic Energy Commission. With this, licensing of nuclear power plants was separated from research activities.

Energy Supply and Environmental Coordination Act of 1974 required that developing energy supplies should be done in compliance with environmental protection policies.

Solar Heating and Cooling Demonstration Act of 1974 provided funds to study combined solar heating and cooling systems.

Geothermal Energy Research, Development, and Demonstration Act of 1974 established the Geothermal Coordination and Management Project to investigate the potential for geothermal energy.

Solar Energy Research, Development, and Demonstration Act of 1974 set up solar energy research and development projects and created the Solar Energy Information Data Bank.

Non-Nuclear Energy Research and Development Act of 1974 set up a program to investigate the potential for a variety of nonnuclear energy sources.

Energy Policy and Conservation Act of 1975 established a policy to maximize domestic production of oil, provided emergency powers to respond to interruptions in imported oil, created mandatory conservation measures, and authorized the creation of the Strategic Petroleum Reserve.

Price-Anderson Extension Act of 1975 extended for ten years federal subsidies for nuclear power accident insurance.

TABLE 3.1. (cont.)

Federal Coal Leasing Act of 1976 required competitive-bidding coal leases be made on all federal lands.

Emergency Natural Gas Act of 1977 gave the President temporary authority to transfer interstate natural gas supplies to areas of the country in need of fuel.

Department of Energy Act of 1977 created a cabinet-level Department of Energy by combining the powers of the Federal Power Commission, the Federal Energy Administration, and the Energy Research and Development Administration, and by absorbing programs from other agencies. It also created, within the Department of Energy, the Federal Energy Regulatory Commission, the Energy Information Administration, and the Office of Energy Research.

Natural Gas Policy Act of 1978 stepped up the process of decontrol of natural gas prices begun in earlier executive orders.

Energy Tax Act of 1978 imposed taxes paid initially by manufacturers on gas-guzzling cars and provided business and residential tax credits for conservation activities. (Originally part of the Carter national energy plan.)

Coal Conservation Act of 1978 required new industrial and utility (especially electric) plants to use coal instead of gas or oil. (Originally part of the Carter national energy plan.)

Public Utility Regulatory Act and Utility Rates Act of 1978 required states to formulate energy conservation programs through rate structures, authorized forms of peak-load pricing, and eliminated heavy-energy-user discount rates. (Originally part of the Carter national energy plan.)

Energy Security Act of 1980 created the U.S. Synthetic Fuels Corporation, authorized the federal government to promote production of alcohol and biomass fuels, and authorized the President to continue the Strategic Petroleum Reserve.

Crude Oil Windfall Profits Tax Act of 1980 imposed a new tax on oil producers from the sale of old domestic oil. Designed to capture a portion of the "windfall profits" oil producers received from decontrol of oil prices.

Pacific Northwest Power Act of 1980 tried to settle a long-standing battle by creating a four-state regional council to make allocation decisions about electricity generated from federal hydroelectric dams and to promote energy conservation in the U.S. Northwest.

PROJECT INDEPENDENCE Stimulated by fears that OPEC could exercise massive influence over the United States by controlling its oil, the federal government, beginning about 1974, embarked on an ambitious plan to become independent of foreign energy sources, especially crude oil. The initial Project Independence report, presented by Federal Energy Administrator John Sawhill but rejected by President Ford, called for major sacrifices by the American people. The report indicated that people would have to conserve more energy resources, even if major life-style changes had to occur as a result. What turned out to be the only lasting component of this project, authorized under the Energy Policy and Conservation Act of 1975, was the Strategic Petroleum Reserve (SPR).

The SPR is a stockpile of crude oil stored in the salt domes of Louisiana and Texas. It was originally intended to consist of one billion barrels of crude

TABLE 3.2. Major Energy Interest Groups

Environmental Groups

Critical Mass
Environmental Action, Inc.
Environmental Policy Center
Friends of the Earth
National Parks and Conservation Association
Natural Resources Defense Council
Public Interest Research Group
Sierra Club
Union of Concerned Scientists

Consumer and Public Interest Groups

Citizen-Labor Energy Coalition
Common Cause
Congress Watch
Consumers Union
Energy Action Committee
Energy Policy Task Force of the Consumer Federation of America
National Taxpayers Union
New Directions
Tax Reform Research Group

Petroleum and Natural Gas Industry Groups

American Gas Association
American Petroleum Institute
American Petroleum Refiners Association
Ashland Oil, Inc.
Clark Oil and Refining Corporation
Council of Active Independent Oil and Gas Producers
Exxon Corporation
Gulf Oil Corporation
National Oil Jobbers Council
National Petroleum Refiners Association
Natural Gas Supply Committee
Shell Oil Corporation
Society of Independent Gas Marketers of America
Sun Company

TABLE 3.2. (cont.)

Electric Power Groups

American Mining Congress
American Nuclear Energy Council
American Public Power Association
Atomic Industrial Forum
Edison Electric Institute
National Association of Electric Companies
National Association of Regulatory Utility Commissioners
National Coal Association
National Rural Electric Cooperative Association

Conservation and Renewable Energy Groups

American Institute of Architects
Consumer Action Now
Institute for Local Self-Reliance
National Association of Home Builders
National Congress for Community Economic Development
Solar Energy Industries Association
United Technologies, Inc.

Labor Unions

AFL-CIO
American Federation of State, County, and Municipal Employees
International Association of Machinists and Aerospace Workers
International Association of Teamsters, Chauffeurs, Warehousemen, and Helpers of America
Oil, Chemical, and Atomic Workers International Union
United Automobile Workers Association
United Mine Workers of America
United Steel Workers of America

Commercial Energy Users Groups

American Public Transit Association
American Trucking Associations, Inc.
Americans for Energy Independence
Association of American Railroads
Business Roundtable
Chamber of Commerce of the United States
Electricity Consumers Resource Council
Industrial Energy Users Forum
Motor Vehicle Manufacturers Association of the U.S.
National Association of Manufacturers
National Farmers Union
Petrochemical Energy Group
Transportation Association of America

Financial Institutions

American Bankers Association
National Savings and Loan League

oil,[12] to be tapped if an emergency interruption of imported oil ever occurred. Yet by 1980, the SPR contained only about 112 million barrels of oil, a little over 10 percent of its goal.[13] Despite President Reagan's initially strong effort to take advantage of subsequent lower oil prices to achieve a doubling of the SPR in his first year in office, his budget since then has not permitted much growth.

THE CARTER NATIONAL ENERGY PLAN   The first really comprehensive proposal formulated to address the energy problem was President Carter's National Energy Plan (1977). It called for major efforts to reduce the amount of oil and natural gas imported to the United States. The plan argued that because the supplies of domestic oil and gas were rather fixed and there were not many alternatives for them, the task was to reduce the quantity of energy demanded by people and industry. The plan called for reductions in energy usage through major conservation efforts, especially in transportation.[14] The principal method suggested for accomplishing this reduction in demand was to decrease consumption by raising prices. The Carter energy plan also involved increased development of nuclear power plants and rebates and tax credits to homeowners installing conservation equipment, such as solar hot-water heaters.

FORMULATION OF THE CARTER ENERGY PLAN   After President Carter's inauguration, one of his first actions was to order the White House staff to produce a comprehensive national energy plan. The staff, under the direction of James Schlesinger, was given 90 days to formulate a plan to be introduced to Congress. The result, which Carter submitted to a joint session of Congress on April 20, 1977, was a massive proposal comprising ten major programs involving dozens of federal agencies. According to Carter's 1977 Message to Congress, by 1985 the programs would

1. Reduce the annual growth rate in energy demand to less than 3 percent;
2. Reduce gasoline consumption by 10 percent;
3. Cut imports of foreign oil by six million barrels a day;
4. Establish a permanent Strategic Petroleum Reserve of one billion barrels of crude oil;
5. Increase coal production by more than two thirds, to over one billion tons per year;

[12] Davis, p. 113.

[13] Michael D. Reagan, "Energy: Government Policy or Market Result?" *Policy Studies Journal,* Vol. 11, No. 3, March 1983, p. 368.

[14] Barry Commoner, *The Politics of Energy* (New York: Knopf, 1979).

6. Help insulate 90 percent of all American homes and all new buildings;
7. Stimulate use of solar and renewable energy in more than 2.5 million homes.[15]

The formation process of Carter's energy plan is perhaps less notable for who was involved than for who was not: apparently, few of the established or emerging organized energy interests were consulted. This was considered desirable in an effort to formulate a policy that would respond more to national needs than to those of special interests, but it only had the effect of shifting the political input of these interests from the formulation stage to the adoption process itself. As a result, when the plan was submitted, Congress was flooded by competing responses from lobbyists representing the petroleum industry, the auto industry, building-trade associations, gasoline and fuel-oil merchants associations, labor, and public interest groups.

CONSIDERATION AND ADOPTION OF PIECES OF THE CARTER ENERGY PLAN   Just as analysts have traditionally dealt with energy policy by looking at each separate energy source, so, too, has Congress. Until fairly recently, there were no standing energy committees in Congress, so when legislation such as the Carter energy plan was introduced into Congress, a decision would have to be made about which of the standing committees had jurisdiction: interior and insular affairs, public works, interstate commerce, or some other committee. However, this was not the experience of the Carter energy plan.

On April 20, 1977, Congress began the process of reviewing what had become known as the National Energy Act. Ordinarily, such a comprehensive piece of legislation would be dissected into numerous component parts, often with each part being sent to a different set of congressional standing committees for review. This was not the case for the Carter energy plan in the House of Representatives. Instead, after initial review by several standing committees, Speaker of the House Thomas "Tip" O'Neill had the bill transmitted to the Ad Hoc Committee on Energy. (It was not until 1978 that the House reorganized to include a standing committee on energy.) This move was apparently designed to prevent the bill from getting bogged down in debate and to ensure that it would be considered as a comprehensive set of interrelated proposals.[16] As a result, the National Energy Act made its way relatively smoothly through the House, where it was easily passed on August 5, 1977.

In the Senate, unlike the House, the bill's proposals were separated and turned over to several standing committees. The Senate Finance Committee

[15]The entire plan is published in Executive Office of the President, *The National Energy Plan* (Cambridge, Mass.: Ballinger Publishing, 1977).

[16]Congressional Quarterly, *Energy Policy*, 2nd ed. (Washington, D.C.: Congressional Quarterly, Inc., 1981), p. 254.

proceeded to kill the Crude Oil Equalization Tax and the "gas-guzzler tax," two very important financial incentives for conservation. And contrary to one of the bill's proposals, the Senate voted to deregulate the price of natural gas. Then a series of proposals were made by Senator Russell Long of Louisiana and others who wanted energy corporations to receive the benefits of increased prices, and by the Carter administration, which wanted the government to receive some of the "windfall profits." This split between members of Congress who were free-market advocates and members who distrusted the free market permeated discussions of the legislation. Such splits were especially evident in the case of the Natural Gas Policy Act of 1978, a component of the Carter energy plan. As a study by Pietro Nivola suggests,

> With Congress torn between legislators who believed ardently in the efficacy and legitimacy of deregulation and an equally large and ardent body of legislators who didn't, it became hard— or almost impossible—to have it both ways.[17]

Eventually, partly because of Carter administration blunders,[18] Congress enacted a National Energy Plan that was considerably different from that proposed originally by Carter. In some sense, the carrot-and-stick logic of tax incentives and price penalties that held the comprehensive energy plan together was rendered meaningless in light of the energy legislation finally enacted by Congress. What was left was a very small carrot with no stick.[19]

ENERGY PLAN UNDER RONALD REAGAN   When Ronald Reagan became President, one of his primary goals was to decontrol and deregulate the American economy. The energy industries were no exception. The Reagan energy policy started with an effort to accelerate the decontrol of natural gas prices that had begun under the Ford and Carter administrations. It also consisted of a promise to eliminate the Department of Energy, as well as an unprecedented divestiture of public lands containing energy resources that could be developed.

In contrast to the Carter energy plan, which proposed to reduce consumption through conservation and higher prices, the Reagan energy policy sought to reduce prices by doing everything possible to give companies a free hand to increase energy supplies.[20] To do this, prices would be decontrolled. Federal

[17] Pietro S. Nivola, "Energy Policy and the Congress: The Politics of the Natural Gas Policy Act of 1978," *Public Policy*, Vol. 28, No. 3, Summer 1980, p. 543.

[18] Charles O. Jones, "Congress and the Making of Energy Policy," in Robert Lawrence, ed., *New Dimensions to Energy Policy* (Lexington, Mass.: Heath, 1979), pp. 185–86.

[19] Commoner, p. 21.

[20] Reagan, p. 368. See also Hanna J. Cortner, "Formulating and Implementing Energy Policy: The Inadequacy of the State Response," *Policy Studies Journal*, Vol. 7, No. 1, Autumn 1978, pp. 24–29.

regulations would be eliminated. And public lands, held by the Interior Department under James Watt, would be brought into the marketplace by being sold off for resource development. Perhaps most important, nearly all of these plans have been effected to varying degrees through administrative rather than legislative action. We will look at some more aspects of these administrative changes when we look at energy policy implementation under President Reagan.

Implementation of Energy Policies

In our examination of studies of energy policy implementation, we will focus on two major areas of analysis. First, we will examine some studies of the administrative arrangements that have been established to put energy legislation into effect. And second, we will look at the analysis of what these agencies have actually done and how they have changed energy policy over time.

THE ENERGY POLICY IMPLEMENTORS   As we have already noted, it wasn't until the energy crisis of the 1970s that our federal and state governments began to develop policies specifically centered on energy. Since that time, many administrative units have been created in the federal and state bureaucracies to deal with energy problems.[21] Initially, during the first fuel shortage of the 1970s, most energy-related activities were the responsibility of the White House Office of Energy Planning (OEP). But when the OEP was abolished in 1973, President Nixon found it necessary to appoint a chief energy adviser and establish the Energy Policy Office (EPO) in the White House.

By December 1973, the EPO all but fell apart because of an internal struggle with other agencies. In the absence of any single energy agency before 1973, several rival centers of power had developed substantial influence over energy issues. And in the early days of the energy crisis, several other federal departments decided that energy problems were sufficiently within their purview to justify their involvement. Specifically, through the Treasury Department, Under-Secretary William E. Simon headed an interdepartmental committee on oil policy. As the energy situation worsened, the influence of this committee grew. At the same time, the Interior Department established an Office of Petroleum Allocation, which also administered pieces of energy policy. It was in this context that the Energy Policy Office attempted to operate.

The intense disagreements between these antagonists over what U.S. energy policy should be led President Nixon to request that Congress create a Federal Energy Administration (FEA), which it eventually did in 1974. In the interim, Nixon replaced the Energy Policy Office with the Federal Energy Office, headed by William Simon. The directors of these various energy offices were

[21] Davis, pp. 105–6.

increasingly given substantial administrative authority over energy industries, especially petroleum. This gave rise to the commonly used term *energy czar* to describe this administrative official.

The Federal Energy Administration remained the principal energy agency in the federal government until 1977. (The only other agencies coexisting with the FEA were the Energy Research and Development Administration and the Nuclear Regulatory Commission, both created in 1974 to focus on nuclear energy issues.) As part of President Carter's original energy plan, the FEA was to be elevated to the status of a cabinet department. As we look at what the implementors do, we will see the ways the implementation of energy policy has changed as these agencies have changed.

Implementation of much of our public policy concerning nuclear energy is the responsibility of a separate agency. As we noted earlier, by about 1951, the Atomic Energy Commission began taking on the responsibility for overseeing the commercial uses of nuclear energy. Conflicts inevitably developed out of the dual role the AEC played: overseeing nuclear energy research and development activities and licensing nuclear facilities. The AEC was believed to be incapable of making objective decisions about licensing of nuclear power plants because it had developed a posture of promoting nuclear power. In 1974, the Nuclear Regulatory Commission was established to take over the licensing responsibility.

Numerous other agencies implement policies that affect energy industries. For example, as we discussed in Chapter 2, the EPA puts constraints on energy industries, especially the electric utility and coal companies, by regulating how much environmental damage (such as strip-mining and air pollution) these companies can create in producing energy sources. The Department of the Interior controls the development of energy resources found on many federally owned lands. It also makes decisions about offshore oil drilling. And the Department of Labor's Occupational Safety and Health Administration (OSHA) attempts to ensure workplace safety, which has direct impacts on the mining activities in the coal industry. But these are not energy policy implementors, since they don't have direct responsibility for carrying out energy legislation.

SO WHAT DO THE ENERGY POLICY IMPLEMENTORS DO? In a general sense, the energy agencies have had responsibility for implementing the legislation adopted by Congress. But, of course, one might argue that they do more than that. The agencies actually give the legislation specific meaning by providing specific interpretations of its language.

Most of the earlier energy agencies, including the Energy Policy Office and the Federal Energy Office, were involved more with intradepartmental problems and interdepartmental conflict than with implementing specific energy policies. In fact, there was little in the way of energy legislation for them to implement. Instead, they began the task of trying to establish their credibility, which they did with little success. For example, taking on the task of projecting oil supply and demand into the future, these agencies repeatedly concluded that major shortages were imminent and that gasoline rationing was advisable. Apparently these conclusions fell on deaf ears.[22]

Perhaps partly because the FEA operated under the threat of extinction from its inception and had manpower shortages, its responsibilities for auditing major oil companies' operations during the Arab oil embargo were not fully carried out until late 1980 (by the Department of Energy).[23] At least according to a study by Rycroft, the operation of the FEA was not only inefficient but inequitable in that it heavily favored large petroleum companies over smaller ones.[24] This contention may not be true for every aspect of FEA activities. Another study of the FEA by Regens and Rycroft focused on the FEA's authority to grant exceptions and appeals. According to existing legislation, the FEA could exempt oil companies from regulation if the regulations created "serious hardship" or "gross inequity." This study found that the FEA's use of its discretionary authority did not seem to provide more favorable exceptions to the larger petroleum companies.[25]

With the establishment of the Department of Energy (DOE) in 1977, major functions supposedly carried out by a variety of other departments and agencies were consolidated. Decisions about petroleum allocation, research, and so on, were placed in the new department. The one major exception to this was the authority of the Secretary of Energy to set fuel prices. Congress preferred to give this responsibility to the independent Federal Energy Regulatory Commission.

What, then, does the DOE do? It actually performs a vast number of tasks. For example, it establishes much of the mineral-leasing policy for public lands, a function it shares with the Department of the Interior. It sets national standards for heating and cooling efficiency, it regulates oil and natural gas pipelines, it collects data and makes projections about fuel production, it monitors the operation of petroleum and gas companies, it conducts research on new and developing fuel sources, and it administers energy conservation programs, including fuel efficiency standards, home and business heating conservation, and so on. We will look at the data collection and projection functions when we examine some studies from the policy prescription approach.

[22] Davis, p. 106.

[23] Richard Corrigan, "Who's in Charge?" *National Journal,* Aug. 8, 1977, p. 1275.

[24] Robert W. Rycroft, "Bureaucratic Performance in Energy Policy Making: An Evaluation of Output Efficiency and Equity in the Federal Energy Administration," *Public Policy,* Vol. 26, No. 4, Fall 1978, pp. 599–627.

[25] James L. Regens and Robert W. Rycroft, "Administrative Discretion in Energy Policy-Making: The Exceptions and Appeals Program of the Federal Energy Administration," *Journal of Politics,* Vol. 43, No. 3, 1981, pp. 875–88.

This data estimation, or projection, function performed by the energy implementors has been heavily criticized. In perhaps the most scathing examination of U.S. energy policy implementation, Wildavsky and Tenenbaum document how the estimates of oil and gas reserves have become "captured" and influenced by different political interests. In their words:

> estimation has become the house that Jack built. The DOE has biases and policy preferences, so Congress creates the Energy Information Agency (EIA) to get the true, hard facts. The EIA is not trusted, so Congress creates a bureau to validate EIA estimates; this bureau is not trusted, so Congress mandates special teams to carry out annual audits. Got it now? Audit teams watch over the bureau that watches the administration that watches the department that is watched by Congress.[26]

In the view of Wildavsky and Tenenbaum, all of these checks on different implementors do not have the effect of improving the implementation of energy policies. Rather, they serve to further politicize the implementation process.

Under the Reagan administration, the DOE has been greatly scaled down. Instead of eliminating the department altogether as had been promised, the department's regulatory role was substantially reduced. Much of its activities now center on the maintenance of the Strategic Petroleum Reserve.

In the field of nuclear power, the Nuclear Regulatory Commission (NRC) exercises implementation responsibility. This agency licenses nuclear-powered electric generators and monitors their operation to ensure safety. The NRC was created in 1974 to take over these functions from the Atomic Energy Commission, which was considered to be such an advocate of nuclear energy that it was more interested in promoting it than ensuring that it was developed safely. Splitting this licensing function away from research and development activities was supposed to remove the motivation for sacrificing safety considerations. In making licensing decisions, the NRC is supposed to make its judgment on the basis of the "need for power," as justified by the developer. It has been argued by Hahn that this phrase continues to be interpreted in favor of the nuclear industry even under the NRC.[27]

U.S. Energy Policy as Distributive Policy

As noted in Chapter 1, one typology of policies commonly applied in policy making process analysis refers to policies as distributive, regulatory, or redistributive. At least one major study of energy policy making argues that energy policy tends to be distributive policy.

---

[26] Aaron Wildavsky and Ellen Tenenbaum, *The Politics of Mistrust: Estimating American Oil and Gas Reserves* (Beverly Hills: Sage Publications, 1980), p. 18.

[27] Robert W. Hahn, "An Assessment of the Determination of Energy Needs: The Case of Nuclear Power," *Policy Sciences,* Vol. 13, 1981, pp. 9-24.

Distributive policies are courses of action followed by governments that have specific characteristics. As Ripley and Franklin stated, "distributive policies are aimed at promoting private activities that are said to be desirable to society as a whole and, at least in theory, would not or could not be undertaken otherwise." This type of policy is usually characterized by congressional involvement at the committee or subcommittee level by a lot of bargaining among competing interests and logrolling so that everyone eventually gains. It is also characterized by relatively stable relations among the actors over time and by very influential private sector interest groups.

Since the 1970s, much of the politics of energy policy has taken place over issues surrounding who will get the benefit and who will bear the costs of developing energy resources. Yet the benefits of energy policies tend to be distributive in the sense that everyone's health can be tied to some aspect of energy availability. The results of this type of policy are often called *public goods*. Unless relatively inexpensive energy sources are available, heat, utilities, transportation, and even food may not be accessible to everyone. Even providing national defense could be a problem. Depending on which types of energy sources are developed, a clean environment may not be available to everyone. It has been argued that thinking of energy policy as distributive policy tends to make it relatively easy for the political system to intervene "too much" in the private energy market. This conclusion has been questioned by Ingram and McCain in the case of one specific regional energy issue.[28]

In terms of political conflict, the issue often comes down to two questions. First, what kind of private benefits necessarily have to be sacrificed in order to provide such public goods? In principle, no group or person would oppose the benefits from inexpensive energy. But some groups might oppose specific ways to obtain inexpensive energy if they think they will bear disproportionate costs. For example, there was very little opposition to nuclear power plants when they promised inexpensive electricity with few risks to people. When people began to perceive that the risks were not so few and were to be borne most by those who live close to the nuclear plants, they began to increasingly oppose such facilities.[29]

Such patterns can also be found in coal policy, where the benefits to major coal companies, Appalachia, the Midwest, and the northern plains must be considered in relation to the costs of danger to the coal miners, damage to the land from strip-mining (where coal is mined from above the ground by stripping the soil and digging the coal), and from air pollution and acid rain that result when

---

[28] Randall Ripley and Grace Franklin, *Congress, the Bureaucracy, and Public Policy* (Homewood, Ill.: Dorsey, 1980), p. 21. See also Helen Ingram and John R. McCain, "Distributive Politics Reconsidered—The Wisdom of the Western Water Ethic in the Contemporary Energy Context," *Policy Studies Journal,* Vol. 7, No. 1, Autumn 1978, pp. 49–58.

[29] Andrew S. McFarland, *Public Interest Lobbies: Decision Making on Energy* (Washington, D.C.: American Enterprise Institute, 1976).

high-sulfur coal is burned. These patterns are also present in oil and natural gas policy, where the benefits to major petroleum and gas companies from decontrol of prices compete with the costs borne by poor people, senior citizens, and many people of the "frost belt," who cannot afford high prices.[30]

In some sense, what has happened since about 1970 is that energy politics has been transformed from being distributive (where everyone benefits) to being regulatory. Before the Arab oil embargo, the different energy producers received the benefits of energy policies. For the most part, the benefits going to producers in one area of energy (petroleum, coal, etc.) did not really reduce the benefits going to other energy producers. That seems to have changed during the 1970s. In a most interesting policy making process study, Chubb argued that the relationships between the new environmental interest groups and the bureaucracy goes a long way toward explaining how this conversion to regulatory policy took place.[31]

CAUSE AND CONSEQUENCE RESEARCH IN ENERGY POLICY

In recent years, there has been a modest amount of policy cause and consequence research done on various aspects of energy policy. Before we discuss some of these, we should refresh our memories about what policy cause and consequence research is. We should also try to explain the general focus of this type of research.

You will remember that in policy cause and consequence research, emphasis is placed on systematically explaining what causes some policy output or outcome or what the consequences of government policy have been. Much of the energy cause and consequence research has centered on economic aspects of energy, especially supply and demand for various energy sources. In this type of research, energy supply and demand are often thought of as factors being influenced or affected by governmental policies. In other words, when our governments decide to pursue some energy policy, it is usually with an eye toward either reducing demand (as with the Carter energy plan) or increasing supplies (as with the Reagan administration's actions). Thus, studies that examine the extent to which changes in supply and demand have occurred as a result of government policy treat energy policies as independent variables.

Other types of energy cause and consequence policy research try to systematically explain why our governments have pursued certain policies rather than others. For example, research has examined why some of the states have

[30] Rosenbaum, pp. 117–61.

[31] John E. Chubb, *Interest Groups and the Bureaucracy: The Politics of Energy* (Stanford: Stanford University Press, 1983).

been more active than others in adopting energy conservation policies. In this kind of research, energy policies are thought of as dependent variables being influenced by other factors, such as the economic, social, and political environments in which the policies are made. We can look at this kind of energy policy analysis first by discussing studies that treat energy policy as the independent variable, then by looking at analyses where energy policy is the dependent variable.

Energy Policy as an Independent Variable

As we have just suggested, much of the cause and consequence research on energy policy deals with economic aspects of various energy sources. Most of this type of research attempts to establish what kind of causal link exists between government policies (such as price controls, higher taxes, or decontrol) and the amount of energy produced (in the jargon of economics, quantity supplied) or used (quantity demanded or consumed). In other words, since decreased consumption (conservation) or increased production seem to be worthwhile goals, studies attempt to discover what kinds of policies seem to best achieve these goals.

STUDIES OF THE EFFECTS OF ENERGY POLICY ON CONSUMPTION AND CONSERVATION Although many studies have looked at how public policies affect energy consumption and conservation, we will briefly describe only a couple of them. This should serve to illustrate the kind of energy cause and consequence research that has been conducted and provide some idea of the kinds of studies that can be conducted in the future.

Two important studies have examined how federal automobile policies have affected gasoline consumption. Koznetsky, Wrather, and Yu focused on the impact of mandatory reductions in the weight of automobiles on gasoline consumption and demand, as well as several other economic characteristics.[32] Similarly, Clotfelter and Hahn studied the effects of the national 55-mile-an-hour speed limit on gasoline consumption.[33] Both analyses showed that governmental policies have significantly decreased the amount of gasoline consumed. If gasoline conservation is a desirable goal to be achieved by energy policy, then the weight limitation and national speed limit seem to have been effective ways to help attain this goal.

Another way of looking at conservation policy is to determine whether government programs have influenced people to change their attitudes and be-

[32] G. Koznetsky, C. Wrather, and P. L. Yu, "The Impacts of an Auto Weight Limitation on Energy, Resources, and the Economy," *Policy Sciences,* Vol. 9, No. 1, Feb. 1978, 97–120.

[33] Charles T. Clotfelter and John C. Hahn, "Assessing the National 55 M.P.H. Speed Limit," *Policy Sciences,* Vol. 9, No. 3, June 1978, 281–94.

havior toward using energy resources. And in a study of people's attitudes, Beck found that tax deductions for residential conservation measures, for example, were identified as being very important incentives for conserving energy.[34]

STUDIES OF THE EFFECTS OF ENERGY POLICY ON ENERGY PRODUCTION

One of the goals of recent U.S. energy policy has been to increase the production of domestic fuel sources so that the importation of oil can be reduced. Many studies have examined the effects of various policies on the amount of energy produced domestically.

For example, Mead, Muraoka, and Sorenson examined the effect that the Crude Oil Windfall Profits Tax has had on corporate profits and production of oil and gas from the outer continental shelf (OCS).[35] They found that the net profits from some 1,223 OCS leases in the Gulf of Mexico were much lower than profits from other manufacturing industries. The study states that the "windfall profits tax reduced the rate of return well below that of manufacturing industries."[36] Because lower profits are translated into less investment in production, the implication is that the Windfall Profits Tax works against the goal of increasing domestic supplies of oil.

Energy Policy as the Dependent Variable

Now that we have a basic idea of the effects of some of our policies, we can take a step backward and ask why we pursue some energy policies rather than others. Although no policy cause and consequence studies have addressed this at the federal level, several studies have done so for individual states. These studies frame the question slightly differently, asking, "Why do some states pursue certain energy policies while others do not?" Answers to this question have been sought by treating energy policy as the dependent variable. In general, the state energy policy dependent variables "explained" in various studies include:

1. The adoption of energy conservation policies;
2. The level of state funding for energy research and development projects;
3. The establishment of a statewide comprehensive energy resource development plan;
4. The creation of state-sponsored demonstration projects;
5. The adoption of tax incentives for industrial conservation;

---

[34] Paul Allen Beck, "Correlates of Energy Conservation," *Public Policy,* Vol. 28, No. 4, Fall 1980, pp. 451–74. See also Ronald D. Brunner and Weston E. Vivian, "Citizen Viewpoints of Energy Policy," *Policy Sciences,* Vol. 12, No. 2, Aug. 1980, pp. 147–74.

[35] Walter J. Mead, Dennis Muraoka, and Philip C. Sorenson, "The Effects of Taxes on the Profitability of U.S. Oil and Gas Production: A Case Study of the Outer Continental Shelf Record," *National Tax Journal,* Vol. 35, No. 1, March 1982, pp. 21–29.

[36] Mead, Muraoka, and Sorenson, p. 27.

6. The adoption of tax incentives for individuals' conservation;
7. The use of energy forecasting and modeling techniques by state agencies;
8. The establishment of interstate cooperative energy resources development agreements;
9. The amount of federal and state funds spent on energy activities;
10. The Common Cause energy conservation index, a composite measure of 14 different state energy conservation measures;
11. The Council of State Governments' rankings of the states in terms of their involvement in energy conservation.

In one study, Perry examined numerous factors that he expected to influence states to adopt conservation policies.[37] This analysis found that states that already had significant consumer protection laws and that have more professional state legislatures are more likely to enact conservation policies, whereas states that produce substantial amounts of coal are less likely to pursue policies of energy conservation. He also found that the level of affluence of the people of the states, how much energy the state consumes, and how energy self-sufficient the state is, have little influence on the enactment of state energy policies.

A recent study by Friedlander and Sawyer examined why some states tend to adopt conservation and renewable energy programs whereas others do not.[38] They expected to find that states that are more vulnerable to large energy price increases and shortages of supplies would be the states that adopt conservation policies, yet they found that this was not the case. Apparently, the most vulnerable states are just as likely as other states to defer to federal policy leadership and to lack the factual information they would need to help them formulate clear policy responses to their vulnerability.

In contrast, Regens examined seven of the items listed above as innovative energy policies.[39] He was interested in asking why some states seem to be more innovative that others in energy policy. Although there were some differences in factors related to the seven policy variables, Regens found a general tendency for states with greater energy consumption and less energy self-sufficiency to be more innovative in adopting these policy options. He found that the level of a state's affluence, industrialization, and saliency of the energy issue, as well as its climate, seemed to have little influence on innovativeness.

In a similar study, Dye and Davidson focused on four energy dependent

[37] Charles S. Perry, "Energy Conservation Policy in the American States: An Attempt at Explanation," *Social Science Quarterly*, Vol. 62, No. 3, Sept. 1981, pp. 540–46.

[38] Susan C. Friedlander and Stephen W. Sawyer, "Innovation Traditions, Energy Conditions, and State Energy Policy Adoption," *Policy Sciences*, Vol. 15, No. 4, Aug. 1983, pp. 307–24.

[39] James L. Regens, "State Policy Responses to the Energy Issue: An Analysis of Innovation," *Social Science Quarterly*, Vol. 61, No. 1, June 1980, pp. 44–57.

variables in the states: the conservation index developed by Common Cause to indicate how active the states are in pursuing some 14 conservation measures; the Council of State Governments' rankings of the states in terms of the numbers of energy functions they perform; the amount of money the state governments spend on energy policies; and the amount of federal money the states receive for energy programs. This study tried to explain these dependent variables by looking at numerous independent variables said to measure the needs of the states for energy conservation, the amount of resources states have to spend, and the capacity of the political systems to respond to these needs. Their findings suggested that "state energy policies are largely 'paper programs'—unrelated to the needs or resources of the states, and unrelated to any notion of political rationality."[40]

We have chosen only a handful of cause and consequence policy studies to illustrate how energy policy has been treated as both an independent and a dependent variable. Clearly, energy policy stands to benefit greatly from expansion of this research approach to many other aspects of energy policy options. With this in mind, we can turn our attention to prescriptive analyses of energy policies.

PRESCRIPTIVE MODELS IN ENERGY POLICY RESEARCH

You will recall that policy prescription research tries to predict explicitly the consequences of any particular governmental action so that a judgment can be made about the "best way" to achieve some desired result in the future. There is probably no field of public policy where prescriptive models have been more widely used than in energy policy. This may be largely the result of the dominant role economists have played in energy policy research, especially of models of energy supply and demand.[41] Such models have often been applied in order to predict how effective any particular governmental course of action is likely to be in promoting the goals of energy conservation or increased energy supplies.

At the same time, our study of energy policy prescription research provides us with a perfect opportunity to examine the relationship between this type of research and the policy making process. We will see that there is considerable evidence that the Carter administration, in devising its national energy plan, arbitrarily altered the existing energy prescription model used by the federal government. We will discuss how and why this was done. But first we should take a brief look at some of the energy policy prescription studies.

[40] Thomas R. Dye and Dorothy K. Davidson, "State Energy Policies: Federal Funds for Paper Programs," *Policy Studies Review*, Vol. 1, No. 2, Nov. 1981, pp. 255–62.

[41] Noel D. Uri, *The Demand for Energy and Conservation in the United States* (Greenwich, Conn.: JAI Press, 1982).

Analyses of Energy-Related
Projects or Programs

Not all policy prescription analyses in energy have been done on supply-and-demand issues. For example, Rasmussen's analysis attempted to assess the health risks associated with commercial nuclear power plants.[42] Another type of analysis, linear programming, has been used to help decide how many nuclear power plants would be needed over time, given the likely demand for power, fuel usage, introduction of new energy technologies, and so on.[43]

Prescriptive analyses have been applied to specific public programs. You might recall that the Energy Policy and Conservation Act of 1975 first established the Strategic Petroleum Reserve, a project designed to stockpile crude oil in Louisiana and Texas salt domes in case of an emergency due to interruptions in the import of oil. A prescriptive study by Kuenne, Higgins, Michaels, and Summerfield investigated stockpiling oil in salt domes versus constructing steel storage tanks and on-site storage.[44] Their analysis took into consideration a very wide range of costs. They concluded that salt dome storage was by far the most economical alternative.

These are brief examples of prescriptive analyses of energy-related projects. We can also look a little more closely at some energy models that are somewhat broader in their perspective.

Energy Models and Policy Prescription

Over the past 15 years or so, numerous policy analysts have developed models of energy in the United States. These models are intended to be used to estimate various market characteristics of energy resources. They usually focus on estimates of the prices of, supply of, or demand for petroleum, coal, or some other source. The results of these models are often combined with large models of the operation of the entire economy. Such models—called econometric—usually consist of mathematical equations that represent the many interrelationships among different sectors of the economy and numerous other factors that both influence and are influenced by how much energy is produced by oil firms, consumed by people and industries, and so on.

In many instances, these models have become tools of energy policy analysis because they permit researchers to examine what might happen if the government decided to alter existing energy policy. For example, if Congress decided

[42] Norman C. Rasmussen, *Reactor Safety Study: An Assessment of Accident Risks in U.S. Commercial Nuclear Power Plants* (Washington, D.C.: Atomic Energy Commission, 1974).

[43] D. E. Deonigi and R. L. Engel, "Linear Programming in Energy Modeling," in Milton F. Searl, ed., *Energy Modeling: Art, Science, Practice* (Washington, D.C.: Resources for the Future, 1973), pp. 144–76.

[44] Robert Kuenne et al., "A Policy to Protect the United States Against Oil Embargoes," *Policy Analysis*, Vol. 1, No. 4, Fall 1975, pp. 571–98.

to levy an additional tax on gasoline consumption (a sales tax), such an energy model could predict what the net effect of the gasoline tax would be on energy usage. While there are numerous econometric models of energy, for the sake of brevity, we will only look at a few models that have been used explicitly as public policy analytic tools.

Energy and the Economy: Some Prescription Model Examples

One of the energy models used in energy policy research is the Short-Term Petroleum Forecasting System (STPFS). This model was developed by analysts at the Federal Energy Administration to help forecast the supply of, demand for, and prices of petroleum products.[45]

Using the STPFS model, along with the Data Resources, Inc. (DRI) model of the entire economy,[46] Askin and Farman examined the effects of the Energy Policy and Conservation Act (EPCA) of 1975.[47] This act was intended to provide phased decontrol of domestically produced crude oil between 1976 and 1978. It also provided for mandatory conservation measures. Askin and Farman attempted to use the STPFS and DRI models to determine whether this act would have the intended short-term effect of increasing the supply of domestic oil while decreasing the quantity of oil demanded. They also wanted to forecast the effects that different EPCA pricing provisions would have on the overall inflation rate, growth in the nation's gross national product, and the unemployment rate. Before the policy was ever implemented, Askin and Farman suggested as a result of their analysis that phased decontrol would have little short-term impact on energy independence or on the general economy, a prediction that looks fairly accurate in retrospect.

Another model widely used by the Federal Energy Administration to project different energy characteristics is known as the Project Independence Evaluation System (PIES). The PIES model has been used to forecast how much domestic energy will be produced, how much will be consumed, how much will be imported, and what the prices of different energy sources will be. Malloy used this model along with the Wharton Annual and Industry Model to look at longer-term effects of various energy policies on the economy.[48] In general, he found

[45] Christopher Alt, *National Petroleum Product Supply and Demand, 1976–1978,* NTIS-PB-254-969 (Springfield, Va.: National Technical Information Service, 1976).

[46] Richard L. Farman and Gerard L. Lagace, "Macroeconomic Simulation of Alternative Energy Scenarios with the DRI Model," in A. Bradley Askin, ed., *How Energy Affects the Economy* (Lexington, Mass.: Heath, 1978), pp. 79–92.

[47] A. Bradley Askin and Richard L. Farman, "Effects of the Energy Policy and Conservation Act on Energy Independence and the National Economy," in Askin, ed. (see Note 46), pp. 51–60.

[48] Arthur J. Malloy, "Simulating Alternative Energy Scenarios with the Wharton Long-Term Model of the U.S. Economy," in Askin, ed. (see Note 46), pp. 61–78.

that pursuing conservation and many other energy policies have little long-term effect on the rate of the nation's economic growth. He did find, however, that increasing the supply of domestic energy sources through various policies would have the long-term effect of expanding the economy.[49]

We have only examined a couple of the many energy models that have been employed for policy analysis. Yet you can begin to see that these models may help us understand what might be the result of any given policy decision. With this in mind, we should look at how such models have actually been used in the policy making process.

Energy Policy Prescription
in the Policy Making Process

The brief descriptions of the energy policy prescription models above may have left you with the impression that they are capable of telling us whether we should pursue any particular set of energy policies. You might even conclude that if only these models could be perfected, they could take the place of politics in making decisions about the best courses of action to pursue.

These prescriptive models do, in fact, provide us with considerable information that is not readily available elsewhere. But as we explained in Chapter 1, many researchers believe that research of this sort can never take precedence over political processes in determining what our policies should be. There is perhaps no better example of how analysis can be subordinated to politics than the example of the FEA's use of the PIES model.

In a discussion of the role of the PIES model in the Carter administration's national energy plan, Commoner argues that the PIES model was manipulated in order to support the administration's policy.[50] We can take a brief look at how and why this seems to have happened.

From the inception of the PIES model in 1974, it was recognized that there could be many problems in its development. As we noted earlier, such models often consist of a series of mathematical equations representing different relationships among factors influencing the energy system. In most cases, these equations are translated into computer programs to produce the specific projections (predictions) for any particular policy options under consideration. These equations and computer programs are often updated as our understanding of the economy changes and as new data become available.

One of the major pitfalls with such models is that mistakes can be made either in formulating the mathematical equations or in translating them into computer language. In other words, the equations may fail to capture the important relationships actually in the economy, or mistakes may be made in converting the equations into computer programs. The only way that such mistakes

---

[49] Malloy, pp. 61–78.
[50] Commoner, Ch. 2.

can be detected is through careful examination by experts. For this reason, Congress created a professional audit team to review the PIES model annually. This, of course, is the process that Wildavsky and Tenenbaum found so ludicrous.[51]

According to Commoner, the review procedures began to break down in 1977. Citing the report from the audit team, Commoner argues that "at the behest of the White House energy staff, the PIES model was so altered that its output supported administration energy policy."[52] The result of the alterations in the model was to overestimate the dependence on imported oil that would occur in the future if the Carter energy plan was not adopted. Once these altered figures became part of the PIES model itself, they had the effect of distorting almost every other aspect of the energy estimates on which the plan was based. Although the model was apparently altered for political reasons, it resulted in changes in the national energy plan that were self-contradictory and unrealistic— and that were fairly easily detected. Even so, this event constitutes a most blatant example of the tension between analysis and politics in the policy making process.

SUMMARIZING THE APPROACHES
TO ENERGY POLICY ANALYSIS

Although we could not discuss all of the energy policy analyses available, we have touched upon some studies representative of the research that has been conducted from each of our three approaches. We should take a few minutes to summarize what we have learned from each type of analysis.

Research from the policy making process approach focused our attention on the energy crisis as problem formation, which led us directly to the OPEC oil embargo as the stimulus for policy change. Policy making process research also examined what responses were forthcoming as a result of this crisis, including Project Independence and Carter's national energy plan. We discussed several studies of the formulation and adoption processes related to aspects of these responses. And we examined numerous studies of the implementation process as applied to specific energy agencies.

Overall, we learned that the American political processes were ill-prepared to respond to the energy crisis of the 1970s. From the trial and error establishment of various energy agencies to the inability of the Carter administration to consolidate congressional support behind its comprehensive energy plan, the energy policy making process experienced very rapid change. And a major component of this change consisted of alterations in both the actors involved in energy policy making, especially in the emergence of new public interest organizations, and the way Congress decided to deal with energy proposals.

[51] Wildavsky and Tenenbaum.
[52] Commoner, p. 13.

Energy policy cause and consequence analyses focused on both national and state energy policy outputs and outcomes. Studies where energy policy outputs and outcomes are treated as the dependent variable began to build a picture of state responses to the energy crisis, especially conservation-related activities. What emerges from this research is a clear picture of some states responding by pursuing conservation policies, but not necessarily because they had greater need for them. The states that responded are those that are better equipped, both economically and politically, to innovate in public policy.

Energy policy cause and consequence studies also investigated how effective energy policies have been in reducing energy consumption (demand) and in increasing energy supplies. In general, policies have been found to be relatively ineffective in producing desirable energy results, with the possible exception of policies related to automobile transportation. The weight limitation and the 55-mph speed limit do seem to have reduced gasoline consumption.

Our examination of energy policy prescription research suggested that policies could perhaps be made more effective in the future. Indeed, several of these studies concluded that energy pricing policies and decontrol might well be able to increase domestic supplies of fuel without causing serious inflation. Even when such policies are combined with conservation measures, there seems to be little detrimental impact predicted for the general economy.

Finally, we saw how the policy making process can involve itself in the conduct of prescriptive policy analysis. We saw that even with precautions and checks built into the process itself, the Carter administration was able to manipulate energy projections to support its proposed policies. Even so, the attempt to do this became transparent to many of the actors in the policy making process.

FURTHER READING

The Energy Policy Making Process

CHUBB, JOHN E. *Interest Groups and the Bureaucracy: The Politics of Energy.* Stanford: Stanford University Press, 1983.
COMMONER, BARRY. *The Politics of Energy.* New York: Knopf, 1979.
DAVIS, DAVID H. *Energy Politics,* 3rd ed. New York: St. Martin's, 1982.
ROSENBAUM, WALTER A. *Energy, Politics, and Public Policy.* Washington, D.C.: Congressional Quarterly Books, 1981.

Energy Policy Causes and Consequences

DYE, THOMAS R., and DOROTHY K. DAVIDSON. "State Energy Policies: Federal Funds for Paper Programs." *Policy Studies Review,* Vol. 1, No. 2, Nov. 1981, pp. 255–62.
KOZNETSKY, G., C. WRATHER, and P. L. YU. "The Impacts of an Auto Weight Limitation on Energy, Resources, and the Economy." *Policy Sciences,* Vol. 9, No. 1, Feb. 1978, pp. 97–120.

MEAD, WALTER J., DENNIS MURAOKA, and PHILIP C. SORENSON. "The Effects of Taxes on the Profitability of U.S. Oil and Gas Production: A Case Study of the Outer Continental Shelf Record." *National Tax Journal,* Vol. 35, No. 1, March 1982, pp. 21–29.

REGENS, JAMES L. "State Policy Responses to the Energy Issue: An Analysis of Innovation." *Social Science Quarterly,* Vol. 61, No. 1, June 1980, pp. 44–57.

Energy Policy Prescription

ASHLEY, HOLT, RICHARD L. RUDMAN, and CHRISTOPHER WHIPPLE, eds. *Energy and the Economy: A Risk-Benefit Approach.* New York: Pergamon, 1976.

ASKIN, A. BRADLEY, ed. *How Energy Affects the Economy.* Lexington, Mass.: Lexington Books, 1978.

DEAN, R. J. "A World Energy Model," in Edward W. Erickson and Leonard Waverman, eds., *The Energy Question: An International Failure of Policy,* Vol. 1. Toronto: University of Toronto Press, 1974, pp. 337–49.

SEARL, MILTON F., ed. *Energy Modeling: Art, Science, Practice.* Washington, D.C.: Resources for the Future, 1973.

CHAPTER FOUR

Approaching Foreign and Defense Policy Analysis

When we study foreign and defense policies, we are actually studying a variety of courses of action in two related areas: relationships between the United States and other nations of the world, and issues of national security. While these two areas of public policy are obviously related to each other, in many ways they are also very different. Analyses of defense policies look at some of the same basic issues as analyses of foreign policy, but they often bring much different perspectives with them.

We will not try to separate foreign and defense policy analyses here. However, when we look at the three approaches to *foreign policy,* we will examine research that considers the questions:

> What are the political and administrative forces that help shape decisions about our relations with other nations?
>
> What seem to be the causes of international conflict (war), and what evidence is there that various policies have the consequence of leading to, or preventing, such conflict?
>
> What seem to be the best ways to prevent international conflict in the future?

When we discuss research from the three approaches to *national defense* or *security policy,* we will focus on the questions:

> What kinds of policy making processes have been involved in increased or decreased emphasis on national defense, especially decisions about the defense budget, and the development of various arms policies, weapon systems, or technologies?
>
> What seem to be the causes of increased or decreased emphasis on national defense (especially domestic defense spending)?
>
> What would be the most effective kinds of responses to future military attacks?

We will only be able to touch on each of these subjects, and there are other important questions of foreign and defense policy that we will not be able to examine at all. But we will begin to see how people can disagree about such important issues as whether contemporary arms policy will ultimately lead to or prevent nuclear holocaust. With this in mind, we can begin looking at some basic foreign and defense policy making process research.

ANALYSIS OF THE FOREIGN AND DEFENSE POLICY MAKING PROCESSES

Over the years, there have been numerous studies of the foreign and defense policy making processes in the United States. Most of these studies examine the roles played by various actors in the political process. Special emphasis is usually placed on the roles of the President, the National Security Council, the career bureaucrats who administer foreign policy in the State Department (especially the Foreign Service), and the Department of Defense.

Some foreign policy studies have focused on the roles played by other, less obvious, actors, such as the independent foreign policy organizations (e.g., the RAND Corporation, the Council on Foreign Relations); still other studies have examined the roles played by the so-called military-industrial complex. It is probably safe to say that studies of defense policy making usually stress the role of Congress and interest groups more than studies of foreign policy making. With this in mind, we can examine some foreign and defense policy making studies.

Foreign and Defense
Policy Making Processes

Most foreign policy making process studies consist of historical analyses of various events[1] or the evolution of certain foreign policy doctrines (such as the Monroe Doctrine).[2] Such studies often begin with a description of the constitutional assignment of the task of conducting foreign affairs to the President in his role as Commander-in-Chief of the Armed Forces.[3] But numerous analyses suggest that the President faces major constraints in exercising this task. For example, Neustadt focuses on the President's ability to persuade rather than command as a factor influencing his ability to make effective foreign policy decisions.[4] Mendel focuses on the many aspects of what he calls the polycentric world of foreign policy. In short, he tells us that the notion of polycentrism in foreign policy "simply means that there are several centers of world power and that no nation, not even the United States or the Soviet Union, can dictate to the others or settle all disputes."[5]

The policy making process stages we have referred to earlier do not apply as nicely to foreign policy making as they do to other areas of public policy. The basic reason for this is that Congress plays such a protracted role in foreign policy formulation and adoption. In other policy areas, we have suggested that there is some correspondence between policy adoption and the actions of Congress, and between policy implementation and the actions of the executive branch bureaucracy.

---

[1] See Graham T. Allison, *Essence of Decision: Explaining the Cuban Missile Crisis* (Boston: Little, Brown, 1971).

[2] Cecil V. Crabb, Jr., *The Doctrines of American Foreign Policy: Their Meaning, Role, and Future* (Baton Rouge: Louisiana State University Press, 1982).

[3] Roger Hilsman, *The Politics of Policy Making in Defense and Foreign Affairs* (New York: Harper & Row, 1971), pp. 17–37.

[4] Richard E. Neustadt, *Presidential Power: The Politics of Leadership* (New York: John Wiley, 1960).

[5] Douglas H. Mendel, Jr., *American Foreign Policy in a Polycentric World,* 2nd ed. (Belmont, Calif.: Dickenson Publishing, 1976).

In foreign policy making, the policy formulation, adoption, and implementation processes all take place more or less within the executive branch of the federal government. As we will see, this is somewhat less true of defense policy making. We will also see that there are instances when Congress has tried to assert itself as an important actor in foreign policy making, but it has done so with limited success. We will also find that the commingling of the stages of foreign policy processes has been a problem and a point of criticism. As we examine foreign and defense policy making, we will focus more on the various actors than on the discrete stages in the process.

The Executive Branch Foreign and Defense Agencies

Within the executive branch of the federal government, numerous agencies play significant roles in foreign policy making. We will look specifically at the State Department—including the Foreign Service and the Arms Control and Disarmament Agency—the Central Intelligence Agency, the Defense Department, and the National Security Council. All of these federal agencies play significant roles in helping to formulate, adopt, and implement foreign and defense policy. [There are other agencies that occasionally play important roles that we will not be able to discuss, for example, the Agency for International Development (AID), the U.S. Information Agency (USIA), and the Atomic Energy Commission (AEC).]

THE DEPARTMENT OF STATE   The State Department is the largest foreign policy agency in the federal government. It is primarily organized around geographic areas of the world, with different divisions having special expertise concerning different nations or regions. Some of the responsibilities of the State Department apply to more than one region and are therefore assigned to functional units, such as the Bureau of Congressional Relations, Economic Affairs, etc.[6] There are eight of these bureaus.

THE FOREIGN SERVICE   Included among the employees of the State Department are the members of the Foreign Service. These are the people who make their careers as diplomats to foreign nations or as contacts to envoys representing other nations in the United States. Over the past decade or two, the Foreign Service has been severely criticized for being an elitist organization, populated by "socialites from effete, Eastern seaboard, upper class families," whose views (and consequent behavior) prevent them from effectively representing the nation.[7]

[6] Hilsman, p. 44.
[7] Hilsman, p. 45.

Perhaps more important, the Foreign Service has been criticized for being unable to carry out the directives of the President. As foreign policy formulators, the Foreign Service has often been intimately involved in making recommendations on foreign policy actions. If the President decides against these recommendations, the Foreign Service has the power to alter, even ignore, his decisions. The Foreign Service has been accused of taking on a life of its own, of deciding for itself which policies (or pieces of policies) it would carry out.[8]

THE ARMS CONTROL AND DISARMAMENT AGENCY   The Arms Control and Disarmament Agency (ACDA), also a division of the State Department, was created in 1961 with the Arms Control and Disarmament Act. The agency's director was made the principal arms control and disarmament advisor to the President and the Secretary of State.[9] The idea was to make ACDA a quasi-independent agency whose director could consult directly with the President. Creation of the agency was, however, the result of a compromise in Congress between advocates of arms control and proponents of peace through military strength.

In practice—although ACDA played a significant role in the first Strategic Arms Limitation Treaty (SALT I) talks—it was "virtually excluded from policy decisions affecting conventional arms transfers and American commercial nuclear exports"[10] until the Carter administration. From 1976 through 1980, ACDA became the focal point for SALT negotiations and acquired substantially more importance in a vast array of arms decisions. Although ACDA has continued to be active in the Reagan administration's Strategic Arms Reduction Treaty talks (START), it seems clear that this area has received a much lower priority than in previous administrations.[11]

THE NATIONAL SECURITY COUNCIL   The belief that some foreign policy agencies have taken on lives of their own is not new, nor is it limited to the Foreign Service. In fact, the National Security Council (NSC) was created by Congress in 1947 to act as a mediator between the agencies dealing with military hardware and agencies involved in foreign policy making.[12] Technically, the NSC

---

[8] I. M. Destler, *Presidents, Bureaucrats, and Foreign Policy* (Princeton: Princeton University Press, 1972). See also Bert Rockman, "America's Departments of State: Irregular and Regular Syndromes of Policy Making," *American Political Science Review*, Vol. 75, No. 4, Dec. 1981, pp. 911–27.

[9] Duncan L. Clarke, *The Politics of Arms Control: The Role and Effectiveness of the U.S. Arms Control and Disarmament Agency* (New York: Free Press, 1979), p. 23.

[10] Clarke, p. 5. See also Graham T. Allison and Peter Szanton, *Remaking Foreign Policy: The Organizational Connections* (New York: Basic Books, 1976), p. 22.

[11] Fred Kaplan, "Missile Envy: Bigness Is Beside the Point," *New Republic*, Vol. 534, No. 3, Oct. 11, 1982, pp. 13–14.

[12] Destler, p. 15.

is part of the Executive Office of the President, not part of the State Department. Since 1947, it has served many different purposes, including providing the President with views on foreign policy matters that have not been homogenized by the State Department.[13] The NSC has also been used to ensure that the President is able to obtain important information that the State Department might find expedient to withhold.[14]

Under President Nixon, the NSC was developed as a sort of substitute State Department, apparently designed in part to bypass the State Department in order to achieve greater responsiveness to his directions.[15] It was also apparently used as a means to keep Congress from meddling in foreign policy making. At one point, Nixon appointed Henry Kissinger as both the National Security Advisor and the Secretary of State. As Secretary of State, Kissinger could be called to testify before Congress to explain and justify his actions. As National Security Advisor, Kissinger was exempt from this scrutiny. Whenever important foreign policy questions were raised by Congress, Kissinger simply declined to answer, claiming executive privilege.

THE CENTRAL INTELLIGENCE AGENCY   The Central Intelligence Agency (CIA) plays a major role in foreign and defense policy making. The National Security Act of 1947 established the CIA as an independent agency that reported to the NSC. It was given the sole responsibility for the conduct of espionage and covert operations.[16] Designed to function largely as a fact-finding organization, the CIA has increasingly been criticized for straying from its original domain: to gather information about other nations that our foreign policy makers needed to help them make well-informed decisions.

The CIA has been accused of actually making major policy decisions on its own (such as leading rebellions and helping to overthrow other nations' governments) and manipulating information it supplied to policy makers to serve its own ends.[17] The basic problem with the CIA has been (and continues to be) one of finding a way to hold accountable an organization whose operations must be secretive in order to be effective.[18] In the spring of 1984, this problem emerged again when CIA Director William Casey was found to have misled the

[13] Destler, pp. 99–100. See also Edward A. Kolodziej, "The National Security Council: Innovations and Implications," *Public Administration Review,* Nov./Dec. 1969, pp. 573–85.

[14] Destler, pp. 131–32. See also Alexander George, "The Case for Multiple Advocacy in Making Foreign Policy," *American Political Science Review,* Vol. 66, No. 3, Sept. 1972, pp. 751–85.

[15] George (see Note 14).

[16] Hilsman, p. 58.

[17] Hilsman, pp. 59–66.

[18] C. L. Cooper, "The CIA and Decision-Making," *Foreign Affairs,* Vol. 50, Jan. 1972, pp. 223–36.

Senate Intelligence Committee about the CIA's role in mining the harbors of Nicaragua. The Senate committee had developed a satisfactory working relationship with the CIA to monitor its operations without violating its secrecy. Casey's actions were seen by the committee and other members of Congress as a breach of trust and an attempt to circumvent congressional supervision.

THE DEPARTMENT OF DEFENSE The Department of Defense is the executive-branch agency that contains the military departments (Army, Navy, and Air Force) and the Joint Chiefs of Staff. It also contains a large civilian staff in the Office of the Secretary of Defense.[19] The department was created by the National Security Act of 1947 and was organizationally modified in 1953 and 1958. It is within this department that major weapon-systems decisions are made. And, as we will see, the relationship between the "military establishment" within this department and the defense industries has been of considerable interest to analysts.[20]

Congress

Traditionally, Congress has tended to defer to the foreign policy making responsibility of the President. But that does not mean that Congress remains completely silent or inactive in foreign affairs. There have been many instances when Congress has asserted itself in specific aspects of foreign policy. And in some cases, congressional activity is affected by interest groups as much in foreign affairs as in other areas of public policy. For example, when in 1981 President Reagan sought the sale of airborne warning and control systems (AWACS) aircraft to Saudi Arabia, lobbying in Congress to support this sale was intense.[21]

Congress's constitutional role in foreign policy making is probably confined to the power of the purse and to the ratification of treaties. Although the use of treaties has almost disappeared, the power of the purse is an important function. It is here that interest groups are most likely to lobby Congress for support of particular policies. For example, in decisions to develop new weapon systems, major governmental contractors play a very important lobbying role.

In practice, however, most important foreign and defense policy matters escape congressional scrutiny. Over the past two decades or so, Congress has occasionally attempted to take an active, formal role in limiting the President's discretion. For example, in 1973, Congress passed the War Powers Act to limit

[19] Alice C. Cole et al., eds., *The Department of Defense: Documents on Establishment and Organization, 1944-1978* (Washington, D.C.: Office of the Secretary of Defense, 1978), Chart 20.

[20] Adam Yarmolinsky, *The Military Establishment: Its Impact on American Society* (New York: Harper & Row, 1971).

[21] *New York Times*, Sept. 18, 1981, pp. 1, 11; Sept. 22, 1981, p. 3.

to 90 days the amount of time American troops can be involved in overseas military conflict without explicit congressional approval.

It is entirely possible that the President could try to ignore this act, although to do so would undoubtedly create a direct constitutional conflict, something which no President has yet been willing to do. Perhaps the instance that comes closest to creating such a confrontation was associated with the 1983 U.S. invasion of the small Caribbean island of Grenada. Apparently, President Reagan was prepared to leave American troops on this island indefinitely without congressional approval in order to stem the flow of Cuban arms to Central America. As it turned out, the troops were withdrawn before the 90-day limit expired.

Congress also attempted to formally influence the President's foreign policy making in Central America. In 1983, Congress enacted legislation that would have tied American military aid to El Salvador to improvements in human rights there. Congress wanted to see military aid made contingent upon the curtailment of what have been called right-wing death squads, which many believed were operated with government approval. The Reagan administration objected to this constraint, and the President vetoed the legislation. Congress could not muster the two-thirds majority necessary to override the veto.

Most congressional influence over foreign policy does not occur through the formal actions of its Foreign Relations and Armed Services committees, rather it occurs through the informal role of critic played by individual senators and representatives. Those individuals who are able to develop expertise in specific areas of foreign policy are often able to play this role well.[22]

The Private Foreign and Defense Policy Organizations

Perhaps more than in any other area, private foreign and defense policy organizations play a significant role in shaping our governmental actions. Possibly the most important of these organizations is the Council on Foreign Relations (CFR).[23] Although many studies of foreign policy making refer to the CFR and other organizations as interest groups, their role in policy making is different from that of interest groups active in most other policy areas.

The CFR has been identified as an organization that plays a significant role in building consensus among experts in formulating the nation's foreign policies. It establishes commissions that investigate numerous aspects of, and set major

[22] Hilsman, pp. 74–76. For a summary of some of this literature, see David Alshire, *The Foreign Policy Makers: President Vs. Congress* (Beverly Hills: Sage Publications, 1979). For more specific discussions, see Alan Platt and Lawrence Weiler, eds., *Congress and Arms Control* (Boulder, Colo.: Westview Press, 1978); Alan Platt, *The U.S. Senate and Strategic Arms Policy, 1969–1977* (Boulder, Colo.: Westview Press, 1978); and Thomas M. Franck and Edward Weisband, *Foreign Policy by Congress* (New York: Oxford University Press, 1979).

[23] Thomas R. Dye, "Oligarchic Tendencies in National Policy-Making: The Role of the Private Policy Planning Organizations," *Journal of Politics,* Vol. 40, No. 2, May 1978, pp. 309–31.

directions for, official foreign and defense policy. In the words of Thomas R. Dye:

> On [the CFR] rests in large measure the decision of when to reassess U.S. foreign or military policy. . . . The history of the CFR accomplishments are [sic] dazzling: It developed the Kellogg Peace Pact in the 1920's, stiffened U.S. opposition to Japanese expansion in the 1930's, designed major portions of the United Nations' charter, and devised the "containment" policy to halt Soviet expansion in Europe after World War II. It also laid the groundwork for the NATO agreement and devised the Marshall Plan for European recovery.[24]

Other private foreign and defense policy organizations include the RAND Corporation, the Institute for Defense Analysis, and the Institute for Strategic Studies. Each of these organizations has occasionally played a similar role in some aspect of foreign or defense policy formulation.

The "Models" of Foreign and Defense Policy Making

Now that we have reviewed some of the major actors involved in the foreign and defense policy process, we can examine several of the more frequently discussed models of the processes themselves. Some researchers have assembled models of these processes to help us understand how the actors interact to make policy.

The most important of these models is often called the *bureaucratic politics* model. It argues that U.S. foreign and defense agencies are so numerous that political influence over policy decisions is extremely fragmented. This model suggests that each agency has developed its own culture (its own way of doing things) and its own policy biases. As a result, different agencies take very different political positions with regard to what should be done in specific situations.

This approach suggests that our official foreign policy is a compromise position resulting from conflict and bargaining among the many agencies. If an analyst wants to develop an understanding of any particular policy decision made in the past, he or she needs only to identify and understand the various positions of the involved agencies. Perhaps most prominent among analysts developing this type of model are Dan Caldwell, I. M. Destler, Morton Halperin, Samuel Huntington, and Graham Allison.[25] Each of these analysts has developed a variation of the bureaucratic politics model.

---

[24] Thomas R. Dye, *Who's Running America?: The Carter Years,* 2nd ed. (Englewood Cliffs, N.J.: Prentice-Hall, 1979), pp. 126-27.

[25] Dan Caldwell, "Bureaucratic Foreign Policy Making," *American Behavioral Scientist,* Vol. 21, Sept./Oct. 1977, pp. 87-110; Destler (see Note 8); Morton H. Halperin, Priscilla Clapp, and Arnold Kanter, *Bureaucratic Politics and Foreign Policy* (Washington, D.C.: Brookings Institution, 1974); Samuel Huntington, *The Common Defense: Strategic Problems in National Politics* (New York: Columbia University Press, 1981); Graham T. Allison and Morton H. Halperin, "Bureaucratic Politics: A Paradigm and Some Policy Implications," *World Politics,* Vol. 24, Spring 1972, pp. 40-80.

Analysts seem to agree that bureaucratic power is an important influence in foreign and defense policy making, but they disagree about just how important it is. In criticizing the model, Perlmutter argues the validity of the "presidential" model, where the President makes the major decisions that guide our foreign and defense policy actions, especially through his choice of staff and cabinet members.[26] This model suggests that when conflict arises among bureaucratic agencies, it is the President who usually resolves it.[27] Other analysts have pointed to the roles of Congress, public opinion, and other interest groups as being important influences within the context of the bureaucratic and presidential models.[28]

Most recently, the bureaucratic politics approach has been found to possess more relevance for crisis decisions, such as the Cuban Missile Crisis, than for more routine policy decisions. For example, Kane suggests that in order to understand most routine foreign and defense policy decisions, such as the 1954-56 decision to establish quotas on sugar imported from Cuba, an analyst must understand elements of all of the models.[29]

Analysis of Defense Policy Making

Up until now, we have focused more on foreign than defense policy making. In our discussion of defense policy making, we will turn our attention to decisions concerning the defense budget, as well as development and deployment of particular weapon systems. We will first look at some attempts to describe what happens in the defense budget-making process. We then will include a discussion of what is known as the military-industrial complex, which some analysts believe provides an accurate description of the defense policy making process. Finally, we will briefly examine some analyses of the processes that led to development of several new weapon systems: the multiple independently targetable reentry vehicle (MIRV) and the cruise missile. Although space does not permit us to look at other weapon systems, many other studies of them exist.

[26] Amos Perlmutter, "The Presidential Political Center and Foreign Policy: A Critique of the Revisionist and Bureaucratic-Political Orientations," *World Politics,* Vol. 27, Oct. 1974, pp. 87-106.

[27] D. J. Ball, "The Blind Men and the Elephant: A Critique of the Bureaucratic Politics Theory," *Australian Outlook,* Vol. 28, April 1974, pp. 71-92; Stephen D. Krasner, "Are Bureaucracies Important? (Or, Allison Wonderland)," *Foreign Policy,* Vol. 7, Summer 1972, pp. 159-79; and Jerel Rosati, "Developing a Decision-Making Framework: Bureaucratic Politics in Perspective," *World Politics,* Vol. 33, Jan. 1981, pp. 234-52.

[28] James A. Robinson, *Congress and Foreign Policy Making* (Homewood, Ill.: Dorsey Press, 1967); and Robert A. Pastor, *Congress and the Politics of U.S. Foreign Economic Policy* (Berkeley: University of California Press, 1980).

[29] N. Stephen Kane, "Reassessing the Bureaucratic Dimension of Foreign Policy Making: A Case Study of the Cuban Sugar Quota Decision, 1954-56," *Social Science Quarterly,* Vol. 64, No. 1, March 1983, pp. 46-65.

ANALYSIS OF THE DEFENSE BUDGETARY PROCESS AND RESULTS

Because issues of defense policy are closely related to finance decisions, the process of making the defense budget has received specific analysis.[30] Perhaps one of the better studies of this type is that by Arnold Kanter,[31] in which he examined numerous line-items, or categories of spending, from 1955 through 1969. He focused mainly on differences in the budget requests from one budget stage to the next and on changes in the allocation of funds among categories of spending between budget stages.[32] He attempted to discern why some defense agencies and functions receive more of what they ask for and others receive less.

What makes Kanter's analysis important is his attempt to infer patterns of organizational behavior from the agency budgets. His results indicated that despite major changes in the budget process between the 1950s and 1960s (such as the introduction of a budget process called Planning, Programming, and Budgeting System, or PPBS), the outcomes of the budget processes were not very different. In his words:

> The rhetoric of defense decision-makers in the 1960s implied dramatic contrasts between their predecessors and themselves in the use of the budget process as a policy instrument. However, an analysis of budget data from the two time periods reveals striking similarity, if not essentially indistinguishable behavior.[33]

In some very important ways, this suggests that the defense budget process resembles the foreign policy making process as conceived by the bureaucratic politics model we examined previously. The similarity comes from the implication that the defense agencies seem to decide what they want their budgets to be, and they manipulate whatever budget process is being used to ensure they achieve that result.

DEFENSE POLICY MAKING AND THE MILITARY-INDUSTRIAL COMPLEX

Despite our previous description of Congress as being somewhat more active in defense than foreign policy making, numerous researchers have described interrelations among key policy making actors that basically exclude Congress. This specific set of interrelations is called the military-industrial complex, which has been described as a pervasive influence on the nature of our national defense policy. Starting with the works of C. Wright Mills in the mid 1950s,[34] much

---

[30] Barry M. Blechman et al., *The Soviet Military Buildup and U.S. Defense Spending* (Washington, D.C.: Brookings Institution, 1977).

[31] Arnold Kanter, *Defense Politics: A Budgetary Perspective* (Chicago: University of Chicago Press, 1979).

[32] Kanter, pp. 6–9.

[33] Kanter, p. 77.

[34] C. Wright Mills, *The Power Elite* (New York: Oxford University Press, 1956).

defense policy making research has directed its attention at this particular set of political relationships. Much of the research on the military-industrial complex argues that the defense establishment, which includes major private defense contractors and industries, works very closely with the military and defense bureaucracy. All of these interests have a stake in high defense spending, especially spending on new weaponry development. Consequently, many studies suggest that our nation ends up spending too much on the military and in a sense is oversupplied with defense hardware.[35]

Several attempts have been made to rigorously examine aspects of the military-industrial complex to see if it exists, and if so, whether it exerts the kind of influence on defense policy some analysts contend. A series of studies reported by Rosen and a reassessment by Sarkesian find that the military and defense industries do indeed enjoy a close working relationship with each other.[36] Although they do not say as much, it is fairly clear that this complex resembles the iron triangles or issue networks we described in Chapter 1.

These studies offer little evidence that this kind of relationship exercises much influence on defense policies themselves. In fact, as we will see momentarily, some new weapon systems are developed despite opposition from the military. The major exception to this is the work by Gordon Adams,[37] who examined the nature of this iron triangle between the private defense industry and military procurement decisions. He contends that these patterns of relationships exert substantial influences on these decisions.

THE PROCESSES OF DEVELOPING AND DEPLOYING NEW WEAPON SYS-TEMS Within the context of defense policy making, many researchers have studied the processes of developing and deploying specific new weapon systems. Although we could look at research on the development of any number of such systems, we will concentrate on two: the multiple independently targetable re-entry vehicle (MIRV) and the cruise missile.

Perhaps one of the better case studies of the development and deployment of a new weapon system is Greenwood's analysis of MIRVs.[38] Greenwood studied numerous aspects of the U.S. Navy and Air Force programs to use MIRVs on their strategic missiles. MIRV technology took existing missiles and

[35] Gabriel Kolko, *The Roots of American Foreign Policy* (Boston: Beacon Press, 1969); Sidney Lens, *The Military-Industrial Complex* (Philadelphia: Pilgrim Press, 1970); Carroll W. Pursell, ed., *The Military-Industrial Complex* (New York: Harper & Row, 1972).

[36] Steven Rosen, ed., *Testing the Theory of the Military-Industrial Complex* (Lexington, Mass.: Lexington Books, 1973); Samuel Sarkesian, *The Military-Industrial Complex: A Reassessment* (Beverly Hills: Sage Publications, 1979).

[37] Gordon Adams, *The Iron Triangle: The Politics of Defense Contracting* (Washington, D.C.: Council on Economic Priorities, 1981).

[38] Ted Greenwood, *Making the MIRV: A Study of Defense Decision Making* (Cambridge, Mass.: Ballinger, 1975).

armed them with multiple warheads, each of which—after launch—could be sent to destroy a different target. In effect, MIRVs converted each existing guided missile into numerous missiles.

As a result of his analysis, Greenwood derived eight propositions describing decisions to develop new weapons technologies and to deploy them as part of our national arsenal. Greenwood concluded:

1. Without adequate political support, a weapons innovation cannot survive to be deployed as part of the force structure;
2. The management, techniques, and style of the Secretary of Defense affect the degree of control he exercises over the weapons acquisition process, and his policy preferences can affect the type of weapons developed and deployed;
3. The critical event in the life of a weapon system is the decision to enter into engineering development;
4. The technical community (scientists and engineers) plays a central role in the weapons acquisition process;
5. Strategic preferences and intelligence projections can have important impacts on weapons choices;
6. Mechanisms exist by which Congress can influence weapons acquisitions decisions;
7. The Arms Control and Disarmament Agency and special interest groups gain influence only through the sufferance of more central actors;
8. Significant unilateral reduction in the rate of modernization of the American offensive strategic forces would be very difficult to achieve.[39]

Perhaps the most important implication from Greenwood's analysis is that once the production of a weapon system is shown to be technically possible, it almost takes on a life of its own. In some respects, this life proceeds regardless of its impact on the real or perceived balance of power unless someone, such as the Secretary of State, intervenes.

Another fairly recent set of decisions relates to developing and deploying cruise missile technology. The cruise missile is relatively small; it can fly fairly great distances; it can be launched from the ground, sea, or air; and it may be very accurate at hitting its target.[40] Perhaps its main advantage over other weapons is that it can fly very close to the ground, easily evading current radar detection.

Several studies have looked intensively at the decision to proceed with the development of this technology. Interestingly, these studies seem to suggest that cruise missile technology was developed and added to the U.S. arsenal despite

[39] Greenwood, pp. 144–51.

[40] John C. Toomay, "Technical Characteristics," in Richard K. Betts, ed., *Cruise Missiles: Technology, Strategy, and Politics* (Washington, D.C.: Brookings Institution, 1981), pp. 31–52.

opposition from the military.[41] Rather, the development of this missile system was promoted by civilian leaders for a variety of reasons. "Secretary of State Henry Kissinger for example wanted it as a bargaining chip to barter away in arms control negotiations with Moscow."[42]

There is also some evidence that the technological possibility of a cruise missile was not the sole driving force behind its development. Art and Ockenden argue, for example, that the technological possibility *and* the political context of the Strategic Arms Limitation Treaty talks (SALT II) exerted pressures for development and deployment in Europe.[43] Between about 1973 and 1977, policy makers came to know that it was technologically possible to develop the cruise missile, but it was their desire to create an incentive for the Soviet Union to engage in the SALT talks that led policy makers to proceed with its development.

"Structural" and "Strategic" Foreign and Defense Policy Making

In the few applications of the policy making process typology to foreign and defense policy, two distinct patterns of policy making have been identified.[44] (A third, crisis policy, has been discussed, but we will not cover it here.) One of these is referred to as structural policy; the other is called strategic policy. We can describe each of these very briefly.

Structural policies very much resemble the distributive policies we described previously. They usually involve weapon systems development, hardware procurement, decisions concerning organizing and deploying military personnel, and so on. These are like distributive policies in that they have very little visibility (except in rare crisis situations) and particular groups (most notably, large defense contractors) can receive benefits without affecting the benefits of others. The main difference between structural and distributive policies is that the former are usually initiated by the executive branch rather than Congress. To a large degree, these are what we have discussed previously as defense policies.

Strategic policies deal with decisions about "the basic military and foreign policy stance of the United States toward other nations."[45] For the most part, these decisions include foreign military and economic aid, decisions about how

---

[41] Richard K. Betts, *Cruise Missiles and U.S. Policy* (Washington, D.C.: Brookings Institution, 1982), pp. 1–3.

[42] Betts, *Cruise Missiles and U.S. Policy,* p. 2.

[43] Robert J. Art and Stephen E. Ockenden, "The Domestic Politics of Cruise Missile Development, 1970–1980," in Betts (see Note 40), pp. 359–413. See also Lawrence D. Freedman, "The European Nuclear Power: Britain and France," in Betts (see Note 40), pp. 443–79.

[44] For the clearest description and summary of these works, see Randall B. Ripley and Grace A. Franklin, *Congress, the Bureaucracy, and Public Policy,* rev. ed. (Homewood, Ill.: Dorsey Press, 1980), Ch. 7.

[45] Ripley and Franklin, p. 27.

to deal with other world superpowers, whether to seek arms control, and so on. In this sense, strategic policies resemble what we have treated as foreign policy. And in general outline, these policies involve processes of the bureaucratic politics sort we described earlier.[46]

A Brief Summary of Foreign and Defense Policy Making

Although we have only begun to scratch the surface of this policy making process approach to foreign and defense policy analysis, we have shown several things. First, there are many very different aspects to making public policy in what we normally refer to as foreign and defense policy. What make these aspects different are the dissimilar processes involved in formulating, adopting, and implementing decisions in each. Decisions about the kind of relations the United States has with other nations have very different political processes than decisions about whether to build a new weapon system.

Second, policy making process analysts disagree about the precise nature of the political patterns in any particular aspect of foreign or defense policy. Some scholars may adhere strongly to the bureaucratic politics description, while others advance plausible and sometimes convincing alternatives.

Finally, it should be clear that the foreign and defense policy making processes are considerably different from the domestic policy processes we have discussed elsewhere. The relations among the various kinds of actors (the President, executive agency officials, Congress, interest groups, etc.) are configured in unique ways. With these general conclusions, we can now turn to the foreign and defense policy cause and consequence approach.

FOREIGN AND DEFENSE POLICY CAUSE AND CONSEQUENCE APPROACH

As noted earlier in this chapter, cause and consequence research in foreign and defense policy has focused on a variety of topics. Due in large part to numerous collective movements and projects—such as the World Event Interaction Survey (WEIS), the Conflict and Peace Data Bank (COPDAB), the Comparative Research on the Events of Nations (CREON), the Dimensionality of Nations Project (DON), the Stanford Studies of International Conflict, and others that we will discuss shortly—our foundation for examining causes and consequences in foreign and defense policy has also expanded.[47]

---

[46] Ripley and Franklin, pp. 197–204.

[47] For a review of many of these projects, see Dina A. Zinnes, "Research Frontiers in the Study of International Politics," in Fred I. Greenstein and Nelson W. Polsby, eds., *International Politics* (Reading, Mass.: Addison-Wesley, 1975), pp. 87–198.

Although we cannot examine every aspect of foreign and defense cause and consequence research, we will look at literature that tries to answer these questions: What seem to be some of the causes of international conflict (especially war)? What seems to be the best way to prevent international conflict? And what causes our government to pursue increased or decreased emphasis on national defense, especially spending? We all have opinions about some of these questions, but let's take a brief look at what the empirical analyses tell us.

Causing and Preventing War

The questions concerning what causes international conflicts, especially armed conflicts, and how such conflicts can be avoided or deterred go directly to the heart of defense and foreign policy doctrines and debates.[48] Numerous logical arguments can be found in literally thousands of treatises on these subjects,[49] and in the past two decades or so, a substantial amount of empirical analysis has been brought to bear on many of these issues. In some important ways, these empirical works have transcended the traditional intuitive arguments as the basis for understanding how effective our policies have been or are likely to be.[50] In other ways, these studies have not nearly lived up to the expectations many held for them.

During this period, studies have sought to identify the factors (variables) that seem to be correlated with nations' involvement in foreign armed conflict. Although some studies explicitly attempt to avoid inferring causation,[51] most of them hope to uncover patterns of international behavior that help us understand the processes whereby wars occur.

One way of categorizing these studies is by the factor or factors they consider to be the primary cause of war,[52] which we can think of as being the dependent public policy variable. In one set of analyses, war is thought to be related to the degree of conflict or disruption within one or another of the warring nations.

Other studies consider a wide range of factors as possible causes of war, among them the kind of military posture and preparedness the nations have before the outbreak of armed hostilities, diplomatic characteristics, and eco-

[48] Crabb.

[49] See Richard A. Brody, "Deterrence Strategies: An Annotated Bibliography," *Conflict Resolution,* Vol. 4, 1960, pp. 443–57.

[50] James N. Rosenau, *The Scientific Study of Foreign Policy,* rev. ed. (New York: Nichols Publishing, 1977), Ch. 8; Lewis Fry Richardson, *Arms and Insecurity: A Mathematical Study of the Causes and Origins of War* (Pittsburgh: Boxwood Press, 1960); and Zinnes, pp. 87–198.

[51] J. David Singer, "The Correlates of War Project: Continuity, Diversity, and Convergence," in Francis W. Hoole and Dina A. Zinnes, eds., *Quantitative International Politics: An Appraisal* (New York: Praeger, 1976), pp. 21–42.

[52] This is the framework used by Zinnes in Greenstein and Polsby (see Note 7).

nomic conditions within the nations. In these studies, public policies that may either cause or prevent (deter) war can be thought of as independent variables. These two sets of studies will be separately summarized.

INTERNAL CONFLICT AS A CAUSE OF WAR   During the period between 1963 and 1973, no fewer than ten major studies of the relationship between internal and external conflict behavior were reported.[53] We can think of these as studies of factors that cause nations to pursue public policies of armed conflict. Most of these studies analyze a large number of nations over some specific period of time to ascertain whether nations going to war seem to have common experiences of internal disarray before getting into war. For example, in two separate studies, Rummel examined the experiences of some 77 nations between 1955 and 1957.[54] In general, most of these analyses have found very little to indicate that internal conflict is correlated with involvement in war with other nations. Only Collins's study of 33 African nations, Burrowes's and Spector's study of Syria from 1961 to 1967, and Hazelwood's study of 74 nations reported such a correlation.[55] In a related issue, Rummel argues that nations where citizens have more economic and political freedom are much less likely to engage in foreign conflicts.[56]

OTHER CAUSES OF WAR   Numerous studies attempt to relate other variables to international conflict. Again, most of these focus on large numbers of nations over a period of time, while others, such as Choucri's study, analyze a *few* nations over a fairly long period of time.[57] Still others look at a sample of wars over a long period. For example, a study by Naroll, Bullough, and Naroll examined 20 wars selected as representative of all wars from 225 B.C. to the present.[58]

[53] Zinnes, pp. 130–38.

[54] Rudolph J. Rummel, "Dimensions of Conflict Behavior Within and Between Nations," *General Systems Yearbook,* Vol. 8, 1963, pp. 1–50; and Rudolph J. Rummel, "Testing Some Possible Predictors of Conflict Behavior Within and Between Nations," *Peace Research Society Papers,* Vol. 1, 1964, pp. 79–111.

[55] John N. Collins, "Foreign Conflict Behavior and Domestic Disorder in Africa," pp. 251–293; Robert Burrowes and Bertram Spector, "The Strength and Direction of Relationships Between Domestic and External Conflict and Cooperation: Syria, 1961–67," pp. 294–321; and Leo A. Hazelwood, "Externalizing Systemic Stress: International Conflict as Adaptive Behavior," pp. 148–190; in Jonathan Wilkenfeld, ed., *Conflict Behavior and Linkage Politics* (New York: David McKay, 1973).

[56] Rudolph J. Rummel, "Libertarianism and International Violence," *Journal of Conflict Resolution,* Vol. 27, No. 1, March 1983, pp. 27–71.

[57] Nazli Choucri, "In Search of Peace Systems: Scandinavia and the Netherlands, 1870–1970," in Bruce Russett, ed., *Peace, War, and Numbers* (Beverly Hills: Sage Publications, 1972).

[58] Raoul Naroll, Vern L. Bullough, and Frada Naroll, *Military Deterrence in History: A Pilot Cross-Historical Survey* (Buffalo: State University of New York Press, 1974).

In general, these studies have found very little that is correlated with conflict. Analyses by Weede and by Rummel suggest that the more powerful a nation is, the more likely it will get into armed conflict with another nation.[59] But the study by Naroll et al. explicitly examined aspects of this relationship and found it to be very weak.[60] In particular, they found that nations taking defensive postures are not less likely to deter war. But their results also suggest that the search for peace and security through arms buildups is likely to be equally ineffective in preventing war.

Another group of studies conducted through an effort commonly known as the Correlates of War (COW) project, directed by J. David Singer, has sought out variables that seem to be correlated with the amount of war present in the international system over a long period of time.[61] Studies by Singer and Small, Wallace, and others looked at whether nations that became part of alliances and defense or neutrality pacts seem to have more or less involvement with war.[62] There seems to be some support for the hypothesis that alliance and neutrality pact participation actually increases the likelihood of being involved in war, although a study by Levy disagreed.[63]

ARMS RACES AND BALANCES OF POWER AS CORRELATES OF WAR

A recurring question in defense policy debates is whether involvement in an arms race (where one nation builds up armaments and another nation responds by building up its armaments) tends to lead to war or peace. One side of the argument says that peace can only be attained through increasing military strength. In this view, war is deterred because of the uncertainty produced when no nation knows exactly how strong a potential enemy's military forces are, while each nation is striving to become stronger. The other side argues that arms races provide the means for nations to fight, that in the long run they increase the tensions that often escalate into armed conflict. In this view, war is best deterred by not getting involved in arms competition.

---

[59] Erich Weede, "Conflict Behavior of Nation States," *Journal of Peace Research,* No. 3, 1970, pp. 229–35.

[60] Naroll, Bullough, and Naroll.

[61] Francis W. Hoole and Dina Zinnes, eds., *Quantitative International Politics: An Appraisal* (New York: Praeger, 1976).

[62] J. David Singer and Melvin Small, "National Alliance Commitments and War Involvement, 1815–1945," *International Peace Research Society Papers,* Vol. 5, 1966, pp. 109–40; Michael Wallace, "Power, Status, and International War," *Journal of Peace Research,* Vol. 1, 1971, pp. 23–36; and R. E. Osgood and R. W. Tucker, *Force, Order, and Justice* (Baltimore: Johns Hopkins University Press, 1967).

[63] Jack S. Levy, "Alliance Formation and War Behavior," *Journal of Conflict Resolution,* Vol. 25, No. 4, Dec. 1981, pp. 581–613.

Analyses by Wallace found substantial support for the latter argument,[64] that participation in arms races indeed makes involvement in war more likely. However, a more recent study by Diehl of the period 1816 to 1970 disputes this finding. In his words:

> Only 25 percent of the disputes preceded by mutual military buildup escalated to war, while 77 percent of the wars were preceded by periods lacking armaments competition.[65]

All of these studies of the possible correlates of war would seem to have implications for the U.S.-Soviet arms race under way today. They say something both to proponents of a U.S. arms buildup (those who support the notion of peace through strength) and to advocates of disarmament. The implication is that, for example, U.S. decisions to pour billions of dollars into building the MX missile system and to deploy Pershing II missiles in Europe probably will not make the world any more or less safe. On the other hand, they also suggest that pursuing unilateral disarmament or nuclear freeze probably will not diminish the chances of U.S. involvement in nuclear war.

The Causes of Increased Emphasis
on National Defense

If we were to take a casual look at American defense spending over the last decade or so, we would probably conclude that there is a considerable fluctuation in how important national defense is viewed to be. But when we look at the matter more closely, we see that there are several different ways of measuring the degree of importance of national defense. For example, we could look at the total amount of money spent on defense (adjusted, of course, for inflation); the amount spent as a proportion of the gross national product; or the amount spent as compared to other nations.

Some analysts try to interpret these expenditures as indicators of national

---

[64] Michael Wallace, "Arms Races and Escalation: Some New Evidence," *Journal of Conflict Resolution,* Vol. 23, No. 1, 1979, pp. 3–16; Michael Wallace, "Some Persistent Findings," *Journal of Conflict Resolution,* Vol. 24, No. 2, 1980, pp. 289–92; Michael Wallace, "Armaments and Escalation," *International Studies Quarterly,* Vol. 26, No. 1, 1982, pp. 37–56. See also Stephen J. Majeski and David L. Jones, "Arms Race Modeling: Causality Analysis and Model Specification," *Journal of Conflict Resolution,* Vol. 25, No. 2, June 1981, pp. 259–88.

[65] Paul F. Diehl, "Arms Races and Escalation: A Closer Look," *Journal of Peace Research,* Vol. 20, No. 3, 1983, pp. 205–12. See also Erich Weede, "Arms Races and Escalation: Some Persistent Doubts," *Journal of Conflict Resolution,* Vol. 24, No. 2, 1980, pp. 285–88. For a theoretical discussion of the conditions that determine whether war or its deterrence will result from arms race involvement, see Michael D. Intriligator and Dagobert L. Brito, "Can Arms Races Lead to the Outbreak of War?" *Journal of Conflict Resolution,* Vol. 28, No. 1, March 1984, pp. 63–84.

security.[66] In this kind of effort, the problem often becomes more complex when one considers exactly what the money is buying. For example, an analyst might consider whether the money is buying potentially very destructive weapons or more limited conventional weapons. In this sense, it is important to know how lethal particular weapons systems are, whether to compare the United States plus its NATO allies to the Soviet Union plus its communist bloc neighbors, and so on.

Investigations of the causes of an increased emphasis on national defense may focus on any of a number of indicators. One study, to which we referred earlier in the foreign and defense policy making process approach, investigated the role of presidential and bureaucratic strategies on various defense budget line items.[67] This study (by Kanter) was interested in explaining the differences between line item budget requests and the appropriations actually made. In particular, Kanter attempted to determine whether making formal changes in the budget process had their intended results. He was most interested in the effects of such reforms as Secretary of Defense Robert McNamara's implementation of a budget process called Planning, Programming, and Budgeting Systems (PPBS).

Comparing the budget requests to the actual spending (policy outputs), Kanter was able to make inferences about whether the changes in the outputs were caused by changes in the process. In general, his analysis showed that budget outputs were not greatly affected simply by making changes in the budgeting process itself. He did find, however, that changes in outputs were brought about through altering the kinds of incentives offered within the defense bureaucracy. In other words, it took more than changes in process to change the budget results.[68]

Perhaps the more common type of analysis of defense spending attempts to relate U.S. spending to a variety of social, political, and economic factors. Most of these studies use some form of longitudinal (time-series) data. Some of the typical variables used to explain U.S. defense spending are the need to stimulate the domestic economy; response to arms buildups by other nations; and the operation of the interest group system, often represented by the military-industrial complex.

Many defense policy studies have tried to link defense spending to the needs of a capitalistic economy. For example, Smith argued that military spending is directly related to the need for policy makers to keep up aggregate demand in our economy.[69] In other words, it is argued that when the business cycle is down, policy makers respond by spending more for defense. This, in turn, has the effect of creating jobs and stimulating the economy. Studies by Nincic and

---

[66] Blechman et al.

[67] Kanter.

[68] Kanter, Chapter 8: "Conclusion."

[69] Ronald P. Smith, "Military Expenditure and Capitalism," *Cambridge Journal of Economics,* Vol. 1, 1977, pp. 61–76.

Cusack and by Cusack and Ward tend to confirm this finding.[70] Nincic and Cusack conclude in their study of defense spending from 1948 to 1976:

> If one removes the effects of war-time mobilization, it is clear that for the U.S. the driving forces in military spending dynamics were (1) the perceived utility of such spending in stabilizing aggregate demand; (2) the political or electoral value of the perceived economic effects arising out of such spending; and (3) the pressures of institutional-constituency demand.[71]

This conclusion has not gone unchallenged: Krell's study found virtually no support for it.[72]

A number of alternative explanations for U.S. defense spending levels have been proposed. For example, Ostrom examined whether defense spending responds to an "arms race model," wherein the U.S. spends more in reaction to spending in the Soviet Union.[73] Alternatively, he wanted to know if spending is driven by the needs of the defense organizations' need for stability and predictability, a theory that parallels Kanter's. Ostrom found little support for either hypothesis.

The operation of the interest group system has been posited as explaining the level of defense spending. An analysis by Cobb sought to determine whether members of the House of Representatives from districts heavily reliant on defense industries were more susceptible to lobbying efforts in support of increased defense spending.[74] He found that this relationship was not very strong, although votes of the more senior representatives (especially people with leadership positions) did seem to be influenced by this factor. However, in an aggregate analysis of this relationship, Krell found virtually no support for its existence over time.[75]

There are numerous types of foreign and defense policy cause and consequence research we have not examined here. For example, there are many studies of the factors that seem to influence the morale and performance of

---

[70] Miroslav Nincic and Thomas R. Cusack, "The Political Economy of U.S. Military Spending," *Journal of Peace Research,* Vol. 16, No. 2, 1979, pp. 101–15; and Thomas R. Cusack and Michael Don Ward, "Military Spending in the U.S., Soviet Union, and the People's Republic of China," *Journal of Conflict Resolution,* Vol. 25, No. 3, Sept. 1981, pp. 429–69.

[71] Nincic and Cusack, p. 101.

[72] Gert Krell, "Capitalism and Armaments: Business Cycles and Defense Spending in the U.S., 1945–1979," *Journal of Peace Research,* Vol. 18, No. 3, 1981, pp. 221–40.

[73] Charles W. Ostrom, "Evaluating Alternative Foreign Policy Models: An Empirical Test Between an Arms Race Model and an Organizational Politics Model," *Journal of Conflict Resolution,* Vol. 21, No. 2, June 1977, pp. 235–65.

[74] Stephen Cobb, "Defense Spending and Defense Voting in the House: An Empirical Study of an Aspect of the Military–Industrial Complex Thesis," *American Journal of Sociology,* Vol. 82, No. 1, July 1976, pp. 163–82.

[75] Krell, pp. 221–40.

military personnel.[76] One important study also examined the unintended consequences of military service in Vietnam for soldiers.[77] There are also studies of the relationship between defense spending and national security. But we have covered some of the better-developed areas of cause and consequence analysis as applied to issues of foreign and defense policy.

PRESCRIPTIVE FOREIGN AND DEFENSE POLICY ANALYSES

Although most foreign policy is not established on the basis of elaborate prescriptive analyses, recent developments in this type of research offer some promise for the future. Initially, we will look at how some prescriptive techniques have been used in strategic analysis. Then we will examine some very specialized models used to simulate actual armed attacks and to prescribe particular courses of action in response. Finally, we will briefly examine the more comprehensive attempts to develop global simulation models, especially directed toward predicting international stability or instability.

Prescriptive Strategic Analyses

Most prescriptive strategic analyses attempt to deal with some very complex issues related to the need for, or desirability of obtaining, various types of new weapon systems. These analyses often begin with an assumption about the goal of defense policy in general. For example, a study might begin its analysis by stating that it assumes the goal of defense policy is to establish some sort of parity with the Soviet Union. The analysis then might proceed to try to determine whether some particular weapon system (such as the MX missile or the B-1 bomber) will provide that parity.

Alternatively, some studies rely on one or another form of benefit–cost, or cost-effectiveness, analysis. Among the literally thousands of such studies, we will look at only a few to illustrate the policy prescription approach. Some of these studies may strike you as being extremely narrow and technical, perhaps even relatively unimportant in terms of overall foreign and defense policy. Yet these studies often lie at the heart of questions about whether our defense capabilities provide a balance of power, or weapons parity, or even whether there is such a thing as weapons superiority. This type of study may also have important implications concerning the justification of the use of force as a defense policy doctrine, since this doctrine implies the ability to use force.

[76] Richard Cooper, *Military Manpower and the All-Volunteer Force* (Santa Monica: RAND Corp., 1977); and Richard Cooper, ed., *Defense Manpower Policy* (Santa Monica: RAND Corp., 1980).

[77] Arthur Egendorf et al., *Legacies of Vietnam: Comparative Adjustments of Veterans and Their Peers* (New York: Vietnam Era Research Project, Center for Policy Research, 1981).

Perhaps the most important characteristic of prescriptive studies is that the value placed on every aspect of a weapon system under analysis must be made explicit. If a particular study makes an error in assessing the benefits to be obtained from one or another alternative weapon, this error may well lead to an erroneous conclusion about what our weapons policy should be. But unlike many other forms of analysis, prescriptive conclusions can be reassessed after errors have been identified and corrected. Keep in mind, however, that the commission of an error in a study does not necessarily make its conclusions wrong. It may be that the conclusions of a study are not sensitive to such an error. Indeed, the critical reading of these studies includes understanding how important specific assessments are to the studies' conclusions.

ANALYSIS OF THE B-1 BOMBER A particularly clear example of this type of study can be found in Francis Hoeber's cost-effectiveness analysis of the B-1 bomber,[78] in which he compares the future development of a B-1 bomber to six alternatives. This analysis is based on the assumptions that the purpose of U.S. strategic policy is to deter nuclear war and that weapons parity or superiority is necessary to maintain this deterrence.[79] Hoeber's six alternatives to building and deploying the B-1 bomber are: (1) building no new bomber, relying instead on ballistic missiles; (2) modifying the currently used B-52 bomber; (3) developing some other new, unspecified bomber; (4) relying only on the currently developed FB-111 as a strategic bomber; (5) substituting air-launched cruise missiles for bombers; and (6) developing some mixture of these alternatives.[80]

After assessing the costs and capabilities of each of these options, Hoeber concludes that the B-1 should be built. A careful reading of this analysis identifies numerous points at which it could be flawed. For example, he states that he has excluded "economic arguments" about the most effective way to create jobs and "social arguments" about the alternative uses of funds for nonmilitary programs because they are "not relevant to the strategic choices before the country."[81] While this is true within the context of Hoeber's assumptions about the need for increased strategic forces, such excluded considerations may well be important to policy makers deciding whether to spend the money. Another example is Hoeber's choice of discount rate. In assessing what is known as the "net present value of the future costs" of various weapons systems, he adopts a 10 percent discount factor[82] with no justification other than it is "reasonable and widely-accepted."[83] If he had adopted another discount rate, such as 12 percent or 7 percent, his results may well have been affected.

[78] Francis P. Hoeber, *Slow to Take Offense: Bombers, Cruise Missiles, and Prudent Deterrence* (Washington, D.C.: Center for Strategic and International Studies, 1977).

[79] Hoeber, p. 2.

[80] Hoeber, pp. 3–6.

[81] Hoeber, p. 6.

[82] Hoeber, pp. 69–70. This refers to what is generally called the *time-value of money*.

[83] Hoeber, p. 70.

ANALYSIS OF THE CRUISE MISSILE In a similar study, John Baker analyzed cruise missiles.[84] His analysis sought to compare the costs of cruise missile systems to other weapon systems designed to perform comparable military missions. His analysis examines three types of cruise missiles—air-launched, ground-launched, and sea-launched—and compares them to the Pershing II missile system and the F-111 and F-16 fighter-bombers. He analyzes the long-term costs through a technique generally known as life-cycle costing, assessing two types of costs: the average cost of producing each weapon; and the average unit flyaway cost (the actual cost of each weapon right off the assembly line).[85] Baker finds that the cruise missile has substantial merit. As he notes:

> On the basis of acquisition costs alone, the [ground- and air-launched] cruise missile systems are the most costly. The conclusion changes dramatically when the long-term operating and support expenses are included; the two cruise missiles then are the *least* expensive on a per warhead basis.[86]

While Baker's analysis is very detailed and technical, he acknowledges that many factors potentially important in making weapons decisions were not considered, and many of the details of the life-cycle costing technique were not presented. For example, Baker didn't discuss the method used to adjust the costs into constant 1981 dollars and what, if any, discount rate was applied. These omissions do not mean the analysis is inaccurate; they simply raise questions, the importance of which an informed reader may wish to investigate.

Nuclear Exchange Analyses

In recent years, various defense analysts have developed different models to prescribe what actions should be taken in response to nuclear attack. These models are often used in an area of public policy research called *nuclear exchange analysis*. Among these models are the Arsenal Exchange Model (AEM), developed for the Air Force, and the Strategic International Relations Nuclear Exchange Model (SIRNEM), developed for the Arms Control and Disarmament Agency. Recently, Baugh reported on another model, which he referred to as NEMATODE.[87] Each of these models is designed to consider numerous important factors in response to specific attacks from various attackers and to allocate defensive and retaliatory resources in a way that would maximize their effectiveness. In other words, these models are used to prescribe the best way to do the most damage with a given set of military capabilities.

[84] John C. Baker, "Program Costs and Comparisons," in Betts (see Note 40), pp. 101–33, 573–95.

[85] Baker, p. 102.

[86] Baker, p. 113.

[87] William H. Baugh, *The Politics of Nuclear Balance: Ambiguity and Continuity in Strategic Policies* (New York: Longman, 1984), pp. 145–46.

FIG. 4.1. AEM9 Arsenal Exchange Simulation Model

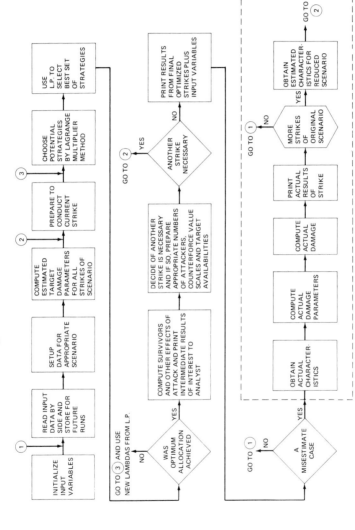

From William H. Baugh, *The Politics of Nuclear Balance: Ambiguity and Continuity in Strategic Policies* (New York: Longman, 1984), p. 142. Reprinted with permission of the publisher.

The AEM9 model (version 9 of the Arsenal Exchange Model) consists of a fairly large computer program that reflects a series of sequential decision steps, depicted as a flow diagram in Figure 4.1. Each block in the diagram reflects a logical step in the complicated process of sorting out many considerations in deciding how to respond to an attack. This flow model has been used to simulate responses to attacks from a single enemy. Obviously a model of this type does not decide anything by itself. It does, however, give decision makers specific estimates and information to be considered when making decisions.

Simply stated, the model begins with a hypothetical attack from some specific enemy. It takes into consideration the source of the attack and damage that may have resulted as it begins to make estimates of the damage that could be inflicted by different strike scenarios (box D of the diagram). The strike is then made on the enemy, and the model then reassesses the damage actually caused to determine whether it was optimum (box H). If the strike was not optimum, the model goes back to point 3 and continues to order strikes until optimization is reached. Once optimality is achieved, it decides whether another strike is necessary (box K). If the answer is yes, it goes back to point 2 and proceeds until another strike is not necessary. Then it assesses the damage, taking into consideration possible errors in earlier estimates of target damage.

Other more elaborate models have been used to simulate responses to more complicated scenarios. For example, the Arms Control and Disarmament Agency has contracted for the development of the SIRNEM. According to Baugh, SIRNEM is capable of taking into consideration numerous detailed factors, including attacks from multiple enemies, the use of many different missile and bomber systems, damage from thermonuclear explosions, and even the geography of potential targets.[88]

Global Simulation Modeling

Not all prescriptive foreign and defense policy analyses are as narrowly focused as the weapon systems or nuclear exchange studies. In fact, attempts have been made to simulate international interactions around the entire world. We will refer to this type of analysis as *global modeling*.[89] These models originated in the late 1950s and early 1960s with the Inter-Nation Simulation (INS) and the Simulated International Processes (SIP) projects at Northwestern University. Since that time, numerous alterations have been made to these models that reflect what Harold Guetzkow refers to as second- and third-generation developments.[90]

[88] Baugh, p. 144.

[89] Harold Guetzkow and Joseph J. Valadez, eds., *Simulated International Processes: Theories and Research in Global Modeling* (Beverly Hills: Sage Publications, 1981).

[90] Harold Guetzkow, "An Incomplete History of Fifteen Short Years in Simulating International Processes," in Hoole and Zinnes (see Note 51), pp. 247–49.

These models are probably the most complicated of all the prescriptive foreign and defense analyses. Each model consists of many submodels, each of which tries to simulate some intra-nation or inter-nation process. The submodels are designed so that when they are put together they interact with each other, that is, what goes on in one submodel is partly dependent on what goes on in the others.

These interactions consist of simulations of international politics and processes, such as a revolution in one nation, a change of government in another, and so on. As a result, elements of any submodel can be changed to assess the effects on other nations and international relations. This sounds very abstract, so let's take a closer look at one of these models to see how it works.

One of the later-generation models is Stuart Bremer's Simulated International Processer (SIPER).[91] The focus of this model is often referred to as the *national decision making unit,* such as a national government. The SIPER model consists of two large components. One of these tries to define the way the political, social, and economic environment is affected by each national decision making unit. The other component tries to specify how the national decision making unit accomplishes its goals in this changing political, social, and economic environment.

The environment of the national decision making unit consists of submodels that represent each of three systems. The first is the international system, reflecting the behavior of other nations. The second is the national economic system, reflecting patterns of consumption, investment, and governmental economic activity. And the third is the national political system, reflecting who is in power and how they make decisions about internal political stability, economic growth, and national security.

It is difficult to summarize the substantive contributions of this type of model in the analysis of foreign and defense policy. To date, much more attention has been paid to criticizing and revising the construction of the submodels than to assessing the policy-relevant results of the models.[92] According to Brewer, however, global simulation models of this type have led us to numerous tentative conclusions not necessarily understood in their absence. For example, one analysis of factors affecting the potential cohesiveness of international alliances using an inter-nation simulation found that if nations provide economic and symbolic benefits, alliances become stronger. If nations threaten potential allies, alliances do not become stronger and may weaken.[93]

[91] Stuart A. Bremer, "The Simulated International ProcessER," in Guetzkow and Valadez (see Note 89), pp. 135–77; and Stuart A. Bremer, *Simulated Worlds: A Computer Model of National Decision-Making* (Princeton: Princeton University Press, 1977).

[92] Stuart J. Thorson, "The Inter-Nation Simulation Project: A Methodological Appraisal," in Hoole and Zinnes (see Note 51), pp. 284–303.

[93] Stuart A. Bremer, "An Appraisal of the Substantive Findings of the Inter-Nation Simulation Project," in Hoole and Zinnes (see Note 51), p. 323.

FIG. 4.2. Amended Flowchart Model of Crisis Decision Process Simulation

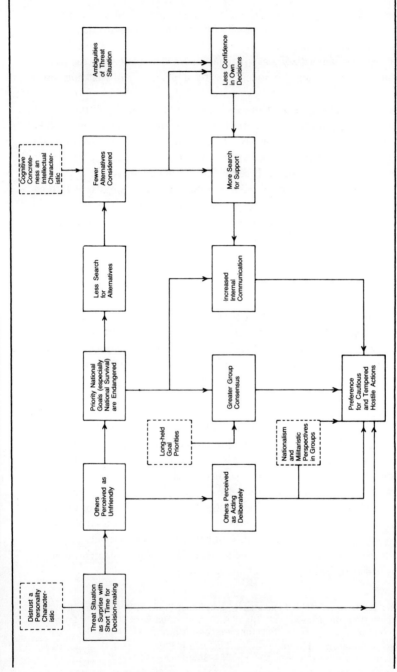

From Harold Guetzkow and Joseph J. Valadez, "International Relations Theory: Contributions of Simulated International Processes," in Harold Guetzkow and Joseph J. Valadez, eds., *Simulated International Processes: Theories and Research in Global Modeling.* (Beverly Hills, Calif.: Sage Publications, 1981), p. 214

Fairly useful substantive findings have come out of the application of the INS models to predict international hostilities.[94] Studies by Alker and Bock and by Driver, to name a few, have incorporated psychological aspects of decision makers into their models.[95] This kind of simulation is depicted by Guetzkow and Valadez as a flow chart of crisis processes. This flow chart, presented in Figure 4.2, shows the relationships among individual cognitive and group characteristics in deciding to take cautious or aggressive actions. These models have undertaken the formidable task of trying to anticipate the effects of psychological factors on decision makers.

We have only been able to take a brief look at a handful of the many prescriptive analyses in foreign and defense policy. We have looked at very narrowly focused studies of weapon systems, at defense simulations of attack situations, and at the very broadly focused global simulations. With this in mind, we should summarize some of the more important points learned from our three approaches to foreign and defense policy analysis.

SUMMARIZING THE APPROACHES TO FOREIGN AND DEFENSE POLICY ANALYSIS

We looked at a considerable number of foreign and defense policy studies from each of our three approaches. We found that the perspectives brought to bear by studies in each approach are very different. We also found that each approach seems to deal with a very different aspect of foreign and defense policy analysis. When we put the findings together, we begin to see the importance of contributions from each approach to our overall understanding of foreign and defense policy.

The foreign and defense policy making approach helped us understand some important aspects of domestic politics. We noted, for example, that Congress's main influence over foreign policy is through the power to authorize and appropriate funds. Individual legislators may play less formal, but nevertheless important, roles by developing personal expertise. We also found that State Department and Defense Department officials play a major role in deter-

[94] Stephen J. Andriole and Robert A. Young, "Toward the Development of an Integrated Crisis Warning System," *International Studies Quarterly,* Vol. 21, March 1977, pp. 107–50.

[95] Hayward R. Alker and P. G. Bock, "Propositions about International Relations: Contributions from the International Encyclopedia of the Social Sciences," in James A. Robinson, ed., *Political Science Annual,* Vol. 3, 1972, pp. 385–495; M. J. Driver, "Individual Differences As Determinants of Aggression in the Inter-Nation Simulation," in M. G. Hermann and T. Milburn, eds., *A Psychological Examination of Political Leaders* (New York: Macmillan, 1977), pp. 337–53; Harold Guetzkow and Joseph J. Valadez, "International Relations Theory: Contributions of Simulated International Processes," in Guetzkow and Valadez, eds., *Simulated International Processes,* pp. 197–251.

mining policies, including relations with other nations, decisions to develop and deploy new weapon systems, and defense spending.

The foreign and defense policy cause and consequence approach focused our attention on the factors that cause nations to go to war and that influence the United States to spend or not spend money on national defense. This research suggested that involvement in an arms race does not necessarily lead to war, nor does it necessarily deter war. Studies also argued that defense spending really does not respond to international threats as much as it responds to domestic economic and political needs.

The foreign and defense policy prescription approach examined three very different topics. The first was whether developing new weapon systems seems to be warranted, compared to their alternatives. The second was the potential effectiveness of various military actions in times of military attack. These exchange models present the sequence of decisions and factors that must be considered in a defense policy of retaliation. The third was a very broad attempt at global simulation modeling. These inter-nation simulations provide the foundation for predicting the effects of foreign policy actions on other nations' domestic conditions and international relations.

FURTHER READING

Foreign and Defense Policy Making Process

DESTLER, I. M. *Presidents, Bureaucrats, and Foreign Policy.* Princeton: Princeton University Press, 1972.
PASTOR, ROBERT A. *Congress and the Politics of U.S. Foreign Economic Policy.* Berkeley: University of California Press, 1980.

Foreign and Defense Causes and Consequences

HOOLE, FRANCIS W., and DINA A. ZINNES, eds. *Quantitative International Politics: An Appraisal.* New York: Praeger, 1976.
WILKENFELD, JONATHAN, ed. *Conflict Behavior and Linkage Politics.* New York: David McKay, 1973.

Foreign and Defense Policy Prescription

GUETZKOW, HAROLD, and JOSEPH J. VALADEZ, eds. *Simulated International Processes: Theories and Research in Global Modeling.* Beverly Hills: Sage Publications, 1981.
HOEBER, FRANCIS P. *Slow to Take Offense: Bombers, Cruise Missiles, and Prudent Deterrence.* Washington, D.C.: Center for Strategic and International Studies, 1977.

CHAPTER FIVE

Approaches to Public Antipoverty and Welfare Policy Analysis

Perhaps no area of public policy has been analyzed more than antipoverty and welfare policy. When we speak of it, we are actually referring to an aggregation of programs and policies designed in one way or another to achieve a common end: to help people who have been categorized as being in poverty or in need.

These antipoverty and welfare programs provide cash transfers called "in-kind transfers" or direct social services to people.[1] In-kind transfers consist of benefits that have cash value or equivalents, although they are usually restricted to use for specific purposes.[2] For example, if a family receives food stamps, it receives coupons that have a particular monetary value but that can only be used for the purchase of food.

There are numerous cash and in-kind benefits provided by our governments to needy people. Many of these benefits are the products of programs that overflow into other policy areas. For example, Social Security is a cash benefit program that provides the single largest transfer of benefits to poor people, even though we often think of it as a program for elderly, disabled and survivors, whether poor or not. Housing subsidies and public housing focus on the shelter needs of poor people, but we often think of them as being part of a general housing policy. Even so, we can begin to look at antipoverty and welfare policy research that is based on our three approaches to public policy analysis. As we do this, we will address several important questions:

> What are the political and social forces that shape the nature of public antipoverty and welfare policies in the United States?
>
> What seem to influence our federal and state governments to pursue specific courses of action in welfare policy?
>
> To what extent have our public welfare and antipoverty policies actually reduced, eliminated, or even increased the level of poverty in the United States?
>
> What seem to be the best ways to alleviate poverty and related miseries in the future, and what are the trade-offs involved with each?

As we examine the research from each of our three policy analysis approaches, we will see that at least partly because of differences in the approaches, researchers can and often do come to very different conclusions about the best way to help poor people.

As we begin our policy making process analysis of antipoverty policies, we will focus on the formulation, adoption, and implementation stages. In our discussions of these stages, we will examine research that analyzes aspects of the

---

[1] Alma W. McMillan and Ann Kallman Bixby, "Social Welfare Expenditures, Fiscal Year 1978," *Social Security Bulletin,* Vol. 43, May 1980, pp. 3–17.

[2] The actual value of in-kind transfers has itself been the subject of debate. See, for example, Timothy Smeeding and Marilyn Moon, "Valuing Government Expenditures: The Case of Medical Care Transfers and Poverty," *Review of Income and Wealth,* Series 26, No. 3, Sept. 1980, pp. 305–24.

political environment of welfare policy making. To accomplish this, we will look at the stages in the process for specific federal programs. Before we do this, we should take a brief look at the programs and actors central to antipoverty and welfare policy.

THE ANTIPOVERTY AND WELFARE POLICY PROGRAMS

When we speak of welfare or antipoverty policy, we are usually referring to specific governmental programs. These programs, as we have already noted, provide cash or in-kind benefits to people who have been determined to be in need. The programs that provide cash benefits include Social Security, Aid to Families with Dependent Children (AFDC), Supplemental Security Income (SSI), Veteran's Assistance, Unemployment Insurance, and Worker's Compensation. The in-kind support programs include Medicare and Medicaid, Food Stamps, housing and public housing subsidies, the women, infants, and children (WIC) nutrition program, and Head Start, a preschool education program. The WIC program also provides some in-kind support. The operations of several other programs, such as the Comprehensive Employment Training Act (CETA), a job-training program, have been terminated, or virtually so, by Congress as a result of Reagan administration initiatives. As we will note later, CETA was replaced by the Job Partnership Training Program, which attempts to shift job-training responsibility to the private sector. Before we begin looking at some of the unique welfare policy making processes associated with many of these programs, we shall briefly look at what these programs are.

Social Security

Social Security—its formal name is Old Age, Survivors, and Disability Insurance (OASDI)—was created by the Social Security Act of 1935. It was not designed as an antipoverty program *per se,* but to guarantee, in part, benefits to people who paid for them through a payroll tax program. As originally enacted, it promised benefits *only* to those who paid into the program. By the time it took effect in 1940, however, it had been altered to provide some benefits based on people's needs. Derthick describes this as a tension of equity- versus adequacy-based benefits.[3] The emphasis has slowly shifted away from equity and toward the adequacy.

Financed out of a payroll tax on earnings, the program was designed to be self-supporting; the revenues collected from the payroll tax were supposed to be the only revenues out of which benefits would be paid. Increases in the

---

[3] Martha Derthick, *Policymaking for Social Security* (Washington, D.C.: Brookings Institution, 1979) and Sar A. Levitan, *Programs in Aid of the Poor for the 1980's,* 4th ed. (Baltimore: Johns Hopkins University Press, 1980), pp. 22–28.

payroll tax were projected that ostensibly would provide the revenues needed to finance a growing demand for benefits. In practice, with the increased emphasis on adequacy-based benefits, the money has come increasingly from general revenues.

Food Stamps

Federal Food Stamps is a classic example of a program designed to achieve several seemingly disparate goals. It was originally formulated and implemented by the U.S. Department of Agriculture in the late 1930s.[4] Although that program ended in 1943, the idea was resurrected by Congress in the late 1950s and put into practice through pilot programs around the country in 1961.

The Food Stamps program was initially developed by the Department of Agriculture more as a kind of commodity program to distribute farm surpluses than to help hungry people. The plan was that agricultural commodities that were overproduced (in surplus) at a given time would be distributed to needy people in order to hold steady the prices of these commodities. It should come as no surprise that this program failed to effectively feed poor people. By 1960, the needy receiving food commodities were obtaining lard, rice, flour, butter, and cheese, the only commodities in surplus.[5]

Under the Kennedy administration, a concerted effort was made to revise and expand the Food Stamps program through pilot projects around the country. In 1963, President Kennedy asked Congress for funds to support an ongoing Food Stamps program. Despite strong support from the Kennedy administration and several members of Congress, the House Agriculture Committee was less than enthusiastic about the program and tabled the proposal in 1964. Through a series of legislative maneuvers, several members of Congress managed to get the bill resuscitated. The result was the passage of the Food Stamp Act, which became law on August 31, 1964. We will look at how this happened when we examine the welfare policy making process.

By the end of the 1960s, there was fairly widespread agreement that the Food Stamps program was not reaching large numbers of needy people. Despite this fact, there was no consensus in Congress about how, or even whether, to reform the program.[6] In 1969 and 1970, the first two years of the Nixon administration, the Department of Agriculture made significant decisions to broaden the eligibility for and increase the level of benefits.[7] These decisions were made through what is often called *administrative rulemaking,* where the Department

[4] Jeffrey M. Berry, *Feeding Hungry People: Rulemaking in the Food Stamp Program* (New Brunswick, N.J.: Rutgers University Press, 1984).
[5] Berry, p. 24.
[6] Lester M. Salamon, *Welfare: The Elusive Consensus* (New York: Praeger, 1978).
[7] Salamon, p. 63.

of Agriculture issued regulations and guidelines that carry the weight of law without a specific act of Congress.[8] In 1970, Congress passed a reform bill that simply ratified what the Department of Agriculture had already done.

Through the 1970s, the Food Stamps program expanded substantially. Whereas in 1969, the program served a monthly average of 2.9 million people, by 1976, it served almost 18 million people. In 1980, under the newly elected Reagan Administration, substantial cuts were made, first by rulemaking in the Department of Agriculture and the Office of Management and Budget, then through the 1981 Omnibus Budget Reconciliation Act, which formalized much stricter eligibility requirements.[9] (In 1985, there were some 20 million people receiving Food Stamps.)

Aid to Families with Dependent Children (AFDC)

AFDC is a joint federal and state funded program established by the Social Security Act and administered by the states. It pays cash assistance to poor families with dependent children. Each state determines eligibility standards and minimum benefit levels. In theory, states are free to pay higher or lower benefit levels, depending on how important welfare is to them, how high the cost of living is, and other factors. But, as we will see later, these factors actually seem to be less influential in determining the average benefit level than how wealthy a particular state is.

AFDC has become increasingly controversial over the past two decades. Some people believe that in some ways AFDC creates a perverse incentive for families to break up—or to never form—and for poor women to have more children in order to qualify for AFDC benefits. Family dissolution occurred because families with an able-bodied man could not qualify for AFDC benefits. And because the amount of benefits is tied to the number of children, the total benefits obtained by a family could be increased by having more children. AFDC qualifications and program operations have been changed to attempt to rectify these problems. For example, in the late 1960s, AFDC was changed so that two-parent families became eligible at the states' option. Currently, about half of the states have exercised this option.

This controversy is also fed by the fact that AFDC is the only major cash assistance program financed out of general funds, which makes it clearly identifiable as a welfare program, one intended to redistribute money from high-income to low-income people. All of this has led to a perception by part of the

---

[8] Berry, pp. 69–70.

[9] Robert X. Browning, "Priorities, Programs, and Presidents: Assessing Patterns of Growth in U.S. Social Welfare Programs, 1949–1990," in Sheldon Danziger and Kent Portney, eds., *The Distributional Impacts of Public Policies* (New York: Associated Faculty Press, 1985).

general public and some policy makers that people can make more money by being on welfare than they can by working.[10]

Beginning about 1967, various work incentive (WIN) requirements have been added to AFDC in pilot programs around the country. These incentives have attempted to encourage people to leave the welfare roles if they could enter the labor force. We will take a look at analyses of whether some of these incentives have been effective in our discussion of policy cause and consequence analyses.

Supplemental Security Income (SSI)

In 1974, Congress amended the Social Security Act to consolidate three income supplement programs to people who are aged, blind, or disabled or to their families. SSI operates to fill the gaps left by other aid programs and brings the aid recipient's total income up to an established level. In other words, SSI uses a means test, taking into consideration all the types of (cash) income received. SSI is financed through general revenues in concert with each of the states. The states may decide to augment the federal contribution with their own funds. As demographic and other conditions have increased the burdens on SSI, policy makers have struggled with ways of stemming the burden of this program on the federal budget.

Medicare

Medicare is a federal program established in 1965 to pay for part of medical care costs for persons 65 years of age or older. It is part of the Social Security program, administered by the Social Security Administration. Medicare usually makes payments to health service providers rather than directly to health service recipients. It may also reimburse recipients for medical care. It is financed out of a Social Security fund that in recent years has been strained because of our rapidly aging population. While Medicare is not specifically targeted at poor people, many of its recipients are poor.[11] Moreover, Medicare is designed to aid those elderly who are not poor but who could easily be thrown into poverty by hospitalization and medical costs in times of illness.

Medicaid

Medicaid is a medical assistance program specifically designed for indigent persons, especially those already receiving AFDC, SSI, or other assistance. It also serves people who are medically indigent, those who cannot qualify for other assistance but who, because of its high costs, cannot afford to pay for essential

---

[10] Ralph Segalman and Asoke Basu, *Poverty in America: The Welfare Dilemma* (Westport, Conn.: Greenwood, 1981).

[11] Segalman and Basu, pp. 242–48.

medical care.[12] Payments made to medical institutions are financed by both the federal and state governments out of general funds.

Job Training

Included among governmental efforts to reduce poverty are those that attempt to remove people from welfare rolls by providing job training. One of the longest-running of these programs was CETA, the Comprehensive Employment Training Act. This program was enacted in 1973 to replace the Manpower Development and Training Act of 1962. It provided federal grants to state and local governments for skills training and job placement of people on other assistance. As we will see in studies of causes and consequences, CETA was not very successful in training the people who needed it the most.

In 1982, Congress replaced CETA with the Job Training Partnership Act (JTPA). This program is designed to involve the private sector directly in training and placement so that job training takes place in occupational areas where business and industry need it. In theory, the program will improve the chance that impoverished job training recipients will find subsequent employment.[13]

THE ANALYSES OF ANTIPOVERTY AND WELFARE POLICY PROCESSES

With these programs in mind, we can now take a brief look at the policy making processes of welfare and its reform. We will see that political conflicts take place over two major issues: the enactment of new legislation and programs; and changes in program implementation, especially administrative changes in the levels of benefits and in eligibility requirements.

Welfare Policy Formulation and Adoption Processes

Traditionally, the federal politics of welfare policy making involve a small group of legislators who favor expanding benefits and a larger group of legislators who oppose or are ambivalent about increased welfare benefits. Welfare legislation is commonly formulated to achieve multiple goals, which often leads some of the welfare opponents to become supporters, because the legislation may also

---

[12] Segalman and Basu, pp. 248-58.

[13] Randall B. Ripley and Grace A. Franklin, "The Private Sector in Public Employment and Training Programs," *Policy Studies Review,* Vol. 2, No. 4, May 1983, pp. 695-714; and Randall B. Ripley and Grace A. Franklin, *Private Sector Involvement in Public Employment and Training Programs* (Washington, D.C.: National Commission for Employment Policy, 1981).

provide benefits to nonrecipients of welfare. Berry's analysis of the Food Stamps program describes a good case in point.[14]

FOOD STAMPS The Food Stamps program was originally designed by the Department of Agriculture both to provide some relief to hungry people and to prevent the prices of surplus commodities from falling. Thus, at least in theory, hungry people would be fed *and* farmers would be protected from the harm caused by large price fluctuations.[15] In its early experience, the program apparently achieved neither goal very well. Nevertheless, the multiple goals present in the program created some incentive for opposing or ambivalent legislators to vote in favor of it.

One of the more in-depth studies of the Food Stamps program adoption process is Randall Ripley's analysis of legislative bargaining.[16] It documents the role of Missouri Representative Lenor Sullivan in convincing Congress to transform the Food Stamps program, at least in part, to aid hungry people rather than simply distribute agricultural surpluses. Ripley described Sullivan as initiating a process of bargaining between Democrats—who tended to favor the transformation—and Republicans—who tended to oppose it—and between Northern supporters and Southern opponents. A bargain was eventually struck in which passage of a wheat-cotton bill, providing benefits to Southern farmers, was linked to passage of the Food Stamp Act.[17]

While examining formally enacted welfare programs provides some insight into welfare policy making, we can also learn a great deal from looking at programs rejected by Congress. One of the more widely studied "rejections" was President Nixon's Family Assistance Plan (FAP). Perhaps ironically, it was the relatively conservative Nixon administration that proposed a rather sweeping reform and expansion of welfare in the United States.

One of Nixon's early actions after taking office consisted of appointing an Urban Affairs Council to prepare a comprehensive policy statement on poverty, hunger, and nutrition. The staff of this council was headed by then Harvard professor, now a senator from New York, Daniel Patrick Moynihan. It was in this role that Moynihan fashioned the Family Assistance Plan.

The plan called for establishment of a negative income tax to replace AFDC and other cash assistance programs. Thus, if individuals or families fell below an established level, not only would they pay no federal income tax, but they would receive a cash payment from the federal government.[18]

---

[14] See Berry.

[15] Berry, Ch. 1.

[16] Randall B. Ripley, "Legislative Bargaining and the Food Stamp Act, 1964," in Frederic N. Cleaveland, ed., *Congress and Urban Problems* (Washington, D.C.: Brookings Institution, 1969), pp. 279–310.

[17] Ripley, pp. 300–6.

[18] Daniel Patrick Moynihan, *The Politics of a Guaranteed Income* (New York: Vintage, 1973).

One might expect the Nixon administration to be rather cool to this idea, but this was not the case. According to Martin Anderson's analysis, Moynihan developed a close working relationship with welfare administrators in the Nixon administration.[19] Anderson argues that Moynihan formulated a proposal with such bureaucratic support that the Nixon administration eventually considered it to be its own, despite the fact that many of these bureaucrats were holdovers from the Johnson administration and that the effect of FAP would have been a considerable expansion of welfare.[20]

FAP legislation was introduced in Congress in 1970 and received fairly quick passage in the House.[21] But the proposal became stalled in the Senate Finance Committee, where conservatives argued that welfare costs would soar and liberals (who ultimately voted for the legislation) thought overall benefits were inadequate.[22] An analysis by Salamon suggests that the main reason why FAP passed in the House but was rejected in the Senate was that Senate leadership failed to give voting cues (guidance) to moderates.[23] Thus, the kind of consensus based on achieving multiple goals, as reflected in the Food Stamps program, seemed to be absent in FAP.

SOCIAL SECURITY Just as the Food Stamps program was designed to achieve multiple goals, so too was Social Security. As noted earlier, much of the political debate over Social Security has centered on the tension between equity and adequacy bases for benefits. The initial legislation in 1935 provoked debate between conservatives and New-Deal liberals.

Generally, the conservatives wanted a self-financing, insurance-like program that benefited only those who paid into the program. It would have been actuarially sound; a pool of money would be created to fund benefits. Self-financing would almost ensure that benefits could not be paid to everyone who needed them. Liberals, on the other hand, wanted the program to provide benefits partly on the basis of need; this could not be supported by the pool of money.[24]

According to Derthick, the political compromise that tied eligibility to the use of a payroll-tax fund allowed conservatives to feel they had achieved their goal of financial soundness. Yet changes were made to provide benefits to people who had not actually paid into the program, including dependents

---

[19] Martin Anderson, *Welfare* (Stanford, Calif.: Hoover Institution, 1978), pp. 5–8.

[20] Theodore Marmor and Martin Rein, "Reforming 'The Welfare Mess': The Fate of the Family Assistance Program," in Alan P. Sindler, ed., *Policy and Politics in America* (Boston: Little, Brown, 1973), pp. 12–13.

[21] M. Kenneth Bowler, *The Nixon Guaranteed Income Proposal: Substance and Process in Policy Change* (Cambridge, Mass.: Ballinger, 1974), p. 71.

[22] Bowler, p. 72.

[23] Salamon, p. 96.

[24] Derthick, passim.

of people who did. Thus, liberals achieved some degree of success by ensuring that benefits would be distributed partly on the basis of need.

As policy makers increasingly responded to added demands for benefits, the program shifted more towards distributing benefits based on need, nearly always in ways that maintained the myth of a self-financing, equity-based program. Today, a great many functions of the Social Security program are financed out of general revenues.

THE ADOPTION OF ANTIPOVERTY POLICIES AS REDISTRIBUTIVE POLI-CIES   According to one strain of policy making process thought, the antipoverty policies and programs have a great deal in common. Based on the policy typology developed by Lowi, which we discussed in Chapter 1, the policies have been termed *redistributive* policies. Although many researchers have attempted to determine how redistribution actually occurs from relatively well-off to relatively poor people, redistributive policies do not require actual redistribution. The key, according to Lowi,[25] and Ripley and Franklin,[26] is whether redistribution is generally perceived by policy makers to be the principal goal of the policies. When the intention is redistributive, we find that the policy making process often involves substantial class conflict (especially between the poor and the wealthy); we also find that the President and upper echelons of the bureaucracy and Congress have substantial influence over what gets done. At the same time, the lower-level agencies and congressional subcommittees tend to have less influence. We have seen at least one major exception to this in Berry's analysis of the Food Stamps program, where the lower-level bureaucracy seemed to play an important role in its development.

One of the important implications that emerges from analyses of welfare as redistributive policy is that it does not look very redistributive at the time when it is adopted. Although we have come to perceive unambiguously that the welfare programs are designed to take from the relatively prosperous and give to the poor, it is not at all clear that this was the case when the programs were developed. When we examined the research on the Food Stamps program, for example, the process through which Food Stamps came to be framed seems to have defined welfare in such a way that numerous groups were helped simultaneously. As long as Food Stamps were designed to help only the poor, the policy makers rejected them. When the nature of perceived benefits was altered to help agricultural interests through the simultaneous adoption of the wheat-cotton bill, then the Food Stamps program was adopted. A similar process was involved with Social Security.

[25] Theodore Lowi, "American Business, Public Policy, Case-Studies, and Political Theory," *World Politics,* Vol. 16, July 1964, pp. 677–715.

[26] Randall B. Ripley and Grace A. Franklin, *Congress, the Bureaucracy, and Public Policy* (Homewood, Ill.: Dorsey, 1979), pp. 21–22.

The Welfare Policy
Implementation Processes

As with many other policy areas, the implementation process of welfare policy is very important to understanding the programs' successes, excesses, and failures. Several studies of welfare program implementation argue that administrative decisions affect such factors as eligibility requirements, the amount of fraud, and who will and who will not ultimately receive benefits.

IMPLEMENTING THE FOOD STAMPS PROGRAM Perhaps the best study of Food Stamps program implementation is Berry's, to which we alluded earlier.[27] This study documents the history of Food Stamps reform through administrative regulations. The expansion of the program in the early 1970s resulted largely from Nixon administration alterations in regulations rather than through congressional action. Generally, congressional action merely ratified decisions already made by the bureaucracy in its rulemaking process. Even in the early 1980s, program contraction was at least initially the result of Reagan administration implementation changes. Of course, Congress put its stamp of approval on these decisions very shortly thereafter.

Early in President Nixon's term, as congressional authorization for the Food Stamps program was due to expire, the newly enacted Urban Affairs Council (a White House advisory panel) was asked to formulate an administrative policy toward welfare. The council found that severe hunger and malnutrition were rampant in the United States, and that previous administrative decisions concerning the price of Food Stamps excluded participation by millions of needy persons. In other words, the amount a poor family had to pay to receive Food Stamps, the result of a decision made within the Department of Agriculture, was set so high that many needy people could not afford them.[28]

In response, the Nixon administration formulated a bill to reform Food Stamps, but it was defeated in Congress. Subsequently, the Department of Agriculture made substantial changes on its own. For example, coupon allotments (the dollar purchasing value of the stamps) were set at a minimum level necessary to provide an "economy diet"; the purchase price of these coupons was reduced; and the program was expanded into areas of the country that were not previously covered.[29] As we noted previously, Congress ratified this action by passing a Food Stamps reform bill in 1970.[30]

Since 1980, the Reagan administration has committed itself to reducing the costs of welfare. This has been accomplished through the major budget cuts

[27] See Berry.
[28] Berry, p. 60.
[29] Berry, p. 63.
[30] Berry, p. 68.

approved by Congress that we discussed in our initial description of the Food
Stamps program.

IMPLEMENTING SUPPLEMENTAL SECURITY INCOME (SSI) We noted
earlier that the SSI program is a part of Social Security, enacted in 1974. Unlike
the traditional form of Social Security, SSI was designed to be a needs-based
supplement to all other forms of income. The job of implementing this program
was given to the Social Security Administration (SSA), an agency that had built
a solid reputation for delivering benefit checks in the right amount to the right
people on time. This new set of tasks created substantial problems for the
agency because the previously used procedures did not work for SSI. As Ripley
and Franklin note:

> The SSI program was intended to provide welfare recipients with an ex-
> tra income, but state and local governments' records on their welfare
> recipients were not complete or accurate, so the SSA had to obtain new
> documentation on an individual basis.[31]

The SSA proceeded to distribute benefits to people without full documen-
tation about their need. As a result, benefits went to some people who were not
qualified and in some cases did not go to people who were. Apparently, several
years of experience did not do much to help the SSA improve administration of
the program.[32]

As if the SSA didn't have enough problems with SSI, in 1977 it was also
given responsibility for Aid to Families with Dependent Children (AFDC). But
AFDC administration faces still a different environment than other welfare programs. It is designed to be implemented by the states and territories. According
to Abe Levine, the main problem with AFDC implementation is the degree of
fragmentation of program responsibility.[33] Not only do the states exercise initial
responsibility, but at least 18 states shift this responsibility to their counties or
cities.[34] Perhaps equally important is the fact that the federal agency that implemented AFDC until 1978 tended to view its administrative role as being very
limited. As Levine notes:

> HEW [the Department of Health, Education and Welfare] has at its
> disposal a number of oft-threatened but seldom displayed fiscal sanc-

---

[31] Randall B. Ripley and Grace A. Franklin, *Bureaucracy and Policy Implementation*
(Homewood, Ill.: Dorsey, 1982), p. 99.

[32] Ripley and Franklin, *Bureaucracy and Policy Implementation*, p. 99.

[33] Abe Levin, "Administration of Public Welfare in the Case of Aid to Families with
Dependent Children," in Salamon, pp. 243–48.

[34] Levin, p. 245.

tions designed by Congress to punish inadequate or illicit state program practices.[35]

Instead, HEW opted to encourage states to develop computerized case load tracking systems that would presumably help minimize fraud and other abuse.[36] With possible exceptions in Florida and Massachusetts, this avoidance of sanctions has remained even after the reorganization establishing the Department of Health and Human Services as program implementor.

The Role of Welfare Rights Organizations in Welfare Policy Implementation

Beginning roughly in the middle 1960s, welfare recipients and proponents emerged as an organized political force in national politics. Perhaps the largest of these groups, the National Welfare Rights Organization (NWRO), was formed in 1966 and lasted until about 1975. During the time of its existence, the organization played a significant role in shaping aspects of antipoverty policy. Yet, apparently because of its inability to broaden its base of support beyond minority women, it increasingly experienced difficulty achieving internal consensus.[37]

The NWRO achieved some notable policy results in its short time of existence. In 1972, for example, it filed a lawsuit against the federal Department of Health, Education, and Welfare over a proposed New York State demonstration project requiring public service employment for welfare recipients. As part of a court-induced agreement, NWRO was built directly into New York's welfare policy implementation process. NWRO's surrogate, the New York City-based Center for Social Welfare Policy and Law, was given the authority to review and comment on state welfare implementation proposals.[38]

In his study of Food Stamps, Berry describes the similar involvement of several major welfare rights and lobbying organizations in the administrative rule-making process. Although they achieved this more through informal than court or legislatively induced involvement, the result was that these organizations were able to play an important part in administrative decisions between 1971 and 1976.[39] This, of course, resembles the iron triangle relationships found in other policy implementation processes.

[35] Levin, p. 244.

[36] Levin, p. 245.

[37] Guida West, *The National Welfare Rights Movement: Social Protest of Poor Women* (New York: Praeger, 1981).

[38] Blanche Bernstein, *The Politics of Welfare: The New York City Experience* (Cambridge, Mass.: Abt Books, 1982), esp. Appendix: "A Case Study in the Politics of Welfare," pp. 165–204.

[39] Berry, pp. 60–68.

What Has the Antipoverty and Welfare Policy Making Process Research Told Us?

The policy making process research on antipoverty policies leaves us with some fairly definite lessons. First, over the past 30 years or so, the antipoverty implementation process has been very important in determining who receives how much benefit. Second, it is clear that in some instances, congressional action on so-called welfare programs was more of a ratification of actions already taken by the welfare agencies in the implementation of programs than a reflection of congressional initiative. This has been especially evident with Food Stamps and AFDC.

Finally, even when the need for welfare is great, the policy making process labors to put its response into a form that avoids making it seem that someone is getting something for nothing. For example, Social Security became palatable when it was designed as a social insurance program where benefits could be distributed as a result of entitlement rather than on the basis of need. The bottom line, then, is that the policy making process, at the adoption stage, has difficulty accepting the notion of distributing benefits to people who need them.

SOME WELFARE POLICY CAUSE AND CONSEQUENCE RESEARCH

Cause and consequence research on public antipoverty and welfare policies has analyzed many important governmental programs. Since the early 1960s, the federal government has financed numerous antipoverty programs, each of which has been analyzed to determine whether it has achieved its desired results. For example, through the 1970s, CETA programs received a great deal of analytic scrutiny to find out whether participation of unskilled persons in this program "caused" an improvement in employability and income status. Similar analyses have been conducted on other federal and federally financed programs, including Food Stamps, AFDC, Project Head Start, and many others.

Another strain of public welfare policy cause and consequence research set out in the late 1960s and early 1970s to answer a question that permeates debates on welfare: whether receiving governmental welfare benefits causes people to lose their incentive to work. Parties in the debates over welfare programs seem to adhere to strong opinions about the answer to this question, but until recently, we had virtually no systematic research to shed light on it. We will look at some of the projects and studies that have sought a systematic answer to this question.

Causes and Consequences Research on Food Stamps, Hunger, and Nutrition

One of the questions addressed in cause and consequence research is whether the Food Stamps program has actually worked. Despite early findings that Food

Stamps were simply not getting to the people who needed them, subsequent program changes would seem to have corrected this problem.[40] But it is also important to learn whether food coupons cause increases in food consumption (reduction of hunger) and improvements in nutrition. Several studies have addressed these issues for specific areas of the country.[41]

A study by Sylvia Lane concentrated on a single county in California to compare Food Stamps recipients with recipients of food distributions and families that were eligible for but received no benefits.[42] Lane used a rather complicated research design in which well over 200 heads of "low-income, Afro-, Mexican-, and Anglo-American" households were interviewed at two points in time. She found that in terms of food consumption, food distribution recipients received more food than they would have purchased with Food Stamps or with their own money.[43] But these people also ended up spending more of their own money on food than the food coupon recipients, apparently because the food distributed was not what the recipients wanted or needed. Food Stamps recipients spent less of their own money, largely because the stamps let them purchase exactly what they wanted or needed in the first place. Lane also found that both Food Stamps and food distribution recipients experienced somewhat better nutrition than poor people who received neither, although Food Stamps led to better nutrition than food distribution. These and similar results indicate indeed that the Food Stamps program seems to be successful in increasing food consumption and improving nutrition.

The Effects of AFDC on Families

AFDC has been criticized over the years because it is thought to have detrimental effects on the structure of families. Because families with an absent father once could qualify for greater benefits, some people felt that AFDC actually created a perverse incentive for families to break up or to never form. It has also been suggested that AFDC created a disincentive to working for a living because the amount of benefits decreased as family earnings increased. These beliefs have received considerable attention in research.

Perhaps beginning with studies in the early 1970s, some evidence began to mount that AFDC did have a perverse effect on family structure. For example, a study by Honig investigated data for a large number of Standard Metropolitan

---

[40] Berry, pp. 62–63.

[41] J. Patrick Madden and Marion D. Yoder, *Food Stamp and Commodity Distribution in Rural Areas of Central Pennsylvania* (University Park: Pennsylvania State University Press, 1972).

[42] Sylvia Lane, "Food Distribution and Food Stamp Program Effects on Food Consumption and Nutritional 'Achievements' of Low Income Persons in Kern County, California," *American Journal of Agricultural Economics,* Vol. 60, Feb. 1978, pp. 108–16.

[43] Lane, p. 114.

Statistical Areas (SMSAs) around the United States.[44] (SMSAs are areas defined by the U.S. Bureau of the Census for the purposes of collecting and reporting census and other data.) In Honig's study, each SMSA was characterized by the average amount of AFDC benefit going to families and the percentage of females over 18 years old who were separated or never married. She found that the SMSAs with the largest AFDC stipend also tended to have the highest rate of separation or singleness. She inferred from this that families receiving larger AFDC payments were more likely to dissolve or never form than families receiving smaller AFDC benefits.

A reanalysis by Minarik and Goldfarb used data from states rather than SMSAs and looked at the relationship between the maximum allowable AFDC payment provided and the percentage of separated or never-married women with children,[45] variables that they argued were somewhat more relevant to the specific question at hand. Their findings, nevertheless, were consistent with those of Honig. In this case, states that provided higher maximum AFDC benefits also tended to have the highest percentage of women-with-children who were separated or never married.

One of the problems with these analyses is that they commit a basic error of social research often referred to as *ecological fallacy*. In short, they use information about collections of people (SMSAs and states, for example) to infer patterns of relationships about individual families. Doing this requires something of a leap of faith. The problem can be stated fairly succinctly. A finding that SMSAs or states offering larger AFDC payments have higher rates of family dissolution tells us about SMSAs or states, but not about specific families. It is possible that the families receiving the AFDC payments are not the same families that have been dissolved, in which case it is difficult to argue that AFDC causes family dissolution. Even so, subsequent steps were taken to alter AFDC to remove the possible incentives for family dissolution.

The Effects of Welfare
on Incentives to Work

A recurring question in welfare policy making is whether providing welfare to people causes them to lose their incentive to earn income through participation in the labor force. This has been such a concern that since 1967, AFDC has at-

---

[44] Marjorie Honig, "AFDC Income, Recipient Rates, and Family Dissolution," *Journal of Human Resources,* Vol. 9, No. 3, Summer 1974, pp. 303–22. For a comprehensive review of studies in this area, see John H. Bishop, "Jobs, Cash Transfers, and Marital Instability: A Review and Synthesis of the Evidence," *Journal of Human Resources,* Vol. 15, No. 3, Summer 1980, pp. 301–34. Also, for a look at the reemergence of the debate on this and related issues, see Charles Murray, *Losing Ground: American Social Policy, 1950–1980* (New York: Basic Books, 1984); and Sheldon Danziger and Peter Gottschalk, "The Poverty of Losing Ground," *Challenge,* May–June 1985, pp. 32–38.

[45] Joseph J. Minarik and Robert S. Goldfarb, "AFDC Income, Recipient Rates, and Family Dissolution: A Comment," *Journal of Human Resources,* Vol. 11, No. 2, Spring 1976, pp. 243–50.

tempted to incorporate various work incentive (WIN) programs or requirements into its operations.

Support for the need to create work incentives for welfare recipients abounds in cause and consequence studies. For example, a study by Durbin in 1974 found that about 40 percent of mothers coming into the AFDC program drop out of the labor force—in other words, lose their incentive to work.[46] She also found that for every ten mothers on AFDC, about two men drop out of the labor force.

A recent analysis by Mead examined the extent to which the expectations of WIN administrators influenced AFDC participants to maintain their work incentive and perform better in jobs they take.[47] His analysis showed that there is an important influence exerted by staff employees in what they tell recipients about their rights and obligations and how they are assigned to the WIN projects. When WIN applicants are assigned to a low-priority category (indicating an expectation that the applicant will be difficult to place and unlikely to hold a job), they tend to understand that expectations of them are low and perform accordingly. The implication here is that some people categorized in the lowest category would very likely obtain employment and perform better if assigned to a higher category.

Numerous reforms of work incentives have been incorporated into AFDC to try to re-establish true incentives. An analysis of the WIN-II program by Ehrenberg and Hewlett found that incentives could be effective in maintaining labor force participation and ultimately in reducing the costs of welfare.[48] And studies of an experimental supported-work program found positive results. In Atlanta, Chicago, Hartford, New York, Newark, Oakland, and the state of Wisconsin, the supported-work program provided welfare recipients with a job for 12 to 18 months, after which they had to leave and seek work elsewhere. Analysis indicated that this type of program leads to improved long-term stability and performance in the job market.[49]

All of these studies point to a general set of conclusions. First, some types of welfare may actually reduce recipients' incentives to work. Second, this loss of incentive does not occur automatically, and programs can be designed to compensate for this loss. And third, it is possible for this incentive to be maintained without excessive additional welfare cost.

[46] Elizabeth Durbin, "Work and Welfare: The Case of Aid to Families with Dependent Children," *Journal of Human Resources,* Vol. 8, No. 5, Supp., 1973, p. 121.

[47] Lawrence M. Mead, "Expenditures and Welfare Work: WIN in New York City," *Policy Studies Review,* Vol. 2, No. 4, May 1983, pp. 648–62.

[48] Ronald Ehrenberg and James G. Hewlett, "The Impact of the WIN-2 Program on Welfare Costs and Recipient Rates," *Journal of Human Resources,* Vol. 11, No. 2, Spring 1976, pp. 219–32.

[49] Stanley Masters, "The Effects of Supported Work on the Earnings and Transfer Payments of its AFDC Target Group," *Journal of Human Resources,* Vol. 16, No. 4, Fall 1981, pp. 600–36. See also Sandra K. Danziger, "Postprogram Changes in the Lives of AFDC Supported Work Participants: A Qualitative Assessment," *Journal of Human Resources,* Vol. 16, No. 4, Fall 1981, pp. 637–48.

Determinants of Welfare Spending
in the American States

An area of analysis that once held the attention of numerous political scientists tries to explain why some states spend more for antipoverty programs than other states. Much of this analysis evolved into a debate about whether political variables are more important determinants of welfare spending than economic or demographic variables. Emerging from the works of V. O. Key[50] is the theory that states that are more democratic (those that have more interparty competition and higher levels of political participation) should be more responsive to the needs of poor people.

As this debate progressed, many studies were conducted to support or refute the ideas proposed by Key. A study by Dawson and Robinson, for example, found little support for Key's theory,[51] but a later analysis by Cnudde and McCrone found evidence of a relationship between party competition and welfare spending in the states.[52] Subsequent analysis by Tompkins attempted to clarify the nature of this relationship, but in the process refuted the finding that there is such a relationship.[53] Despite this, there is some evidence that the differences in findings may be attributed to differences in the methods employed and the variables used to measure party competition and welfare spending.[54] And Dye has argued that the differences in the studies are largely the result of differences in the professional biases brought to the analyses by people in the various disciplines.[55] In particular, he argues that many pluralist political scientists misinterpret empirical research results in order to support their values that political system characteristics are important influences on public policy.

Preschooling for the Disadvantaged:
The Effectiveness of Project Head Start

As we noted earlier, Congress enacted in 1965 the Head Start program, a project designed to help disadvantaged young children by compensating very early for their educational deficiencies. Many studies indicated that because children of

---

[50] V. O. Key, Jr., *American State Politics* (New York: Knopf, 1956).

[51] Richard E. Dawson and James A. Robinson, "Inter-Party Competition, Economic Variables, and Welfare Policies in the American States," *Journal of Politics*, Vol. 25, May 1963, pp. 265–89.

[52] Charles F. Cnudde and Donald J. McCrone, "Party Competition and Welfare Policies in the American States," *American Political Science Review*, Vol. 63, Sept. 1969, pp. 858–66.

[53] Gary L. Tompkins, "A Causal Model of State Welfare Expenditures," *Journal of Politics*, Vol. 37, May 1975, pp. 392–416.

[54] Michael S. Lewis-Beck, "The Relative Importance of Socioeconomic and Political Variables for Public Policy," *American Political Science Review*, Vol. 71, June 1977, pp. 559–66.

[55] Thomas R. Dye, *Policy Analysis* (University, Ala.: University of Alabama Press, 1976), pp. 30–35.

poverty are disadvantaged from the beginning, they receive fewer benefits from public education once they start school. And as the years go by, the effects of this disadvantage multiply.[56] Does Head Start provide a mechanism to help equalize the benefits that can be obtained from education? The program has been evaluated using many criteria, including the impact on poor communities, on the social development of participating children,[57] and others.

The evaluations of Head Start illustrate one of the problems with relying on cause and consequence research results to assist in public policy formulation. According to a summary study by Lois-ellin Datta, evaluations of Head Start projects have shifted their conclusions at least three times between 1965 (the program's inception) and 1979.[58] So there is still no clear-cut answer to the question of whether Head Start has been effective.

Studies up until 1968 generally concluded that Head Start produced definite short-term and long-term benefits for disadvantaged children. Between 1969 and 1974, evaluations tended to suggest that Head Start was a failure, both because of design flaws and implementation problems. From 1975 through 1979, studies again pointed to positive effects of the program. And since 1980, with the virtual elimination of the program through budget cuts, the issue has almost been forgotten.

Characteristic of the early set of positive findings were studies by Duntemann et al. and by Coulsen et al.[59] These studies examined the IQs and the readiness of children entering primary schools. In almost every instance, the studies found that Head Start children were better prepared and had higher IQs than their counterparts who did not attend Head Start. A study by Kirschner Associates even showed that communities and their institutions (government departments, schools, parents' councils, etc.) became sensitized to the needs of disadvantaged children and altered the delivery of their services in response.[60] Thus, Head Start had a secondary effect beyond the possible direct benefits provided to the children in the program.

The tone of the findings shifted with what is probably the best-known

[56] Edward Zigler and Jeanette Valentine, eds., *Project Head Start: A Legacy of the War on Poverty* (New York: Free Press, 1979), pp. 12–17.

[57] A. J. Mann et al., *A Review of Head Start Research, 1969 to 1976: An Annotated Bibliography* (Washington, D.C.: Social Research Group, George Washington University, 1977).

[58] Lois-ellin Datta, "Another Spring and Other Hopes: Some Findings from National Evaluations of Project Head Start," in Zigler and Valentine, pp. 405–32.

[59] G. Duntemann et al., *A Report on Two National Samples of Head Start Classes: Some Aspects of Child Development of Participants in Full Year 1967-1968 and 1968-1969 Programs* (Research Triangle, N.C.: Research Triangle Institute, 1972); and J. M. Coulsen et al., *Effects of Different Head Start Program Approaches on Children of Different Characteristics: Report on Analyses of Data from 1966-67 and 1967-68 National Evaluations* (Santa Monica, Calif: Rand Corp., 1972).

[60] Kirschner Associates, *A National Survey of the Impacts of Head Start Centers on Community Institutions* (Albuquerque: Kirschner Associates, 1970).

Head Start evaluation, conducted by the Westinghouse Learning Corporation.[61] This study indicated that Head Start children did not improve their performance on standardized tests. These findings were criticized both because of problems in the analysis of the data[62] and because the evaluation process itself became "politicized."[63]

An example of a study whose conclusions reflect a shift toward finding more positive effects from Head Start is that by Weisberg and Haney.[64] This study tracked students who participated in the Head Start follow-through program and compared them with national averages and with Head Start children who did not participate in the follow-through program. They found, among other things, that follow-through participants, while losing ground over time to the national average on standardized educational achievement tests, did better each year than Head Start children who did not participate in follow-through.

We can see from the Head Start evaluations that it is not easy to make blanket pronouncements about whether a program has worked. The results are more likely to provide information about specific ways the program has been successful and ways in which it has failed. Without question, the assessment of whether achieving the successes is worth the failures must be a value-based one.

Do Antipoverty Policies Reduce
the Overall Level of Poverty?

One of the broader questions addressed in welfare policy analysis is whether antipoverty policies have had the effect of reducing the overall level of poverty. Actually, the question can be divided into two related questions: Does increasing public welfare reduce the level of poverty? and, Does decreasing public welfare increase the level of poverty? While the answers to these questions may seem obvious, many people argue that increasing welfare does not reduce poverty. And as reflected in Reagan administration sentiment, there are those who believe that major cuts in welfare can be made without causing an increase in the level of poverty, largely because of the belief that many people who are not poor receive welfare program benefits. Because this issue can become so emotional, it is important that we reiterate that we are interested in the results of analyses rather than impressionistic, intuitive, or anecdotal accounts.

Some of the more rigorous analyses of this issue suggest that increasing

---

[61] Westinghouse Learning Corp., *The Impact of Head Start: An Evaluation of the Effects of Head Start on Children's Cognitive and Affective Development* (Washington, D.C.: Clearinghouse for Federal Scientific and Technical Information, 1969).

[62] Datta, pp. 417–19.

[63] See Walter Williams and John W. Evans, "The Politics of Evaluation: The Case of Head Start," *Annals of the American Academy of Political and Social Sciences,* Vol. 385, Sept. 1969, pp. 118–32.

[64] H. I. Weisberg and W. Haney, *Longitudinal Evaluation of Head Start Planned Variation and Follow Through* (Cambridge, Mass.: Huron Institute, 1977).

welfare does decrease the level of poverty. Several important studies have recently documented the effects of antipoverty programs on the overall level of poverty. Clearly, there are differences in studies' findings because of the way poverty and the value of in-kind transfers are measured.[65] Even so, analyses by Sheldon Danziger, Peter Gottschalk, Robert Haveman, Timothy Smeeding, and Robert Plotnick, to name a few, have addressed this type of question.[66] In general, the studies indicate that since about 1975, poverty has been increasing in the United States. But these studies show that the level of poverty is growing at a slower rate than would be the case in the absence of federal antipoverty programs. As Danziger notes, although the antipoverty effects of federal income transfer policies have declined in recent years, they still significantly reduce the level of poverty, perhaps by as much as 20 percent.[67]

Analysis of the Reagan "Safety Net"

After the 1980 election, President Reagan proposed to cut welfare spending without affecting the truly poor by making changes in the levels of benefits and eligibility.[68] The Reagan administration argued that these cuts could be made while maintaining a "safety net" that would catch the truly needy. Several analyses have attempted to assess whether such a safety net existed after the cuts were made, and if it did, whether some poor people still fell through it.[69]

One of the more comprehensive studies of this is MacDonald's assessment of how the many welfare programs interact in providing—or failing to provide—aid to truly needy people.[70] He looked at six major transfer programs—Food Stamps, AFDC, Unemployment Compensation, Old Age Survivors and Disability Insurance (Social Security), and Medicaid—to see how the poorest people have

[65] Carol Fender and Mollie Orshansky, "Improving the Poverty Definition," *Proceedings of the American Statistical Association,* 1979; and Marie Osmond and Mary Durkin, "Measuring Family Poverty," *Social Science Quarterly,* Vol. 6, No. 1, 1979, pp. 87-95. See also Timothy Smeeding, "Reagan, the Recession, and Poverty," in Danziger and Portney, *The Distributional Impacts of Public Policies* (forthcoming), 1986.

[66] A small sampling of these studies includes Sheldon Danziger, Robert Haveman, and Robert Plotnick, "How Income Transfer Programs Affect Work, Savings, and the Distribution of Income: A Critical Review," *Journal of Economic Literature,* Vol. 19, 1981, pp. 975-1028; Robert Plotnick and Felicity Skidmore, *Progress Against Poverty* (New York: Academic Press, 1975); and Timothy Smeeding, "The Antipoverty Effects of In-Kind Transfers," *Policy Studies Journal,* Vol. 10, No. 3, March 1982, pp. 499-521.

[67] Sheldon Danziger, "Recent Trends in Poverty and the Antipoverty Effectiveness of Income Transfers," in Danziger and Portney (forthcoming).

[68] See John L. Palmer and Isabel V. Sawhill, eds., *The Reagan Experiment: An Examination of Economic and Social Policies under the Reagan Administration* (Washington, D.C.: Urban Institute, 1982), Ch. by Michael Gutowski and Jeffrey Koshal.

[69] Richard Nathan et al., *The Consequences of Cuts: The Effects of the Reagan Domestic Program on State and Local Governments* (Princeton, N.J.: Princeton University Press, 1983).

[70] Maurice MacDonald, "Multiple Benefits and the Safety Net," in Danziger and Portney (forthcoming).

been affected by Reagan administration program cuts. His findings confirmed the administration's contention that there is a safety net. But he also demonstrated that the effect of Reagan cuts has been to lower the safety net to a point where it does not really catch people until they fall below roughly half of the official poverty line. Thus, many people live below the poverty line without being able to qualify for welfare benefits.

Analyses of Job Training's Effects on Poverty Reduction

As we noted earlier, in 1973 Congress enacted the Comprehensive Employment and Training Act (CETA), a job-training program for the chronically unemployed. The idea underlying CETA was that a large number of people are poor because they are unemployed or unemployable; and they are unemployable because they have no job skills to offer. So CETA was enacted in order to provide training to unskilled, unemployed persons and to provide job placement for those who had received training.

Analyses of CETA have centered on two major questions: Did the program succeed in training and placing people who were most in need? And, did CETA participants increase their income *because* of the program? These are not easy questions to answer, although numerous cause and consequence studies have tried. We can take a look at some of them.

We might expect that the better a job-training program was able to involve the chronically unemployed, the better it would be able to alleviate poverty. So the initial question is whether the program involved the people most in need of job training.

Analyses of CETA implementation by Van Horn and by Mirengoff and Rindler[71] show fairly clearly that because the people selecting the CETA participants were cognizant of the necessity of placing their trainees in jobs, they tended to select participants for whom they knew they could get jobs. Thus, there was a tendency for CETA programs to train people who were not the most in need of training, but who were employable before participating in job training. This pattern persisted despite attempts by Congress in 1976 and 1978 to tighten eligibility requirements.

The question about whether CETA participation improved participants' income is somewhat more difficult to answer. Most of the studies of this issue are interested in what happens to CETA participants' incomes years after involvement in the program. Have CETA participants experienced long-term increases in their earning power as a result of their training? The four major studies of this question all show that, except for white men, CETA improved earnings for participants. There is considerable evidence from these studies that women,

---

[71] Carl Van Horn, "Implementing CETA: The Federal Role," *Policy Analysis*, Vol. 4, Spring 1978, pp. 159–83; and W. Mirengoff and I. Rindler, *CETA: Manpower Programs under Local Control* (Washington, D.C.: National Academy of Sciences, 1978).

especially minority women, improved their earnings far above what they would have achieved without CETA participation.[72] And a recent study by Bassi argues that the job-training portion of CETA (but not the placement activities) was highly cost-effective—in other words, the amount of increased earnings going to participants more than exceeded the cost to taxpayers.[73]

Despite its benefits, Congress decided in 1982 to replace CETA with the Job Training Partnership Act. This program is designed to foster private involvement in job training by offering tax credits to companies. Although it is probably much too early to make any sort of definitive assessment, a summary analysis by Ripley and Franklin indicates, however, that private sector involvement is not likely to produce better results in employing poor people than did CETA.[74]

Analyses of a Guaranteed Annual Income

Although never enacted, President Nixon's Family Assistance Plan included a proposal to substitute a negative income tax for AFDC, Food Stamps, and several other welfare programs. This was an appealing welfare reform to some people, but it raised questions about whether it would reduce poverty and whether it might cause undesirable, unanticipated side effects. For example, some people feared that a negative income tax, regardless of the way it "forgave" earned income, would destroy people's incentives to work. Major experiments were undertaken to try out various negative income tax programs and to assess their effects.

In 1968, the Office of Economic Opportunity (OEO) sponsored a three-year experiment involving over 1300 familes in New Jersey and Pennsylvania.[75] This project, commonly known as the New Jersey Guaranteed Income Experiments, established four levels of income and different schedules for forgiving earned income, that is, reducing the negative income tax payment going to families if they earn income from other sources. Some families had their benefits reduced by 30 percent of their outside earned income, others had their benefits reduced by 50 percent, and still others by 70 percent. These families were also compared to a control group of families that received no payments.

[72] Laurie Bassi, "The Effect of CETA on the Post-Program Earnings of Participants," *Journal of Human Resources,* Vol. 18, No. 4, Fall 1984, pp. 539–56; Congressional Budget Office, *CETA Training Programs—Do They Work for Adults?* (Washington, D.C.: Congressional Budget Office, 1982); Westat, *The Impact of CETA on 1978 Earnings: Participants in Selected Program Activities Who Entered CETA During Fiscal Year 1978; Report to the Employment and Training Administration* (Washington, D.C.: Westat, 1982).

[73] Laurie Bassi, "CETA—Did It Work?" *Policy Studies Journal,* Vol. 12, No. 1, Sept. 1983, pp. 106–18.

[74] Ripley and Franklin, "The Private Sector in Public Employment and Training Programs," pp. 695–714.

[75] David Kershaw and Jerilyn Fair, *The New Jersey Income-Maintenance Experiment, Vol. I: Operations, Surveys, and Administration* (New York: Academic Press, 1977).

Subsequent income experiments were conducted in Gary, Indiana, Denver, Colorado, and Seattle, Washington.[76] Each of these experiments incorporated improved methodologies and attempted to assess wider ranges of impacts than the New Jersey experiment. Some of these studies came very close to using true experimental designs with random assignment.

The New Jersey study generated an immense amount of data about people's life-styles, consumer behavior, and so on. The results of the study provided some hard evidence that guaranteed incomes create neither great perversions in behavior nor model citizens.[77] In general, the study found that the lives of the vast majority of people receiving guaranteed incomes were unaffected with respect to health, social activities, and family structure. The money received from the government was spent pretty much the same way as money from any other source would have been spent. The single exception to this was that families receiving a guaranteed income were more likely to improve the quality of their housing, especially through home purchases.

The experiments in Seattle and Denver (often referred to as SIME/DIME for Seattle/Denver Income Maintenance Experiment) used a design similar to the one used in New Jersey.[78] The SIME/DIME project used three levels of guaranteed income. It focused on the effects of this income on decisions about working; psychological job satisfaction or distress among those who worked; marital dissolution; decisions about whether to have children; decisions to move (change residence); the use of subsidized housing; and several other factors.

The results of these experiments suggested that the heads of families receiving increased income reduced participation in the job market.[79] It also suggested that children between the ages of 10 and 21 in such families also reduced their work participation.[80] Employed women, but not employed men, in families receiving a guaranteed income seemed to experience some improvement in satisfaction with their jobs and less job-related distress.[81] The negative income tax seemed to stabilize some families and destabilize others.[82] And the negative income tax reduced the likelihood that families would rely on subsidized housing.[83]

[76] Philip K. Robins et al., eds., *A Guaranteed Annual Income: Evidence from a Social Experiment* (New York: Academic Press, 1980). See also the entire issue of *Journal of Human Resources*, Vol. 15, No. 5, Fall 1980, which is devoted to analyses of SIME/DIME.

[77] William J. Baumol, "An Overview of the Results," in Harold W. Watts and Albert Rees, eds., *The New Jersey Income-Maintenance Experiment, Vol. III: Expenditures, Health, and Social Behavior; and the Quality of the Evidence* (New York: Academic Press, 1977), p. 14.

[78] Robins et al.

[79] Philip K. Robins, "Labor Supply Responses of Family Heads and Implications for a National Program," in Robins et al., Ch. 3.

[80] Richard W. West, "Labor Supply Responses of Youth," in Robins et al., Ch. 4.

[81] Philip K. Robins, "Job Satisfaction," in Robins et al., Ch. 7.

[82] Lyle P. Groenveld, Nancy Brandon Tume, and Michael T. Hannan, "Marital Dissolution and Remarriage," in Robins et al., Ch. 9.

[83] Marcy E. Avrin, "Utilization of Subsidized Housing," in Robins et al., Ch. 16.

Public Antipoverty Cause and Consequence Research: A Summary

We have looked at numerous cause and consequence studies of welfare and anti-poverty policies. Yet, there are many topics addressed by such research that we could not examine. It should be fairly clear, however, that cause and consequence research on welfare issues is somewhat more sophisticated than it is in other areas. For example, the use of experimental designs seems considerably more prevalent in welfare policy analyses than elsewhere.

Several points emerge from much of this research. First, there is considerable empirical evidence that common wisdom about welfare does not necessarily hold. The income maintenance experiments, for example, provide a great deal of evidence that welfare probably does not automatically destroy people's incentives to work. Second, many studies seem quite optimistic about the potential for pursuing antipoverty policies that avoid producing negative consequences. At the same time, however, cause and consequence research seems to offer something for everyone. Proponents of welfare can point to studies of Head Start, AFDC supported-work, and other programs as producing significant, measurable benefits. Welfare foes can identify other, negative consequences of welfare policies and programs. It seems clear, however, that cause and consequence studies have gone a long way toward enhancing our knowledge of government's role in social welfare and raising the level of public debates on such issues.

PRESCRIPTIVE ANTIPOVERTY POLICY ANALYSES

Many of the techniques of public policy prescription analysis were not applied to antipoverty problems until fairly recently. Until about 1970, usable data were simply not available to permit this type of analysis. Since that time, however, the application of many of these techniques to welfare policy has advanced rapidly.

Perhaps one of the more common uses of prescriptive analysis examines the Social Security and retirement system. Although the retirement portion of Social Security is not a welfare program per se, many prescriptive analyses have emphasized its antipoverty effects. Prescriptive studies of Social Security have been responsible for many of the alarming reports that program bankruptcy is imminent. Other studies of Social Security have tried to assess the future effects of different reforms to avert such bankruptcy.

Prescriptive analyses have also been applied to other welfare programs. For example, several simulation models have been developed to assess the future effects of different kinds of income transfer policies.[84] Recently, another simula-

---

[84] Robert H. Haveman and Kevin Hollenbeck, eds., *Microeconomic Simulation Modeling for Public Policy Analysis, Vol. 1: Distributional Impacts* (New York: Academic Press, 1980). See also Herman P. Miller and Roger A. Herriot, "Microsimulation: A Technique for Measuring the Impact of Federal Income Assistance Programs," in Salamon, pp. 249–52.

tion model has been developed to examine the effects of several Supplemental Security Income reforms on low-income elderly people.[85] Although these are not the only issues addressed in policy prescription studies of welfare policies and programs, they represent some of the more important applications.

Prescriptive Social Security Analysis: The Prophets of Doom and Reform

Although predictions of financial difficulty for Social Security retirement and other accounts have been made for the last 30 years, analyses since the mid-1970s have increased our awareness of the problems these programs face. Perhaps the most notable of these analyses are those conducted by actuaries of the Social Security Administration for its board of trustees. (Actuaries are statisticians who are trained to make projections about insurance risk, premiums, etc. in order to help ensure the solvency of insurance programs.)

One of the more explicit analyses of this sort is that reported by A. Haeworth Robertson, once the chief actuary for the Social Security Administration.[86] Robertson conducted a fairly comprehensive, although nontechnical, analysis of the problems faced by Social Security from 1979 through the middle of the 21st century. His projections deal separately with disability insurance, hospital insurance, and supplemental medical insurance, all part of Social Security.

In order to make these projections, Robertson had to make numerous assumptions about different economic conditions. For example, projecting the amount of money Social Security would take in from the payroll tax required that he make an assumption about what wages will be in the future, what the employment rate will be, and so on. In making these assumptions, Robertson relied on three different sets of possible events. He called them his "optimistic, pessimistic, and intermediate" alternatives.[87] The set of optimistic assumptions are those that produce the least burden on, or most contributions to, the various Social Security funds.

Robertson's analysis indicated that without payroll tax increases between 1987 and 2015, Social Security payments are likely to exceed revenues by a considerable amount;[88] the hospital insurance program will run a deficit from 1980 on; and the supplemental medical insurance program, already partly financed out of general public revenues, will continue to require increased contributions.[89] Many reforms have been proposed, including increasing payroll taxes, to

---

[85] Roger Pupp and John Menefee, "Public Transfer Support and Income Adequacy among the Low-Income Aged," *Policy Studies Journal,* Vol. 12, No. 1, Sept. 1983, pp. 62–78.

[86] A. Haeworth Robertson, *The Coming Revolution in Social Security* (McLean, Va.: Security Press, 1981).

[87] Robertson, p. 348.

[88] Robertson, pp. 83–84.

[89] Robertson, pp. 84, 88, 95.

combat these fiscal problems. One of the causes often cited for Social Security's current problems is the congressional decision in 1973 to automatically adjust benefits according to changes in the consumer price index (CPI), a measure of inflation. In an effort to assess the effects of some proposed alternatives to this method of adjusting benefits, Baum and Sjogren conducted a prescriptive analysis.[90] They examined seven alternative indexing schemes for Social Security and made estimates about the impact of each on the incomes and levels of poverty of the elderly. These schemes call for tying benefit changes to indexes other than the overall CPI, including indexes of wage increase only, the cost of living for the elderly only, personal consumption expenditures, and others.[91]

The analysis conducted by Baum and Sjogren shows that all of the alternative indexing schemes cause the cost of Social Security to increase more slowly than using the overall CPI, yet they do so at the expense of the well-being of many elderly Social Security recipients. The analysis shows that under all of the proposals, the incidence of poverty would increase substantially for widows and other unmarried women.[92]

Simulations of Income Transfers

One developing method of analyzing future consequences of antipoverty policy reforms relies on the simulation of income transfers. There are several models used by policy analysts to assess who would be helped or hurt, and by how much, under various specific proposals. For example, during the 1970s, researchers at the Urban Institute in Washington, D.C., developed the Transfer Income Model (TRIM) for the U.S. Department of Health, Education, and Welfare. A later Urban Institute model, the Dynamic Simulation of Income Model (DYNASIM), has also been used for analyses of income transfer programs. These models were originally developed to analyze various negative income tax proposals, but they have been adapted to other income transfer policies as well. Another of these models is the MATH model, developed by the Mathematica Policy Research Group, Inc. It was also developed to analyze negative income taxes and has been since used by the Congressional Budget Office.[93]

Each of these models uses a technique called microsimulation, which means that the data used in the analysis consist of characteristics for individual people or families. The assessment of future impacts is accomplished by examining how each person or family would be affected by the specific proposal under

---

[90] Sandra R. Baum and Jane Sjogren, "Alternative Social Security Indexing Schemes and Poverty among the Elderly," *Policy Studies Journal,* Vol. 12, No. 1, Sept. 1983, pp. 79–90.

[91] Baum and Sjogren, pp. 84–85.

[92] Baum and Sjogren, p. 87.

[93] Herman P. Miller and Roger A. Herriot, "Microsimulation: A Technique for Measuring the Impact of Federal Income Assistance Programs," in Salamon, pp. 249–52.

consideration. Overall impacts are usually assessed by looking at aggregations, or summaries, of the individual impacts.

These models also are said to be dynamic, which means that they try to account for changes in people's characteristics over time. For example, if an analyst wants to project the impact of a welfare program to the year 2000, then the population in question must be "aged." In other words, the model has to take into consideration the fact that the characteristics of people, such as age, change over time. (Due to the repetitive nature of the calculations necessary to make these assessments, a computer is almost always used.) With these points in mind, we can take a brief look at the DYNASIM model, understanding that there are limits to how technical we can get.

Perhaps one of the better descriptions of the DYNASIM model as applied to income transfer programs is that by Orcutt, Caldwell, and Wertheimer.[94] This analysis demonstrates the simulation of Social Security, retirement pensions, Unemployment Insurance, AFDC, SSI, and Food Stamps. Although specific policy reform proposals are generally not analyzed, this study provides a fairly clear description of the potential the DYNASIM model possesses for such analyses.

DYNASIM consists of a fairly complex set of mathematical equations that are constructed based on the theoretical and empirical relationships found in previous research. The equations are arranged in subsets, and each subset is used to project a different variable or group of variables expected to eventually contribute to some aspect of the public program or policy in question.

As an example, before an analyst can make projections about the cost of AFDC, he/she must begin by projecting how many people would be eligible for, and participate in, AFDC. In order to know this, the analyst would have to project the sizes of the populations of people who meet specified eligibility requirements. Thus, DYNASIM has a subset of equations to project population growth by age, sex, income class, and so on, for each year. In order to accomplish this, of course, assumptions have to be made about what the birth and death rates will be. But these assumptions can be varied to assess how the population size would differ if these rates turned out to be different from the originally assumed rates.

DYNASIM actually has four large subsets of equations, one dealing with demographic characteristics (births, deaths, marriages, divorces, education, etc.), labor and employment (wage rates, labor force participation, earnings, etc.), transfers themselves (Social Security and retirement programs, Unemployment Compensation, AFDC, SSI, Food Stamps, etc.), and taxation and wealth (wealth income, savings, earned income, and federal income taxes). The subsets of equations are connected in such a way that if an analyst changes an assumption in one subset, other subsets take this change into consideration. For example, one

[94] Guy H. Orcutt, Steven Caldwell, and Richard Wertheimer II, *Policy Exploration Through Microanalytic Simulation* (Washington, D.C.: Urban Institute, 1976), Ch. 9.

can investigate what would happen to a welfare program's cost if the birth rate steadily increased over the next ten years. One set of equations would use this change in birth rate to calculate how large the population would be in the future. Other subsets of equations that use this population information would then automatically take this change into account in their respective calculations.

This model has been used to help analyze many different public programs. For the most part, it has been used to assess what would happen to the costs of public programs if changes occur in the rates of birth, death, divorce, female-headed family, and female labor force participation. Recently Orcutt et al. reported on some specific analyses of these kinds of changes on Social Security, AFDC, Unemployment Insurance, and taxes, as well as the impact on the elderly population.[95]

The Simulation of In-Kind Transfers

These microsimulation models have also been used to analyze in-kind transfer policies. Perhaps the most succinct description of this type of application is Beebout's analysis of the Food Stamps program using the MATH model.[96] His analysis focuses on the total costs that would arise from making changes in program eligibility. This type of question is not easy to answer because changes made in one program often lead to changes in other programs. For example, if Food Stamps eligibility is changed, this would have an effect on other welfare programs, such as AFDC. Thus the MATH model attempts to account for all of these program interactions.[97] Beebout's analysis shows that changing the Food Stamps program to eliminate the purchase requirement would increase the number of stamp recipients by about 15 percent and increase the total cost by about 9 percent.

What Do These Models Tell Us?

In some sense, these models help us understand what might be the best ways to alleviate poverty (or to achieve any other welfare-related goal). They do so, however, only to the extent that we can decide on the types of trade-offs we are willing to accept in achieving particular goals. Indeed, perhaps the most important contribution of the models to date is an explicit delineation of the trade-offs involved in making policy or program changes.

What do we mean by trade-offs? We mean that in order to achieve any particular goal, we may be forced to sacrifice the achievement of some other goal. We may sincerely wish to provide benefits to everyone who needs them

[95] Guy H. Orcutt et al., "Microanalytic Modeling and the Analysis of Public Transfer Policies," in Haveman and Hollenbeck, pp. 81–106.

[96] Harold Beebout, "Food Stamp Policy Modeling: An Application of MATH," in Haveman and Hollenbeck, pp. 45–72.

[97] Beebout, pp. 65–70.

and at the same time reduce the costs of welfare. But such models help us understand the extent to which achieving both of these goals simultaneously is impossible. We can often make public programs more efficient (less costly), but we can usually do so only at the expense of making some people worse off than they would be under a less efficient program. Thus, these models (especially the MATH model) are very useful for projecting how many people would be worse off by improving program efficiency by, say, 10 percent. In simulations of Social Security, the trade-off is explicit: between maintaining program solvency and taxing people in various income classes to achieve that solvency.

SUMMARIZING THE APPROACHES TO ANTIPOVERTY ANALYSIS

We have reviewed studies of antipoverty and welfare policy from each of the three approaches to policy analysis. Each of these approaches leads us to focus on different aspects of antipoverty policy, and each provides a very different perspective. We should take a couple of minutes to summarize and contrast the contributions from each.

The policy making process analyses of antipoverty policies begin to give us some insight into how many of our antipoverty programs are formulated, adopted, and implemented. The welfare policy formulation processes are generally influenced by the federal agencies having responsibility for implementation. Key congresspersons and the President are generally very important actors in the formulation process, while congressional committees and subcommittees seem to be much less important. The antipoverty policy adoption process may reflect a congressional ratification of policies already pursued by various federal agencies. In some sense, this implies that adoption really takes place in the agencies rather than in Congress. This seems to have been true with Food Stamps, but not necessarily in other areas, where Congress has played a much more pronounced role. And as is often the case with other policies and programs, the implementation process is exceedingly important in antipoverty programs. Many of the decisions about eligibility criteria and benefit levels are decided through administrative rulemaking by the federal agencies.

The antipoverty policy cause and consequence analyses attempted to answer some very important questions related to our welfare policies. Such studies of guaranteed incomes or negative income tax programs looked at what happens to people when they receive direct cash payments from the government. They found, for example, that people do not seem to lose their incentives to work and generally do not change a great deal because of receiving the subsidies. Although AFDC recipients did seem to have developed a disincentive to work in previous times, reforms in the program since the early 1970s appear to have minimized this disincentive.

The antipoverty policy cause and consequence studies indicate fairly clearly that federal programs can have a positive effect on people's lives. Although there is considerable debate about these issues, there seems to be some evidence that programs such as Food Stamps, CETA, and Head Start produced positive results for relatively disadvantaged people. Cause and consequence studies also provided us with a picture of how people have been affected by many Reagan administration reforms. The Reagan safety net can be said to exist, although many people who seem to be very needy are not caught by it. Thus, whether you believe the Reagan reforms have been successful depends on whether you think the people at about one half of the official poverty line deserve assistance.

We also learned that the antipoverty policy prescription approach has developed many ways of analyzing future reforms of our policies. Prescriptive studies have shown that various parts of Social Security soon will not be able to produce the revenue needed to finance benefits. Automatic cost-of-living benefit increases and the changing U.S. demography combine to deplete the funds that finance hospital insurance, supplemental medical insurance, and SSI. Future policies will have to increase revenues, decrease benefits, or both. Antipoverty policy prescription studies also examined other transfer programs to assess how people would probably be affected by changes in Food Stamps, AFDC, and other programs. In general, these studies seem to indicate that further cuts in these programs through changing eligibility criteria or through reducing benefit levels will have the effect of substantially increasing the level of poverty.

FURTHER READING

Antipoverty Policy Making Processes

BERNSTEIN, BLANCHE. *The Politics of Welfare: The New York City Experience.* Cambridge, Mass.: Abt Books, 1982.

BERRY, JEFFREY M. *Feeding Hungry People: Rulemaking in the Food Stamp Program.* New Brunswick, N.J.: Rutgers University Press, 1984.

DERTHICK, MARTHA. *Policymaking for Social Security.* Washington, D.C.: Brookings Institution, 1979.

MOYNIHAN, DANIEL PATRICK. *The Politics of a Guaranteed Annual Income.* New York: Vintage, 1973.

Antipoverty Cause and Consequence Research

KERSHAW, DAVID, and JERILYN FAIR. *The New Jersey Income Maintenance Experiment.* New York: Academic Press, 1977.

ROBINS, PHILIP K., et al., eds. *A Guaranteed Annual Income: Evidence from a Social Experiment.* New York: Academic Press, 1980.

ZIGLER, EDWARD, and JEANETTE VALENTINE, eds. *Project Head Start: A Legacy of the War on Poverty.* New York: Free Press, 1979.

Antipoverty Policy Prescription Analysis

HAVEMAN, ROBERT H., and KEVIN HOLLENBECK, eds. *Microeconomic Simulation Modeling for Public Policy Analysis, Vol. 1: Distributional Impacts.* New York: Academic Press, 1980.

ORCUTT, GUY H., STEVEN CALDWELL, and RICHARD WERTHEIMER II. *Policy Exploration through Microanalytic Simulation.* Washington, D.C.: Urban Institute, 1976, esp. Ch. 9.

CHAPTER SIX

Approaches to Public Physical and Mental Health Policy Analysis

Public health policies, dealing with aspects of our physical and mental health, do not seem to be as well developed as other policies, that is, the United States has tended to think of health as a personal issue and has resisted comprehensive governmental intrusion into these areas. Nevertheless, we do have public health policies in the United States.

Much of what we consider here to be part of health policy may also be thought of as part of other policy areas. For example, in this chapter we will address Medicaid as part of our public health policy, but it is often considered to be part of public welfare policy. Questions of stemming the rising costs of health services, especially services paid for by governments, may be thought of as being related to either health policy or public finance policy, as discussed in Chapter 7. Whether we discuss these issues as part of health policy or some other policy is largely determined by how much emphasis we think they should receive. Here we have made the decision to address a variety of health-related issues together.

Although public health policies may not appear to be as well developed as other policy areas, aspects of our federal and state health programs have been analyzed using all three of our approaches to policy analysis. As we examine a number of studies that represent these three approaches, we will focus on a number of important topics of public physical health policy:

The on-going debate about national health insurance;
Medicare and Medicaid;
Regulation of the health and medical industry, especially hospitals, private and medical insurance, and the pharmaceutical companies;
The efforts to contain the rising costs of medical care.

As we discuss public mental health policies, we will focus primarily on

The community mental health movement; and
Deinstitutionalization of the mentally disabled.

As we look at health studies in each of our three approaches, we should begin to understand some of the reasons why we have the public health programs and policies we have, as well as what potential there is for future government policy in the health field. We will find that health policy research is dominated by policy making process and policy cause and consequence studies, with somewhat less reliance on policy prescription techniques. We shall begin by looking at some of the major public health programs that compose our public policy toward health.

THE HEALTH POLICY PROGRAMS

When we think of public health programs, those which come most readily to mind are Medicare and Medicaid. These are programs designed to directly affect the health care that people receive. Since the federal government does not operate medical facilities as part of these programs, they provide transfers to people or health care providers so that medical services can be purchased.

Medicare, considered to be a social insurance program, was enacted into law in 1965 as a Social Security Act amendment. It provides compulsory hospital insurance for the elderly, including in-patient and surgical coverage for all those who are eligible for Social Security retirement benefits. It also provides subsidized voluntary medical insurance, mainly to cover out-patient doctor visits and post-hospitalization care in skilled-nursing or home-care facilities.

Medicaid is a program designed to provide medical services to people who cannot otherwise afford them. To some people, this makes it a form of socialized medicine. We will see that this distinction between public medical insurance and socialized medicine has played a significant role in the politics of public health policy.

While these are the two most recognized public health programs, there are many others. The Hill-Burton Act of 1946, for example, initiated a federal program to stimulate and subsidize hospital construction so that people could be assured access to medical care. During the 1970s and 1980s, as hospital and medical care costs soared, the federal government made a number of efforts to try to slow this growth. In the early 1970s, for example, efforts were made to stimulate the use of prepaid medical plans, now called health maintenance organizations (HMOs). And in the late 1970s, Congress enacted the Health Professions Educational Assistance Act to address shortages of particular types of medical personnel, especially doctors in general and family practice.

There are many other governmental efforts to affect public health. In fact, a 1970 congressional report noted that during the Johnson administration alone, Congress enacted perhaps 50 pieces of health-related legislation.[1] This legislation established programs administered in many different federal agencies, usually as part of some other benefit program targeted at specific groups of people (such as children in urban areas or refugees).

Public mental health policy adds another dimension to our discussion of health policy. Although mental health policy is in some ways incorporated into the health programs we have already noted, two separate areas of mental health policy deserve attention. Federal and state involvement in the community mental health movement through the policy of deinstitutionalization—where many patients in large state-run mental hospitals are released into various community settings—is another area to be discussed. We will look at the roots of this policy and what its consequences have been for patients and communities. Initially, we can begin with a look at the public health policy making process approach.

---

[1] U.S. Congress, Senate, Committee on Government Operations, Subcommittee on Executive Reorganization and Government Research, *Federal Role in Health.* S.R. 809, 91st Cong., 2nd sess., p. 18.

ANALYSES OF HEALTH
POLICY MAKING APPROACHES

In recent years, much debate has centered on whether governments ought to be involved in public health at all. This debate has roots that go back at least to the mid-1940s, long before proposals were put forth to provide subsidies for health care through Medicare or Medicaid. The debate continues, however, and in the last two decades or so, public sentiment favoring government intervention has mounted as the costs of private health care and insurance have grown at a rate much higher than overall inflation. We will look at this debate, initially focusing on how these questions get on the public agenda in the first place.

One characteristic will emerge from the studies as being very important in understanding the public health policy making process: the extreme fragmentation of decision making in health policy. The number and variety of actors involved in the process is quite high compared to other policy areas we have examined. A graphic representation of this fragmentation is provided for us by Brown in his analysis of the health policy making process (Figure 6.1). Here we can see that health policy, located toward the middle of the figure, is influenced by numerous institutions, agencies, and political interests. For example, we see

FIG. 6.1.   Major Influences on Health Care Policy

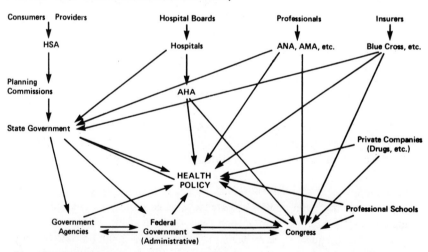

Reprinted, by permission of the author, from J.H.U. Brown, *The Politics of Health Care* (Cambridge, Mass.: Ballinger, 1978)

HSA = Health Service Agencies
AHA = American Hospital Association
ANA = American Nurses Association
AMA = American Medical Association

that federal and state government agencies are depicted as playing a role, along with hospitals, professional associations, private companies, professional schools, and health care consumers. We will begin to understand the mechanisms through which many of these actors affect public health policy.

Putting Health Policy Proposals on the Public Policy Agenda

Public financing and involvement in medical care has been a recurring issue for decades. Unlike many other policy issues, however, public health does not seem to have the same sort of crises as other policy issues (such as energy, the environment, etc.) to serve as an impetus to a policy response. In other words, the policy making process in health would seem to lack the kind of events that we often think of as influencing our policy makers to begin a process of formulating a public response. Thus, we must begin by asking how these health issues have become part of the public agenda in the first place. When we ask this question, we are really inquiring about the health policy problem formation and policy formulation processes.

Recently, Kingdon provided us with some specific insight into these processes where health issues have evolved into national concerns for public policy.[2] Kingdon's analysis addressed several different policy areas. In the area of health, he was mainly interested in finding out how some issues become part of the public agenda while others do not, and how they become part of the agenda at a given time when they were previously ignored. Kingdon's analysis relies on interviews with well over 100 congressional staff, executive agency, and nongovernmental actors involved in health-related decisions or policy advocacy.

Kingdon points to three components of the agenda-setting process. One component is what he calls "the march of problems pressing in on the system,"[3] which means that problems may emerge slowly over time, often gaining broad attention as the result of a prominent event (not necessarily a crisis). The second component of the agenda-setting process is the gradual accumulation of knowledge among specialists in a given policy area. These specialists then formulate policy proposals based on the state of this knowledge. The third component is formed by a variety of political (partisan) influences, that is, changes brought about directly or indirectly through electoral results, such as changes in the composition of Congress, the election of a new President, and so on.

Kingdon's analysis differs substantially from several previous studies that, in essence, argue that health care crises, the events that are often thought to help shape the public health policy agenda, are really the creations of various interest

[2] John W. Kingdon, *Agendas, Alternatives, and Public Policies* (Boston: Little, Brown, 1984).

[3] Kingdon, p. 17.

groups. In separate studies by Alford[4] and Mechanic,[5] evidence is presented in support of the idea that pro-medical establishment interest groups work to create crises, such as a revelation of Medicaid fraud, in order to attain their goals.

AGENDA SETTING FOR MEDICAID AND MEDICARE   You might wonder how these general statements about agenda setting apply to health policy. Kingdon tells us that these processes lead to placement of issues on the public agenda through what he calls policy windows.[6] He suggests that the policy window represents an opportunity for advocates of particular policy proposals to have their alternatives seriously considered. The policy window often is not predictable, and when opened, stays open only a short time. Medicare and Medicaid slipped onto the policy agenda with a new fervor after the election of 1964 opened such a window. It was during this short period that Congress took seriously the proposals to develop health care coverage for many people who needed it. In Kingdon's words:

> Policy windows open infrequently, and do not stay open long. Despite this rarity, the major changes in public policy result from the appearance of these opportunities. In 1965-66, for instance, the fortuitous appearance of extra liberal Democratic seats in Congress brought about by the Goldwater debacle opened a window for the Johnson administration that resulted in the enactment of Medicare, Medicaid . . . and all the other programs collected into Johnson's Great Society initiatives.[7]

Of course, not all open policy windows result in policy adoptions. They do, however, provide the opportunity for policy advocates to have their proposals put on the public agenda and discussed seriously. In this sense, they are a necessary but not sufficient condition for policy adoption.

NATIONAL HEALTH INSURANCE AND THE PUBLIC AGENDA   After the 1976 election, in which Jimmy Carter was elected, a policy window seemed to be open for national health insurance.[8] During Carter's term (1977-1979), many proposals were discussed and introduced in Congress. Yet no national health insurance program was ever adopted. According to Kingdon, some proponents of national health insurance, such as the United Automobile Workers union,

---

[4] Robert R. Alford, *Health Care Politics: Ideological and Interest Group Barriers to Reform* (Chicago: University of Chicago Press, 1975).

[5] David Mechanic, *Public Expectations and Health Care: Essays on the Changing Organization of Health Services* (New York: John Wiley, 1972).

[6] Kingdon.

[7] Kingdon, p. 175.

[8] Kingdon, pp. 7-9.

Senator Edward Kennedy, and other labor representatives, could not reach agreement with the Carter administration over the form of such a policy. The Kennedy-labor group favored a program with universal coverage and comprehensive benefits. The Carter administration preferred a much more limited program. Despite the fact that national health insurance was clearly on the public agenda, no policy was adopted. By 1980, when Ronald Reagan gained the White House and the composition of Congress changed, the policy window had apparently closed.

HEALTH COST CONTAINMENT AND THE PUBLIC AGENDA Since about 1970, the federal government has become very concerned about the cost of health care in the United States. The cost of medical care rose much faster than the overall inflation rate and put tremendous pressure on the Medicare and Medicaid budgets.[9] By 1970, as this became recognized, health cost containment became a major issue on the public agenda. Initially, this took the form of federal incentives for prepaid health plans, or Health Maintenance Organizations.[10] This issue later re-emerged on the public agenda, this time prompting a more focused federal response. We will take a look at the Carter administration's proposed legislation to directly control the rising costs of health care when we examine policy proposals that have failed to be enacted.

The Medicare and Medicaid Policy Adoption Processes

It is difficult to ignore the contention that the adoptions of Medicare and Medicaid in 1965 represented a major change, perhaps even an aberration, in the direction of public health policy. Never before (or after) have our federal or state governments been charged with responsibility for health care of large segments of the American public.

In a discussion of the process of adopting Medicare and Medicaid, Stevens and Stevens provide a fairly detailed description of the disagreements between advocates of national health insurance and the American Medical Association (AMA) and the Health Insurance Institute (HII).[11] During the early 1960s, the evidence began to mount that elderly Americans were increasingly unable to provide for their own health care. Despite this, the AMA and the HII argued that health care had to be privately provided to be effectively delivered.[12] In the

---

[9] See Martin Feldstein, "An Econometric Model of the Medicare System," *Quarterly Journal of Economics,* Vol. 85, No. 1, Feb. 1971, pp. 1–20.

[10] Kingdon, pp. 6–7.

[11] Robert Stevens and Rosemary Stevens, *Welfare Medicine in America: A Case Study of Medicaid* (New York: Free Press, 1974).

[12] Stevens and Stevens, p. 46.

debates over Medicare—the highest priority health proposal of the Johnson administration—discussion focused on whether workers' contributions to the program should be voluntary or compulsory, whether prolonged hospital stays should be covered, and how payments would be made from the program to hospitals and physicians.

When the House Ways and Means Committee finished its hearings on national health insurance, it produced not a single bill but a composite of three rather disparate proposals.[13] As finally enacted, the three proposals represented a compromise among the various policy advocates. One of the proposals became the basic Medicare program, providing benefits to the elderly who qualified by participating in the Social Security retirement system. A second proposal provided federal subsidies so that the elderly could voluntarily participate in a health insurance program to cover what are often called out-of-pocket doctor bills. The third proposal called for extending medical care to the non-elderly poor and medically indigent through federal grants to the states. This proposal became known as Medicaid.

In some sense, the final Medicare proposal reflects the influence of private health insurance. As eventually adopted, both the compulsory and voluntary parts of Medicare contained deductibles and coinsurance, two features widely found in private insurance. Deductibles refer to the fact that a patient must initially pay some amount of the bill, after which Medicare takes over payments. Coinsurance requires that a patient pay a daily flat fee for extended hospital stays.[14] Although these provisions were proposed because they were thought to create a disincentive for patient abuse of the system and overinsurance, they also ensure that the very poorest people would still be unable to obtain health care.

It was in this context that Medicaid, a program aimed at providing medical coverage for the indigent, was also adopted. Stevens and Stevens suggest that concern over whether this would lead to an even more comprehensive form of national health insurance or even socialized medicine had a definite impact on the final program.

In a sense, this concern both "Americanized" the program (so that it did not resemble the socialized medicine programs in other nations, such as Great Britain) and almost ensured that it would be less than fully successful. In particular, the decision to finance and administer Medicaid through the states made it a direct extension of the existing welfare system. As we will see later, Medicaid is designed in a way that probably causes inefficiency in the health care industry and inflation of health care costs. We will also see that both Medicare and Medicaid have been implemented in ways that permit the medical community to retain most of the health care decision-making authority.

[13] Stevens and Stevens, p. 47.
[14] Stevens and Stevens, p. 49.

Attempting to Adopt Health Care
Cost Containment

Containing the costs of health care has been on the public agenda since at least the late 1960s. Despite this fact, very little public policy has been adopted to deal directly with the issue. Perhaps the most notable attempt to do so was made by the Carter administration between 1977 and 1980. Although the massive effort of the administration did not result in adoption of health cost containment legislation, we can learn something from looking at several studies of what happened in the process.

In April of 1977, President Carter proposed a health cost containment program centered on limiting hospital price increases. Targeting the area where it felt the greatest cost inflation had occurred, the Carter administration decided to propose controls on the prices charged by hospitals for in-patient care only. The proposal called for a 9 percent increase the first year after the bill's passage, with smaller increases in subsequent years. This, of course, was considerably less than the double-digit rate of health care cost inflation and the overall cost of living. The ultimate goal of the Carter administration apparently was to replace the existing system of paying for health care with some alternative system.[15]

The fate of this hospital cost containment bill can be tied, in part, to the way it was formulated. According to Jones, the U.S. Department of Health, Education and Welfare was the place where the bill was developed and drafted. In the process, hospitals and medical associations were excluded from the process,[16] and the bill, if enacted, would have required the medical industry to bear the financial costs. The medical industry, represented by the American Medical Association, the Federation of American Hospitals, and the American Hospital Association, argued that the quality of health care would necessarily suffer if the bill were enacted.[17]

To make matters more difficult for the bill, Congress was not ideally organized to deal with health legislation. There are two Senate and two House committees, each of which maintains some jurisdiction over health matters. The Senate Committee on Human Resources' Subcommittee on Health and Scientific Research and the Senate Committee on Finance's Subcommittee on Health shared health jurisdiction with the House Committee on Interstate and Foreign Commerce's Subcommittee on Health and Environment and the House Ways and Means Committee's Subcommittee on Health.[18]

---

[15] Congressional Quarterly, *Health Policy: The Legislative Agenda* (Washington, D.C.: Congressional Quarterly, Inc., 1980), p. 23.

[16] Charles O. Jones, *An Introduction to the Study of Public Policy,* 3rd ed. (Monterey, Calif.: Brooks/Cole, 1984), pp. 100–1.

[17] Congressional Quarterly, pp. 24–25.

[18] Jones, pp. 101–2.

The significance of this is that each of these committees deals with many issues other than health. Perhaps more important, the various committees possess different perspectives on what, if anything, would constitute acceptable health policy changes. For example, the House Ways and Means Committee's Subcommittee on Health is somewhat more likely to focus on the financial and budgetary aspects of health rather than medical aspects. And each of these committees provides substantial opportunity for a variety of interest groups that oppose the legislation to gain access to the health policy making process. Under these conditions, we would probably expect a consensus to be very difficult to achieve. Indeed, none was ever achieved over this bill, and the presidential term of Jimmy Carter ended with no health cost containment legislation enacted.

Public Mental Health Policy Adoptions

Public mental health policy has not received quite as much attention as have other areas of public health policy. One reason for this is that we have very little in the way of public mental health policy.[19] Another reason is undoubtedly the belief that mental health research has not been all that successful in finding effective treatments or cures for mental illness. Even so, we do find some significant federal and state government involvement in mental health policy.

It was not until roughly 1946 that mental health problems began to become recognized as legitimate targets of public policy. In the National Mental Health Act of 1946, Congress established the National Institute of Mental Health to work on improving the state of knowledge about mental health treatment through the provision of research grants.

Beginning probably in the late 1950s, mental health professionals began to push the idea that the most effective forms of treatment for most mentally ill persons included some type of community-based care.[20] Up until that time, public mental health care mainly consisted of patients being committed to often prolonged stays in state-operated mental hospitals. In part, the community mental health movement fostered the idea that some form of halfway, or aftercare, facility was necessary to ease the return of mental hospital patients to society.

We often think of state mental health hospitals as facilities housing only those patients who cannot be rehabilitated. On the contrary, until at least the mid-1960s, state hospitals often were a kind of dumping ground for people who were in need of mental health care but who could not afford private treatment and had nowhere else to go.[21] The community mental health movement sought

---

[19] D. A. Regier, L. D. Goldberg, and C. A. Taube, "The De Facto U.S. Mental Health Services System: A Public Health Perspective," *Archives of General Psychiatry,* Vol. 35, No. 6, June 1978, pp. 685-92.

[20] Jack R. Ewalt, "The Birth of the Community Mental Health Movement," in Walter E. Barton and Charlotte J. Sanborn, eds., *An Assessment of the Community Mental Health Movement* (Lexington, Mass.: Lexington Books, 1977), pp. 13-20.

[21] B. J. Ennis, *Prisoners of Psychiatry: Mental Patients, Psychiatrists, and the Law* (New York: Harcourt, Brace, Jovanovich, 1972).

to help establish a place for many of the patients to receive treatment while maintaining contact with the outside world.

Congress began to help fulfill this need in 1963, with the enactment of the Kennedy administration's Mental Retardation Facilities Act and Community Mental Health Centers Construction Act. It did so, at least in part, with the hope that state mental hospitals would no longer function as mere custodial institutions for large numbers of people with legitimate needs for treatment.[22]

The enactment of Medicare and Medicaid also included provisions for financing mental health care. In an effort to keep program costs relatively low, Congress decided that in the case of Medicaid only the costs of in-patient mental health care would be covered. Thus, the states often found that they could recover the costs of providing mental health care from the federal government only by institutionalizing (hospitalizing) patients. Many of the patients who were institutionalized were apparently not particularly appropriate candidates for such care. This problem was rectified by the Social Security Act amendments of 1975, which extended coverage to include treatment in various types of community-based facilities. Of course, this increased the program's costs.

Deinstitutionalization of Mental Health Patients

As a logical extension of the community mental health movement, the late 1960s and 1970s saw states pursuing a set of mental health policies that we commonly refer to as deinstitutionalization. These policies were apparently fostered both by legislators who wanted to keep the costs of public mental health services down and by a series of court suits.

Throughout the 1970s and into the 1980s, mental health practitioners sought to discourage the use of state mental hospitals as custodial institutions, where no one received much real treatment. They did so by becoming—and urging others to become—parties to civil lawsuits in an attempt to establish that mental health patients have a right to treatment.[23] By the late 1970s, the results of these suits seem to have gone a long way toward establishing treatment as a right. However, in 1981, the Supreme Court seemed to begin backing away from this concept.[24] The idea was that deinstitutionalization was preferable to institutionalization, even if it produced no better treatment results, because it is less a violation of people's constitutional rights.[25]

[22] Murray Levine, *The History and Politics of Community Mental Health* (New York: Oxford University Press, 1981), esp. Ch. 3.

[23] Edward Kaufman, "The Right to Treatment Suit As an Agent of Change," *American Journal of Psychiatry*, Vol. 136, No. 11, Nov. 1979, pp. 1428-32. See also Paul Lerman, *Deinstitutionalization and the Welfare State* (New Brunswick, N.J.: Rutgers University Press, 1982), esp. pp. 86-104, for a discussion of California's experiences.

[24] Levine, pp. 129-39.

[25] Lerman (see Note 23), Ch. 9.

This co-optation of the courts for the purpose of forcing changes in public policy again demonstrates the difficulty with this tactic. The parties in the civil suits seem to have expected that establishing the right to treatment would force the states, through their mental hospitals, to provide high-quality treatment. Instead, the states avoided the high cost of providing such treatment. The result was a wholesale release of mental patients into the community.[26] In most instances, this release was not accompanied by any sort of increase in community-based facilities.[27]

Implementing Health Policy:
The Case of Medicare

We discussed some problems of implementing Medicare as a problem of welfare policy in Chapter 5, but it also has health-related implications, of course. Until 1965, when the newly enacted Medicare program was turned over to the Social Security Administration, the SSA principally had responsibility for providing pension and disability benefits to people it determined to be eligible. With Medicare, the SSA was being asked to take on a very different set of tasks, involving the improvement of the quality of people's health.

In a study of the process that the SSA followed in deciding how to implement Medicare, Feder provides a clear description of the competing considerations.[28] In particular, she describes how the SSA avoided getting involved with taking actions that improved, or even assessed, the quality of health care. Instead, it opted to focus on the payment of claims filed by health providers (hospitals, doctors, etc.), simply deciding whether the claims were appropriate and, if so, paying them. According to Feder, part of the reason why the SSA chose this path was in response to the political pressures of the medical establishment. Apparently, the SSA felt that if it had become involved in trying to determine whether specific treatments were warranted, the medical establishment would have done its best to ensure the failure of the program.[29]

---

[26] A. A. Stone, "Recent Mental Health Litigation: A Critical Perspective," *American Journal of Psychiatry*, Vol. 134, No. 3, March 1977, pp. 273–779; and Kaufman, pp. 1428–32.

[27] Robert L. Okin, "The Future of State Mental Health Programs for the Chronic Psychiatric Patient in the Community," *American Journal of Psychiatry*, Vol. 135, No. 11, Nov. 11, Nov. 1978, pp. 1355–58.

[28] Judith M. Feder, "The Social Security Administration and Medicine: A Strategy of Implementation," in Kenneth M. Friedman and Stuart H. Rakoff, eds., *Toward a National Health Policy: Public Policy and the Control of Health-Care Costs* (Lexington, Mass.: Lexington Books, 1977). See also Judith M. Feder, *Medicine: The Politics of Federal Hospital Insurance* (Lexington, Mass.: Lexington Books, 1977).

[29] Feder, *Medicine*, p. 19.

Implementing Health Policy: The Case
of Pharmaceutical Regulation

Another important area of health policy implementation deals with federal efforts to regulate the industry that produces our medicine; the pharmaceutical industry. Analyses of the regulation of this industry provide lessons both for people who generally favor deregulation and for people who propose regulation as a panacea.

The license and manufacture of drugs is regulated by the Food and Drug Administration (FDA). This federal agency has had a rocky existence since its establishment in the 1930s.[30] Many of the activities of the FDA seem more closely related to agricultural policy (its food inspection functions), to consumer product safety, and even to nutrition policy (its food-labeling function). But principal among its tasks is the charge to license drugs developed by private companies and to decide which medicines will be available only through prescription. In this respect, much of the FDA's activities relate directly to public health.

Beginning with the Food, Drug, and Cosmetic Act of 1938 and its 1962 amendments, the FDA was given responsibility for ensuring that licensed drugs are both safe and effective. As a result, the FDA faces the tasks of trying to ensure that people will not be harmed by specific drugs and of determining whether specific drugs actually work. The way the FDA accomplishes these tasks has been the source of much controversy and subsequently considerable public policy making process research.

Problems with FDA decision making with respect to drug licensing began to emerge as public issues during the middle and late 1950s with the revelations about birth defects attributed to a drug approved as safe by the FDA. The drug Thalidomide, used as a tranquilizer for pregnant women, was approved by the FDA despite increasing evidence that the drug was not safe.[31] Other similarly disturbing decisions have been made by the FDA, and analysts have tried to understand how and why these decisions were made. Common wisdom suggests that agency capture by the industry they regulate is the reason for these decisions. But analysts have pointed to other factors. Analysis by Moore suggests that indecision about scheduling drugs to be controlled substances was at least partly the result of disagreements with other agencies.[32] Even so, the way the FDA made its decisions has been tied to a more fundamental problem.

---

[30] Paul J. Quirk, "Food and Drug Administration," in James Q. Wilson, ed., *The Politics of Regulation* (New York: Basic Books, 1980), pp. 191–235.

[31] See Francis E. Rourke, *Bureaucracy, Politics, and Public Policy*, 3rd ed. (Boston: Little, Brown, 1984), p. 51.

[32] Mark H. Moore, "Reorganization Plan 2 Reviewed: Problems in Implementing a Strategy to Reduce the Supply of Drugs to Illicit Markets in the United States," *Public Policy*, Vol. 26, No. 2, Spring 1978, p. 239.

For the most part, the FDA's decision-making process in licensing new drugs tended to err on the side of benefiting the drug companies at the possible expense of people's safety. FDA personnel were often cognizant of the financial impact their decisions would have on the drug companies. In some instances, the FDA's decision to grant or not grant a license for a particular drug determined whether the drug's manufacturer would be able to continue to operate.

The apparent reasons for the FDA's decisions were twofold: first, the FDA staff often accepted at face value the laboratory research submitted to it by the drug companies designating their drugs safe; second, the FDA developed a sort of revolving door of employment with the pharmaceutical industry, that is, FDA employees often looked to the drug companies for employment when leaving government service, and the FDA's new employees were often hired straight out of the pharmaceutical industry. Over time, this had the effect of staffing the FDA with people whose philosophies and values often mirrored those of people in the drug industry. The result was that FDA decision makers tended to err on the side of industry. The revolving door was partially closed after the passage of the 1978 Ethics in Government Act, which requires a two-year wait by federal employees before taking jobs in industries with which they worked closely.[33]

Analysis by Quirk argues that agency capture is less responsible than other factors for problems of drug regulation. In particular, he points to what he calls an intractable congressionally imposed policy dilemma.[34] He suggests that the FDA is required to scrutinize the drug development process in private industry, but in doing so, it imposes heavy burdens on the drug industry. The result is that new drugs become available less often, therefore denying people the benefits of the drugs. The FDA, according to Quirk, understands this dilemma but cannot hope to resolve it to everyone's satisfaction.

The concern in 1984 over the widespread use of possibly harmful dyes in foods demonstrates the fact that the FDA continues to experience problems. Apparently, poor coordination between the FDA and the Department of Agriculture was at least partly responsible for the lack of action in banning the use of such dyes as coloring agents. Despite the regulatory reforms, the FDA continues to be fairly widely perceived as making decisions that benefit the drug industry at the possible expense of people's health.

[33] Congressional Quarterly, *1978 CQ Almanac* (Washington, D.C.: Congressional Quarterly, Inc., 1978), pp. 840–41; and Congressional Quarterly, *1979 CQ Almanac* (Washington, D.C.: Congressional Quarterly, Inc., 1979), pp. 543–45.

[34] Quirk, pp. 191–235; Sam Peltzman, *Regulation of Pharmaceutical Innovation* (Washington, D.C.: American Enterprise Institute, 1974); and Henry G. Grabowski, *Drug Regulation and Innovation: Empirical Evidence and Policy Options* (Washington, D.C.: American Enterprise Institute, 1976). See also Robert S. Friedman, "Representation in Regulatory Decision Making: Scientific, Industrial, and Consumer Inputs to the FDA," *Public Administration Review*, May/June 1978, pp. 205–14.

The Institutionalized Health Service
Control Process: PSROs and HSAs
as Evaluators and Feedback Machines

In an effort to partially meet the need for greater cost control in health services, Congress enacted legislation in 1972 that required the establishment of what are called Professional Standards Review Organizations (PSROs) throughout the country.[35] PSROs consist of local boards composed of physicians who are supposed to monitor the use of hospital facilities and services. The congressional intent was to provide some mechanism to ensure that Medicare and Medicaid patients were not being required to stay in hospitals longer than necessary. But the legislation sought to do this without preempting the influence of physicians in making the individual decisions about what is necessary treatment.

If hospitals in a given area of the country desired to admit patients receiving Medicaid or Medicare benefits, there would first have to be a functioning PSRO. If a local area refused to establish a PSRO, the Department of Health, Education and Welfare (now Health and Human Services) was given authority to establish one. This acted as an incentive for the doctors in local areas to create their own PSRO. Despite this fact, the medical community generally reacted unfavorably to this perceived incursion into the realm of individual physicians' decision making.[36]

PSROs were designed to act as a major influence in the health policy making process. They were supposed to conduct utilization review of hospital services, a process whereby a committee designated by the PSRO decides, patient by patient, whether prescribed treatment is warranted.[37] The idea was to provide routine feedback on the quality, effectiveness, and costs of health care and to ensure that government programs were not paying for unneeded medical services. In fact, there is some evidence that the utilization review has had little influence on eliminating unnecessary treatment. There is also some evidence that the costs of running PSROs exceeds that of the unnecessary treatment Congress intended to control.[38]

Another attempt to coordinate the fragmented health care system in the United States was made through the National Health Planning and Resources Act of 1974. This act required states to establish Health Services Agencies

---

[35] J.H.U. Brown, *The Politics of Health Care* (Cambridge, Mass.: Ballinger Books, 1978), pp. 44–45. See also Clark C. Havighurst and James F. Blumstein, "Coping with Quality/Cost Tradeoffs in Medical Care: The Role of PSRO's," *Northwestern University Law Review*, Vol. 70, No. 1, March/April 1975, pp. 9–25.

[36] Jane Cassels Record, "Medical Politics and Medical Prices: The Relation Between Who Decides and How Much It Costs," in Friedman and Rakoff (see Note 28), pp. 71–106.

[37] Record, pp. 81–82.

[38] Record, pp. 82–83. See also Brown, pp. 47–50.

(HSAs) to evaluate the need for hospital and health facilities. HSAs are boards that report to statewide health agencies that are usually appointed by governors.[39] The intent was for HSAs to ensure that new facilities were actually needed in parts of the states before being built. The goal was to provide systematic evaluation of the need for new facilities to prevent the maldistribution of services within a state and to prevent the cost increases brought about by unnecessary new construction. Again, there is some evidence that HSAs have not had much impact on the control of health care costs. Apparently, HSAs find it somewhat easier to respond to the health care establishment (of which hospitals wishing to construct new facilities are a part) than to health consumers.

CAUSE AND CONSEQUENCE RESEARCH
ON HEALTH POLICY

While the policy making process research on public health policy begins to provide us with an idea of the complex political environment, there are many important questions we have not yet tackled. For example, we have not directly addressed the question of whether public health policies actually can be said to improve people's health. In terms of the economics of health, we have not yet looked at studies of the factors, including public policies, that seem to influence the rapidly increasing price of health care. These are among the health policy issues that have been studied using cause and consequence approaches to public policy analysis.

As in other policy areas, we will look at studies that treat public health policy as the conceptual independent variable (the variable causing some desirable or undesirable result). For example, we will look at studies of Medicare and Medicaid as causes of improved access to health care, as well as studies that argue that Medicare and Medicaid are the principal causes of health cost inflation. Unlike many other policy areas, there is very little research that treats public health policy as the conceptual dependent variable. With this in mind, let's look at what studies have to tell us about the health-related consequences of public health policies.

The Health Consequences
of Medicare and Medicaid

Perhaps the single most important health policy cause and consequence issue is whether public health programs can be said to cause people to be physically better off than they would be without such programs. There are at least three specific questions related to this issue. First, do Medicaid and Medicare increase health insurance coverage among people who otherwise would not be able to obtain private health insurance? Second, do Medicare and Medicaid increase

[39] Brown, p. 42. See also Havighurst and Blumstein (Note 35), pp. 9–25.

access and usage of health services for those who otherwise would find medical services inaccessible? And third, are people actually healthier because of Medicaid and Medicare? Numerous studies have attempted to answer these questions.

The earliest studies of population coverage indicated that the enactment of Medicare and Medicaid may have doubled the number of people in the United States covered by health insurance during the first few years of its existence.[40] Despite this increased coverage, the advent of Medicare does not seem to have created a massive increase in actual use of medical services by the elderly. For example, in a study of Medicare utilization rates, Gornick found that over the period 1967-1973 there was virtually no change in elderly Medicare recipients' use of medical services.[41] In other words, once Medicare increased coverage, it did not seem to create an ever increasing demand for health care services.

However, several studies of access to health services show that major gaps exist in the extent to which certain specific groups of people actually take advantage of the coverage. Indeed, the issue of overall utilization or access rates may be less important than the rates for specific subgroups of the population, such as poor people or racial minorities.

In studies of the role of Medicaid and Medicare in stimulating health service usage by the elderly, Davis and Reynolds found what they considered to be major problems.[42] Based on the 1969 Health Interview Study, a general population survey that asked people about their health experiences, Davis and Reynolds found that even controlling for differences in health status, Medicare and Medicaid had generally failed to eliminate major race- and income-related inequities in the frequency of use of medical services by the elderly. In particular, they found that racial minorities and people of low incomes were less likely to use government subsidized medical services than whites and people with higher incomes. However, a similar study over a longer period of time (1969 to 1976) by Link, Long, and Settle found that racial and income differences in Medicare utilization rates had nearly disappeared by the end of this period.[43]

[40] Harold S. Luft, *Poverty and Health: Causes and Consequences of Health Problems* (Cambridge, Mass.: Ballinger Books, 1978), p. 3.

[41] Marian Gornick, "Ten Years of Medicare: Impact on the Covered Population," *Social Security Bulletin,* Vol. 41, July 1976, pp. 3-21. See also D. Rabin and F. Schach, "Medicaid, Morbidity, and Physician Use," *Medical Care,* Vol. 13, 1975, p. 68; and John A. Butler and Richard K. Scotch, "Medicaid and Children: Some Recent Lessons and Reasonable Next Steps," *Public Policy,* Vol. 26, No. 1, Winter 1978, pp. 3-27.

[42] See Karen Davis and Roger Reynolds, "Medicine and the Utilization of Health Care Services by the Elderly," *Journal of Human Resources,* Vol. 10, Summer 1975, pp. 361-77; Karen Davis and Roger Reynolds, "The Impact of Medicare and Medicaid on Access to Medical Care," in Richard N. Rosett, ed., *The Role of Health Insurance in the Health Services Sector* (New York: National Bureau of Economic Research, 1976); and Karen Davis and Cathy Schoen, *Health and the War on Poverty: A Ten Year Appraisal* (Washington, D.C.: Brookings Institution, 1978).

[43] Charles R. Link, Stephen H. Long, and Russell F. Settle, "Equity and the Utilization of Health Care Services by the Medicare Elderly," *Journal of Human Resources,* Vol. 17, No. 2, Spring 1982, pp. 195-212.

Unfortunately, these analysts provide little explanation for what could have happened in the interim to account for this change.

In a related vein, the issue to some is what the public policies have done, if anything, to reduce disparities that already existed in the American health care system. For example, Martin Feldstein (former chairman of the President's Council of Economic Advisors) suggests that Medicare created substantial income and racial biases beyond those that already existed.[44] Conversely, Vogel and Morrall found evidence that when you consider Medicare and Medicaid together, the latter goes a long way toward offsetting the discriminatory effects of the former.[45] Analysis by Stuart shows that disparities in the distribution of Medicaid benefits to poor people have become more pronounced under Medicaid.[46]

The final question is what many people consider to be the bottom-line criterion on which to judge the success of public health programs: are people healthier because of Medicaid and Medicare? Interestingly, the weight of the evidence calls into question whether people really are better off as a result of greater health insurance coverage and access. On its face, the question would seem to be rather straightforward. But it has at least two parts. First, are people physically healthier with Medicare and Medicaid? And second, what are people giving up to obtain the increased coverage and access? We will deal with some studies of this first issue here; we will defer a discussion of the second issue to the next section, where we look at the inflationary effects of health insurance.

The consensus about the Medicare and Medicaid health effects research parallels the findings related to the health effects of general access to medical resources. Most studies seem to suggest that access to medical resources, public and private, has very little impact on how healthy we are.[47] Instead, our health is primarily influenced by our personal life-style. Since Medicare and Medicaid are designed simply to provide *access* to medical care, these programs by themselves do not seem to have much influence on health quality or on improving participants' life-styles.[48]

Before we state this conclusion too emphatically, we should note that there is some evidence pointing in the other direction. One of the more compre-

[44] Martin Feldstein, "An Econometric Model of the Medicare System," *Quarterly Journal of Economics*, Vol. 85, No. 1, Feb. 1971, pp. 1–20.

[45] Ronald J. Vogel and John F. Morrall, "The Impact of Medicaid on State and Local Health and Hospitals Expenditures, with Special Reference to Blacks," *Journal of Human Resources*, Vol. 8, No. 2, 1973, pp. 202–11.

[46] Bruce Stuart, "Equity and Medicaid," *Journal of Human Resources*, Vol. 7, No. 2, Spring 1972, pp. 162–78.

[47] Victor R. Fuchs, ed., *Essays in the Economics of Health and Medical Care* (New York: Columbia University Press, 1972); and Victor R. Fuchs, *Who Shall Live?* (New York: Basic Books, 1974).

[48] Joseph P. Newhouse and Lindy J. Friedlander, "The Relationship between Medical Resources and Measures of Health: Some Additional Evidence," *Journal of Human Resources*, Vol. 15, No. 2, Spring 1980, pp. 200–18.

hensive studies of the relationship between access to health care and the quality of people's health is by Hadley.[49] His analysis focused on access to all types of health care, public and private, as conceptual independent variables, with explicit attention paid to Medicare and Medicaid. He attempted to assess whether areas of the country that had greater use of Medicaid and Medicare also had better health as measured by numerous variables, including adult, neonatal, and infant mortality (death) rates, rates of disease, and so on. His results indicate that Medicare and Medicaid do seem to improve health, especially in areas with greater concentrations of white men between the ages of 45 and 64 and of black women.

The Effects of Medicare and Medicaid on Health Price and Cost Inflation

One of the more compelling arguments against any sort of national health insurance is that government-sponsored health subsidies have been found to result in higher health service costs and prices. Indeed, it has been suggested that existing public health insurance programs—such as Medicare (and possibly Medicaid), as well as many state-initiated programs—are major fuels in the health price inflationary fire. It has also been suggested that such programs increase the *costs* of operating health facilities, which in part explains how they can cause increases in the *prices* charged the recipients of health services. There are many studies of these relationships, and we can take a brief look at some of them.

Perhaps most notable among researchers finding that public health insurance programs are inflationary is Martin Feldstein. He argues in several studies that what he calls overinsurance is responsible for the massive price and cost increases in health care.[50] Overinsurance is not solely the result of Medicare and Medicaid. Private health insurance, in Feldstein's view, is also partly to blame. But in terms of public policy, Medicare and Medicaid constitute perhaps the most direct contributors to health price inflation. Feldstein contends that if health cost or price inflation is to be reduced, it must be done largely through discouraging overinsurance. In addition to pursuing methods of discouraging the use of Medicare and Medicaid, Feldstein proposes, as we will see shortly, methods of affecting private overinsurance through changes in the federal tax system.

Several other studies have narrowed the focus of research to factors that cause health cost or price inflation. A study by Davis, for example, examined

[49] Jack Hadley, *More Medical Care, Better Health? An Economic Analysis of Mortality Rates* (Washington, D.C.: Urban Institute, 1982). Hadley's findings support the results found in Davis and Schoen's *Health and the War on Poverty* (see Note 42); they provide substantial evidence that access to health care *has* improved the health status of the poor and disadvantaged.

[50] Martin Feldstein, *Hospital Costs and Health Insurance* (Cambridge, Mass.: Harvard University Press, 1981); Martin Feldstein, "The Welfare Loss of Excessive Health Insurance," *Journal of Political Economy,* Vol. 81, No. 1, March/April 1973, pp. 251-80.

the relationship between Medicare and the wages paid by hospitals to staff workers.[51] Wages, of course, are primary contributors to the costs hospitals must bear in providing health care. Davis found that Medicare does seem to play a fairly significant role in increasing hospital costs by contributing to higher hospital worker wages.

A study by Sloan narrowed the focus specifically to the fees or prices charged by private physicians.[52] He analyzed the relationship between the Medicare and Medicaid fee schedules and the follow-up office visit fees charged by the doctors, while controlling for other factors that might confound this relationship. His results showed fairly strong correlations: as the Medicare and Medicaid fee schedule provides higher levels of reimbursement, doctors' office visit fees for all patients increase even more. This is further evidence of the inflationary effects of national public health insurance programs.

There is not perfect agreement about whether Medicare and Medicaid can be said to be principal causes of health cost or price inflation. Studies by Newhouse and others, for example, argue that while Medicare and Medicaid contribute to the rising cost of health care, they do so by no means alone.[53] Without explicitly studying alternative causes of health cost inflation, the implication is that Medicare and Medicaid are being blamed for a more widespread problem. We can turn to this issue for some more detailed evidence.

Other Causes of Health Price and Cost Inflation

While Medicare and Medicaid certainly seem to be major contributors to rising health care costs, there are other factors that have been studied. The three most prominently identified influences are: (1) the growth in all types of health insurance, public and private; (2) rapid advances in very expensive medical treatment technologies; and (3) the marked increase in medical malpractice lawsuits and the consequent increases in the use and price of malpractice insurance for doctors.

In his study of cost inflation, Feldstein argues persuasively that all of these influences are not independent of one another. He presents evidence that the growth in sophistication and complexity of medical technology has been caused

[51] Karen Davis, "Theories of Hospital Inflation," *Journal of Human Resources,* Vol. 8, No. 2, Spring 1973, pp. 181–201.

[52] Frank A. Sloan, "Effects of Health Insurance on Physicians' Fees," *Journal of Human Resources,* Vol. 17, No. 4, Fall 1982, pp. 533–57.

[53] Joseph Newhouse, Charles E. Phelps, and William B. Schwartz, "Policy Options and the Impact of National Health Insurance," *New England Journal of Medicine,* Vol. 290, June 13, 1974, pp. 1345–59; Joseph Newhouse, "Inflation and Health Insurance," in Michael Zubkoff, ed., *Health: A Victim or Cause of Inflation* (New York: Milbank Memorial Fund, 1976), pp. 210–24.

by the growth in health insurance, both public and private.[54] In his analysis, Feldstein argues that the growth in health insurance coverage has influenced people to seek medical care even when they do not need it. Accordingly, he concludes, the key to reducing health costs is to reduce coverage from health insurance.[55] Once this is accomplished, only people who really need health care will seek it, and health care costs will take care of themselves. Thus, health care cost inflation, theoretically, would be curbed without people's health necessarily suffering.

Tax Policies as Influences on "Overinsurance"

If overinsurance constitutes such a profound influence on health price and cost inflation, then why do people overinsure and what can be done to intervene? Again, Martin Feldstein's work provides the primary basis for answers to these questions.

Feldstein has studied the relationship between the federal tax system and the tendency for Americans to overinsure against health problems.[56] In particular, he examined provisions in federal personal and corporate income taxes that exempt payments for private health insurance from taxation. We can say that these exemptions in a sense provide government subsidies of the private health insurance system. Feldstein's analysis examines the effects of these subsidies on several specific dependent variables. First, he argues that health insurance tax exemptions create a substantial loss of federal tax revenue. Second, the exemption encourages many people to buy more insurance than they really need or could otherwise afford, given the level of health risks they actually face. Third, those who are overinsured tend to overutilize health services, which in turn causes the price of health care to escalate. And fourth, those who are overinsured and who tend to overutilize health services tend to be disproportionately concentrated among higher-income families, those who ostensibly need the services the least.

---

[54] Feldstein, *Hospital Costs and Health Insurance*, pp. 1–6; and Martin Feldstein, "A New Approach to National Health Insurance," *Public Interest*, Vol. 23, Spring 1971, pp. 93–105.

[55] Feldstein, *Hospital Costs and Health Insurance*, pp. 1–6; and Feldstein, "A New Approach to National Health Insurance," pp. 93–105.

[56] Martin Feldstein and Elizabeth Allison, "Tax Subsidies and Private Health Insurance: Distributions, Revenue Loss, and Effects," in Feldstein, *Hospital Costs and Health Insurance*, pp. 205–20. See also Bridger Mitchell and Ronald Vogel, "Health Taxes: An Assessment of the Medical Deduction," *Southern Economics Journal*, Vol. 41, No. 4, April 1975, pp. 660–72; and Ronald J. Vogel, "The Tax Treatment of Health Insurance Premiums As a Cause of Overinsurance," in Mark V. Pauly, ed., *National Health Insurance: What Now, What Later, What Never?* (Washington, D.C.: American Enterprise Institute, 1980), pp. 220–49.

Perhaps the most significant implication of these findings is that this type of incentive to overinsure may actually make people worse off. In a separate study, Feldstein argues that overinsurance results in an overall loss of welfare to society because the purchased insurance does not really produce improved health. Instead, the emphasis on health insurance causes higher health prices and influences the health industry to develop and use more sophisticated and costly services.[57] As prices of health care increase, people feel the need to acquire more insurance, which they often can afford because the tax exemption permits them to pay only part of the price. In Feldstein's view, public policy should attempt to discourage overinsurance by eliminating tax subsidies and generally making the price of health insurance higher.[58]

The Causes and Consequences
of Pharmaceutical Regulation

Earlier in this chapter, we looked at some studies of the pharmaceutical regulatory process involving the Food and Drug Administration. We raised the issue then of whether the FDA's decisions on licensing new drugs reflects pressure brought by the drug industry itself. This can be thought of as a question requiring a cause and consequence policy study. From this perspective, the question becomes, What is it that causes the FDA to make decisions the way it does?

A study by Grabowski is important because it approaches this issue from a rather explicit cause and consequence perspective.[59] In other words, it addresses the results of a specific regulatory *process* using the cause and consequence approach. Grabowski's study attempts to explain the level of regulation the FDA imposes. In general, the evidence suggests that market pressures influence the FDA to impose greater restrictions on the licensing of new drugs. These restrictions actually work to the benefit of those companies having already licensed drugs, since most new license applications are from competing companies for drugs that are comparable to, but chemically different from, these drugs.[60]

Just as the causes of FDA decisions have been subjected to study, so, too, have their consequences. There have been several important analyses of the impact of the FDA's regulations on the drug industry. For example, Peltzman conducted a time-series analysis to investigate how FDA decisions have influenced the drug industry's development of new drugs over time.[61] By comparing the

[57] Feldstein, "The Welfare Loss of Excess Health Insurance" (see Note 50), pp. 251–52.

[58] Feldstein, "The Welfare Loss of Excess Health Insurance" (see Note 50), pp. 251–52.

[59] Grabowski (see Note 34).

[60] Grabowski (see Note 34).

[61] Peltzman (see Note 34). See also Henry G. Grabowski and John M. Vernon, *The Regulation of Pharmaceuticals: Balancing the Benefits and Risks* (Washington, D.C.: American Enterprise Institute, 1983), esp. Ch. 3; and Henry G. Grabowski, John M. Vernon, and Lucy G. Thomas, "Estimating the Effects of Regulation on Innovation: An International Comparative Analysis of the Pharmaceutical Industry," *Journal of Law and Economics*, Vol. 21, No. 1, April 1978, pp. 133–64.

number of new drugs developed by pharmaceutical companies before 1962—when the Food, Drug, and Cosmetic Act Amendments were passed by Congress—to the number of new drugs developed since 1962, he made an effort to infer the effect of regulation.

The analysis indicates that there has been a substantial decline in the number of new drugs developed, which Peltzman attributes to increased regulations imposed by the FDA. He argues that this is an exceedingly high price to pay because it denies people the potential benefits of new drugs while providing only the smallest improvements in safety. Because Peltzman's results show that the decline in the number of drugs developed actually started sometime before 1962, some have argued that the decline has nothing to do with the FDA's actions, but rather it has more to do with technological difficulties faced by the pharmaceutical companies.

The Causes and Consequences
of Deinstitutionalization

Up until now, all of the policy cause and consequence analyses have focused on physical health. But studies of the consequences of mental health policies have also been widely conducted. One subject that has received substantial treatment is deinstitutionalization, which we discussed earlier. In particular, analysts have endeavored to discover why some states pursue deinstitutionalization more than others and whether mental health has been improved by deinstitutionalizing patients, as was intended by many in the community mental health movement.

The mental health policy of deinstitutionalization has been followed to some degree by all of the states. But recent research has revealed that some states carry it to an extreme, while others prefer to give it a much more limited role. In an effort to discover why such variations exist, Sigelman, Roeder, and Sigelman analyzed a number of factors.[62]

Using the 1977 Survey of Community Residential Facilities (a nationwide compilation of mental health treatment facilities), Sigelman, Roeder, and Sigelman focused on the percentage of each state's mentally retarded persons who were placed in community residences. They assessed the relative role played by a number of socioeconomic, demographic, and political factors in explaining the difference among states. Their results showed that several characteristics of the political/institutional system of the states (legislative professionalism and political culture) seemed to constitute major influences. States with more professional legislatures were more likely to pursue deinstitutionalization than other states. Thus, the authors see deinstitutionalization as a specific form of policy innovation in treatment rather than simply a method of reducing the states' budgets.

As we noted earlier, deinstitutionalization was never founded on the

[62] Lee Sigelman, Phillip W. Roeder, and Carol K. Sigelman, "Social Service Innovation in the American States: Deinstitutionalization of the Mentally Retarded," *Social Science Quarterly,* Vol. 62, No. 3, Sept. 1981, pp. 503–15.

notion that it would necessarily facilitate effective treatment; the policy was preferred because it was thought to be at least as effective as institutional treatment and did not violate patients' personal rights. As a result, analyses of deinstitutionalization's consequences have focused on the size of the institutional population and on public mental health costs. A study by Aviram, Syme, and Cohen showed rather dramatic reductions in the sizes of mental health institutions' patient populations.[63] But Lerman argues that the states' costs of mental health care actually increased, an effect opposite to that anticipated by many policy makers.[64]

HEALTH POLICY PRESCRIPTION RESEARCH

The analysis of health policy has made use of a variety of prescriptive models or techniques. Perhaps largely because cost considerations have become so important in health policy, the need to assess the future impacts of policy changes has inspired the development of at least three major econometric models, micro-simulation models of the sort we discussed previously. In this case, the ultimate goal is to assess various financial considerations. Each of these models is designed to assess the future financial impacts of different kinds of policy changes. We shall take a look at what these models consist of, what they have been used for, and how useful they have been as instruments of health policy analysis.

The National Health Insurance Simulation Model

Perhaps the best-known health policy prescription model is the National Health Insurance Simulation (NHIS) model, developed by Feldstein and Friedman.[65] The NHIS model attempts to predict how household demand for health services is influenced by supply and price considerations. Its most notable application has been the assessment of the effects of a future national health insurance program on the costs and prices of medical services. The model consists of a series of equations relating families' hospital and medical expenditures to the prices of such services. The model also considers the differences among families' household characteristics, such as ages and genders, whether or not the families have health insurance, and the amount of any insurance deductibles. When the data on the families having these various characteristics are analyzed, one can then

---

[63] U. Aviram, L. S. Syme, and J. B. Cohen, "The Effects of Policies and Programs on Reduction of Medical Hospitalization," *Social Science and Medicine,* Vol. 10, 1976, pp. 571–77.

[64] Lerman (see Note 23), pp. 94–97.

[65] Martin Feldstein and Bernard Friedman, "The Effect of National Health Insurance on the Price and Quantity of Medical Care," in Rosett (see Note 42). See also Feldstein, *Hospital Costs and Health Insurance.*

project the impact of policy changes on consumers' health service behavior, health care prices, total program costs to the government, and so on.

Feldstein and Friedman applied this model to an analysis of two national health insurance plans proposed in the late 1970s.[66] In the first instance, they analyzed a national health insurance proposal with low deductibles: $50 a year for hospital care and $50 a year for other medical services. This proposal also carried a coinsurance rate of 10 percent. This simply means that the prospective patient pays the first $50 and pays 10 percent of the cost over $50. In the second plan, the deductible is also $50, but the coinsurance rate is raised to 20 percent. And each family's total medical bill during a year is limited to 10 percent of the total family income. This represents a sort of catastrophic-illness insurance. Where families' health expenditures exceed 20 percent of total family income, the government pays the difference.

Analysis of these proposals revealed some important patterns. Under the first plan, people's health expenditures would increase 38 percent over what they were with no national health insurance plan. Much of the increase was due to price inflation that the plan itself caused. Under plan two, we might expect the higher coinsurance rate to decrease expenditures and ultimately cost the government less than plan one. But because of the limit at 10 percent of total family income, the second plan ends up costing the government more. The model reveals that the price of medical services increases over time as a result of the health insurance program. As these prices increase, families' health service expenditures increasingly exceed the 10 percent limit. As a result the government actually pays more under plan two than under plan one.

The Human Resources Research Center
Health Care Sector Model

Another microsimulation model developed for the purpose of analyzing public health care policy is the Health Care Sector (HCS) model developed by the Human Resources Research Center.[67] The HCS model has been used to assess a variety of future policy impacts, and according to its developers, it is ideally suited to analyzing the distributional impacts (who benefits a lot, who benefits a little, etc.) that future policies may produce.

The HCS model actually consists of five submodels, each of which is designed to depict a different major component in the production or delivery of health care. Figure 6.2 is a simple version of the block diagram showing the dif-

[66] Feldstein and Friedman, pp. 292–305.

[67] Donald E. Yett et al., "The HRRC Health Care Sector Simulation Model," in Robert H. Haveman and Kevin Hollenbeck, eds., *Microeconomic Simulation Models for Public Policy Analysis, Vol. 1: Distributional Impacts* (New York: Academic Press, 1980), pp. 231–69. See also Donald E. Yett et al., *A Forecasting and Policy Simulation Model of the Health Care Sector: The HRRC Prototype Microeconometric Model* (Lexington, Mass.: Lexington Books, 1979), Ch. 9.

FIG. 6.2.   The HRRC Health Care Sector Microeconomic Model

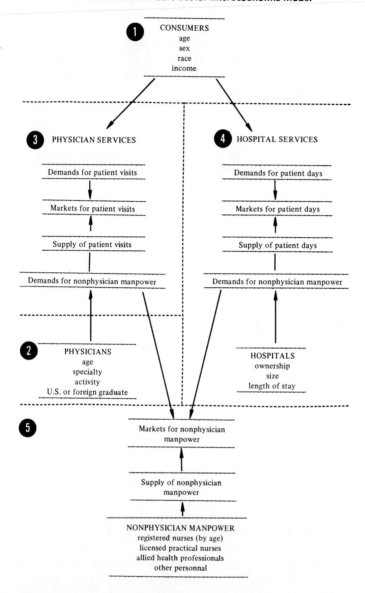

From D. Yett et al., "The HRRC Health Care Sector Simulation Model," in R. Haveman and K. Hollenbeck, eds., *Microeconomic Simulation Models for Public Policy Analysis, Vol. 1, Distributional Impacts* (New York: Academic Press, 1983), p. 235. Reprinted with permission of the Institute for Research on Poverty, University of Wisconsin, Madison.

ferent components and how they interact with one another. As this figure indicates, the submodels of the HCS model are: (1) the nature of the consumers of health services (age, gender, race, and income); (2) the character of medical physicians (age, area of medical specialty, level of activity, and type of medical school attended); (3) the quantities and prices of physicians' services; (4) the quantities and prices of hospital services; and (5) the supply of nonphysician medical personnel (such as nurses).

Perhaps the most important characteristic of the model is that it permits fairly long-term impacts to be assessed. If public policy alters aspects of one of the model's components, an assessment can be made of how those alterations affect other model components. For example, if a public policy were being considered that would stimulate the supply of doctors (for instance, increasing the number of medical school students), the model could assess the effect of this on the supply of medical services, the prices consumers pay for various medical services, and so on. Accordingly, the model has been used to analyze many different prospective health policy proposals.

One example of the model's use is the application to a proposed national health insurance (NHI) program. Yett et al. use this model to assess several hypothetical NHI programs with different levels of coinsurance (the amount that the prospective consumer of health services must pay). In this example, the model first assesses the impact of a program with an average coinsurance rate of 20 percent. The program calls for a lower-than-average coinsurance rate for poorer families, an average coinsurance rate for middle-income families, and a higher-than-average rate for families with higher incomes. Then the model is used to assess an alternative program with coinsurance rates set at half of what they are under the first program. The results of the model compare these two programs in terms of a variety of impacts measuring utilization of different types of health services. It reveals, for example, that the lower coinsurance rate would be expected to produce about 10 percent more demand for hospital services than the higher rate, and this increase in demand would be disproportionately concentrated among the very young and the very old, among white men, and among the relatively poor.

A Linear Programming Health Manpower Model

An alternative approach, with perhaps a more limited purpose, has been developed by Detsky.[68] His model represents a modification of other models used in health care planning.[69] The purpose of Detsky's model is to permit estimates

[68] Allan S. Detsky, *The Economic Foundations of National Health Policy* (Cambridge, Mass.: Ballinger, 1978).

[69] For example, Larry Shuman, John Young and Eliezar Naddor, "Manpower Mix for Health Services: A Prescriptive Regional Planning Model," *Health Services Research*, Vol. 6, No. 2, Summer 1971, pp. 103–19.

of the need for physicians in specific isolated health care markets. Detsky relies on a technique called linear programming, which is used to estimate the most efficient (optimum) mix of inputs needed to produce a desired level or range of outputs. In Detsky's model, the output that he wishes to optimize is the needed level of health services in a particular market area. The inputs consist of all of the technically feasible methods of delivering health care to people. Ultimately, the question is how many doctors, nurses, and other health personnel and re-sources would be required to optimally produce the needed level of health ser-vices, the idea being that it would be inefficient to have too many doctors and not enough hospital beds or too few support people, and so on.

This linear programming model permits analysis of various public policies designed to improve the quality or optimize the quantity of health care person-nel. Detsky provides an analysis of the 1976 Health Professions Educational Assistance Act, comparing it to other health manpower proposals in their abili-ties to attain specific goals.[70] In particular, the legislation is analyzed to deter-mine whether it is likely to achieve the stated goals: (1) increasing availability of health care facilities and services in geographic areas that are underserved; (2) increasing concentrations of doctors in primary care subfields or specialties, such as family medicine; (3) increasing medical education opportunities; and (4) decreasing the number of foreign students attending U.S. medical schools. In a rather detailed analysis, Detsky suggests that the Health Professions Educa-tional Assistance Act could not produce much progress in reaching these goals.

Many other public health policy prescription models have been devel-oped.[71] This description should provide a glimpse at the policy conclusions drawn from several important models. It should also give you a taste of the difference between this approach to public health policy analysis and other approaches.

SUMMARIZING THE APPROACHES
TO HEALTH POLICY RESEARCH

In our coverage of a substantial amount of public health policy research, we have seen that the focus of policy making process research is much different from cause and consequence and policy prescription research. We have learned, too, that there are many political interests active in the public health policy making process. Except perhaps for a short time in the mid-1960s, when Medicare and Medicaid were enacted by Congress, the medical profession has succeeded in retaining the decision-making power over the quantity, quality, distribution, and

---

[70] Detsky, pp. 198–215.

[71] For a good review of other prescriptive models and studies, see Duncan Boldy, ed., *Operational Research Applied to Health Services* (New York: St. Martin's, 1981).

form of health care delivery. Public health policy changes have been made possible only during times when policy windows have opened, that is, those fairly short periods of opportunity that often result from factors over which policy makers exercise very little direct influence.

In an effort to combat the extremely high health price and cost inflation of the 1960s and 1970s, Congress attempted several policy interventions. It fostered the development of health maintenance organizations and subsequently mandated various forms of institutional review and feedback from the medical establishment. For example, Congress required the establishment of professional standards review committees. When all else failed, the Carter administration proposed direct cost controls, which the medical establishment helped influence Congress to reject.

In mental health, we learned that much of what constitutes our public policy is a reflection of the community mental health movement. However, policy makers carried the community care idea to its extreme by pursuing the deinstitutionalization of chronic mental care patients, including the mentally retarded. This was done at least partly because of the potential cost savings to the states.

When we looked at research on the implementation stage of the public health policy making process, we found that the political interests in health policy have sometimes been viewed as fairly successful at exercising influence. For example, we saw that the Social Security Administration intentionally administered Medicare in a way that ignored explicit health quality considerations. And we saw that the Food and Drug Administration's regulation of the pharmaceutical industry is thought to have been influenced partly by the industry itself, as well as by the nearly impossible task of ensuring drug safety without destroying the drug industry.

In the public health policy cause and consequence research, we learned that Medicare and Medicaid seem to have produced a rather profound improvement in health insurance coverage and access to medical services. There is also some evidence that Medicaid helps to reduce some of the income and racial biases in the private and Medicare health systems. Despite these effects, it is not entirely clear that these programs have improved people's health.

Public health policy cause and consequence research also argued persuasively that health insurance, public and private alike, constitutes a major cause of the rapid health service price and cost increases. And public policies in non-health-related areas, such as taxation, create incentives for people to overinsure against health problems, which itself contributes to the price and cost increases. The implication is that health price and cost inflation can only be controlled through discouraging overinsurance.

Public health policy cause and consequence research concerning mental health suggested that the states most heavily relying on deinstitutionalization are the most innovative states and the ones with the most professional legislatures. Yet, other cause and consequence research revealed how ineffective de-institutionalization has been as a treatment technique.

Our look at public health policy prescription analysis focused on three models. The first of these, the Feldstein and Friedman National Health Insurance Simulation Model, clearly demonstrated the unexpected prospective influence of public health insurance programs on the federal budget through increasing prices. The Human Resources Research Center's Health Care Sector simulation model provides the ability to assess the future effects of policy changes on the quality, prices, and quantity of health care services available to consumers. And the Detsky linear programming model permits an assessment of how to deliver public health services most efficiently within a given geographic region.

With all of the topics and studies we have examined, there is much more that we have ignored. One or another of our three approaches to public health policy analysis has been applied to issues we did not address. For example, there have been studies of health maintenance organizations, of other forms of community health programs, and of the role of medical personnel unionization. There have also been many studies on topics of environmental health,[72] although we discussed some aspects of this in our look at environmental policy studies in Chapter 2.

Policy making process research has analyzed the tension between government promotion of cigarettes through subsidies to the tobacco industry and their efforts to reduce the known detrimental health effects of smoking tobacco products.[73] Research has also addressed additional questions of mental health policy, such as the process and impact of including psychiatric services in Medicare and Medicaid coverage.[74] All of these constitute important public health topics where a great deal of research has been conducted using our three analytical approaches.

FURTHER READING

Public Health Policy Making Process Studies

KINGDON, JOHN W. *Agendas, Alternatives, and Public Policies.* Boston: Little, Brown, 1984.
LEVINE, MURRAY. *From State Hospitals to Psychiatric Center: The Implementation of Planned Organizational Change.* Lexington, Mass.: Lexington Books, 1980.

[72] Lester B. Lave and Eugene P. Seskin, *Air Pollution and Human Health* (Baltimore: Johns Hopkins University Press, 1977).

[73] A. Lee Fritschler, *Smoking and Politics: Policymaking and the Federal Bureaucracy,* 3rd ed. (Englewood Cliffs, N.J.: Prentice-Hall, 1983).

[74] T. G. McGuire, "National Health Insurance for Private Psychiatric Care: A Study in the Distribution of Income," *Public Finance Quarterly,* Vol. 9, No. 2, 1981, pp. 183-96.

LEVINE, MURRAY. *The History and Politics of Community Mental Health.* New York: Oxford University Press, 1981.
STEVENS, ROBERT, and ROSEMARY STEVENS. *Welfare Medicine in America: A Case Study of Medicaid.* New York: Free Press, 1974.

Public Health Policy Cause and Consequence Analyses

DAVIS, KAREN, and CATHY SCHOEN. *Health and the War on Poverty: A Ten Year Appraisal.* Washington, D.C.: Brookings Institution, 1978.
FELDSTEIN, MARTIN. *Hospital Costs and Health Insurance.* Cambridge, Mass.: Harvard University Press, 1981.
GRABOWSKI, HENRY G. *Drug Regulation and Innovation: Empirical Evidence and Policy Options.* Washington, D.C.: American Enterprise Institute, 1976.

Public Health Policy Prescription Studies

DETSKY, ALLAN S. *The Economic Foundations of National Health Policy.* Cambridge, Mass.: Ballinger, 1978.
FELDSTEIN, MARTIN, and BERNARD FRIEDMAN. "The Effects of National Health Insurance on the Price and Quantity of Medical Care," in Richard Rosett, ed., *The Role of Health Insurance in the Health Services Sector.* New York: National Bureau of Economic Research, 1976.
YETT, DONALD, et al. *A Forecasting and Policy Simulation Model of the Health Care Sector: The HRRC Prototype Microeconometric Model.* Lexington, Mass.: Lexington Books, 1979.

CHAPTER SEVEN

Analyses of Public Tax and Revenue Policies

Up until now, all of our substantive discussions have involved studies of public policy areas where our governments spend tax revenues. Policy analysts are equally interested in how our governments raise the monies they spend, so their studies also focus on the various taxes our governments levy. Most of the studies analyze the different tax instruments (personal income, corporate income, and property taxes, for example) to assess why we use them, how economically efficient they are, who ultimately pays them, and what effects they have on people's lives. In particular, when we apply our three approaches to the study of tax and revenue policy, we will examine studies of:

> The political influences on decisions to use or not use various taxes, including the tax limitation movement;
>
> Who ultimately pays the different taxes. For example, do corporations really pay the corporate income tax? Do middle-income people bear the greatest burden of the federal personal income tax?
>
> What the consequences are of the different taxes on the operation of the overall economy. For example, does the federal personal income tax reduce capital investment, increase inflation, etc.?
>
> What the effects are of our taxes on society in general. For example, do people paying higher income taxes lose their incentive to earn more? Do state and local taxes influence business and residential location decisions? Does the local property tax affect the quality of public education?
>
> What the tax limitation movement has tried to achieve and whether it has been successful.
>
> What the result would be if we tried to make changes in existing taxes. For example, what would happen if we eliminated the mortgage interest deduction from the federal personal income tax?

As you can see, we will examine studies of a relatively large number of topics. In our examination, we will see that, because most of the tax and revenue policy research has been conducted by economists, analyses of the policy making processes are relatively few. Even so, there are some very important tax policy making process studies. Before we look at them, we should review some characteristics of the federal, state, and local tax systems in the United States.

AN OUTLINE OF THE FEDERAL, STATE, AND LOCAL TAX AND REVENUE SYSTEMS

The U.S. tax and revenue systems are composed of a relatively large number of tax instruments. The federal government relies on the personal individual income tax, enacted by Congress through ratification of the Sixteenth Amendment to the Constitution in 1913. While this is clearly the most important federal tax from the standpoint of the amount of revenue raised, the federal government also receives considerable revenues from corporate income, gift, and estate taxes.

The states rely on a variety of taxes. Some states use a single instrument to raise needed revenues, such as a general or limited tax on retail sales, personal income taxes, or corporate income taxes. Other states prefer to rely on some combination of these.

Local governments rely heavily on real estate property taxes and personal property taxes (such as a motor vehicle tax), although many large cities have adopted city income or wage taxes and a variety of user fees to produce what they consider to be needed levels of revenue. Other units of local government may also impose taxes, including special districts (fire districts, school districts, etc.) and counties. These governmental units are usually limited to collecting revenues through property taxes or user fees.

We have referred to tax reliance as a concept that distinguishes the different tax instruments. When we speak of tax reliance, we are referring to something fairly specific: the percentage of total revenues a unit of government raises from a particular tax. For example, the extent to which we rely on the federal income tax is measured by the percentage of total federal revenue raised by the income tax. With this in mind, we can take a brief look at the actual extent of reliance on the various taxes we have mentioned.

At the federal level, about half of the tax revenues raised comes from the individual income tax. By contrast, only about 7.7 percent is derived from the corporate income tax. Overall, the state and local governments are much less reliant on any single tax. Sales taxes and property taxes contribute the greatest portion, although there is substantial variation in this from state to state.

Since the early 1960s, reliance on the various taxes has remained surprisingly constant. Our reliance on the federal individual income tax has slightly increased, while the reliance on property taxes by state and local governments has diminished. With these basics in mind, we can now turn to the tax policy making process research.

ANALYSES OF TAX AND REVENUE
POLICY MAKING PROCESSES

Perhaps the most obvious thing that can be said about tax and revenue policies is that our legislators really do not want to raise taxes or enact new taxes, especially during election years. With this said, however, one might wonder how and why taxes have been increased to the point where many Americans apparently feel they need to join a tax rebellion. The answer is that taxes result from different types of compromises, from a balancing among different goals and priorities. And many of our taxes have been enacted in such a way that they raise more revenue as personal income goes up without requiring legislators to take any action at all. To economists, as we will see later, this type of tax is referred to as a revenue-elastic tax with respect to income. In the case of personal income taxes, the average taxpayer may recognize this as bracket creep.

The Roots of Conflict:
The Competing Values in Tax Policy

Before we begin to examine some studies of specific tax policies, we should explain some of the competing values that underlie most tax policy debates. In general, there are competing notions of what tax reform should be, that is, what constitutes a fair tax. Another set of root values relates to the purposes (goals) of taxation. Often our tax system is used to achieve goals well beyond simply collecting money.

COMPETING NOTIONS OF FEDERAL TAX REFORM   Over the years, many attempts have been made to change the federal tax system. Since about 1950, well over two dozen major changes have been made in the federal tax system. Congress is constantly making changes in the system, providing reduced tax liabilities to some groups of people and increased liabilities to others. Many of these changes have been directed at correcting errors in the tax code or in trying to make federal taxes conform to some legislator's conception of fairness.

There are at least two competing notions of fairness that underlie the changes in the federal income tax. At any given time, either or both of these notions of fairness may be included under the rubric of tax reform. In the first instance, tax reform is based on the notion that too much of the tax burden is placed on lower- and middle-income taxpayers, not enough on the very wealthy. So many people advocate reforming the tax system to close loopholes for the wealthy and to restructure the tax in other ways. In the second notion, the idea is to simplify the federal personal income tax. Although simplification would seem to lead to the same end (the elimination of loopholes would be a necessary element of simplification), it is more common that simplification is seen by its advocates as a way of equalizing the tax rate paid by all income classes. It usually calls for the establishment of a so-called flat tax, with a common or similar tax rate for everyone.

Ultimately, the difference between these competing notions comes down to one's definition of fairness. To some people, a fair tax would have the lowest-income earners paying a *smaller percentage* of their incomes in taxes and the highest-income earners paying a *higher percentage* of their incomes in taxes. This type of tax is referred to as a progressive income tax. Other people believe that asking different types of taxpayers to pay different rates is unfair. They argue that all taxpayers should pay the same rate, regardless of their level of income. A flat or proportional tax relies on this type of rate structure. Thus, tax simplification through the creation of a flat tax constitutes an attempt to make the tax less progressive.

In other reforms, the net result has been increases or decreases in specific tax breaks, often referred to as tax expenditures. Tax expenditures represent the amount of revenue not collected from the federal personal income tax because some group of taxpayers was given special consideration. For example, when Congress provided tax deductions for people who installed solar water-heating systems, it was treating them in a special way. Of course, the justification for this special treatment was that the nation would be better off in the long run by foregoing the revenue in order to help stimulate energy independence (see Chapter 3). Pechman's comprehensive assessment of the extent of tax expenditures indicates that there were at least 107 such tax provisions in the income tax code as of 1982.[1] These tax expenditures amounted to a total of well over $300 billion, or about 40 percent of total federal outlays.[2]

THE USES OF FEDERAL TAX POLICY As is often the case with other public policies, federal tax policy has become a vehicle to achieve a variety of political, economic, and social goals. There is little question but that the principal purpose of federal taxes is to bring in the money that the federal government needs to do its work. To economists, this means transferring resources from the private to the public sector.

However, along with raising revenue are several additional goals that persist as justifications for making changes in the tax system. First, many people see the federal income tax as an instrument for helping determine our nation's fiscal and monetary policy. In other words, some people think of federal taxes as mechanisms to be used to control economic growth, inflation, interest rates, unemployment, and so on.

Second, other people see the federal tax system as a means to achieve a redistribution of wealth in society. In this view, it is appropriate to require wealthier people to pay more taxes than the relatively poorer people. As we will see, achievement of these two goals and others constitute important elements in the federal tax policy making process.

The Federal Personal Income Tax

By far the most robust revenue-raising tax instrument is the federal personal income tax. It is the oldest major tax in existence, enacted through the Sixteenth Amendment to the Constitution in 1913. It was controversial then, and it has become more so in the decades that followed.

The Political Processes
of Changing Federal Taxes

Before we examine specific studies of the policy making processes associated with specific tax legislation, we should take a look at the actors in the processes. These actors are not always involved in tax legislation, but there is a tendency

---

[1] Joseph A. Pechman, *Federal Tax Policy,* 4th ed. (Washington, D.C.: Brookings Institution, 1983).

[2] Pechman, pp. 341–48.

for them to repeatedly play roles in changes. As we have in the past, we can characterize these actors as being formulators, adopters, or implementors.

THE FEDERAL INCOME TAX FORMULATORS   In some respects, the President must be considered a major actor in the formulation of tax and revenue proposals. Generally, however, the President delegates the development of tax reform proposals to others within the executive branch. For the most part, the people who play pronounced roles as formulators of tax policy changes reside in the Department of the Treasury, which has three separate staffs of analysts to perform this function. One of these is the Office of Tax Analysis, consisting of a group of some 35 economists and statistical analysts who assess alternative ways of changing the tax. A second staff, the Office of the Tax Legislative Counsel, consists of about 20 tax lawyers who principally convert the economists' proposals into legislative language. The third staff is the Office of International Tax Counsel, a fairly small group of lawyers expert in issues of taxing income from sources outside of the United States.[3]

It is probably safe to say that the expertise of the economists in the Department of the Treasury is rarely utilized to its fullest, at least in terms of helping to make the federal income tax more efficient. Often the role economists play is one of trying to discover ways of providing needed marginal or incremental changes in the tax system without giving up too much revenue.

Another very important group of tax formulators and initiators can be found in Congress itself. Perhaps largely because the U.S. Constitution clearly specifies that "all bills for raising revenue shall originate in the House of Representatives," Congress has played a somewhat more extensive role as policy formulators than it has in other policy areas. The group of legislators in the House of Representatives that historically has been most important as formulators is the House Ways and Means Committee. In recent years, Congress has come to rely on the staff of the Congressional Budget Office to help prepare and formulate proposals for tax alterations.

In addition to these institutional tax policy formulators, private policy making organizations have occasionally performed this function. Among these are the Brookings Institution in Washington, D.C., and the Hoover Institution in Stanford, California. And, of course, the tax policy formulation function has also been performed by private special interest groups, such as the National Association of Manufacturers and the American Petroleum Institute, among many others.

THE FEDERAL TAX POLICY ADOPTERS   As in most other policy areas, the principal adopters in tax policy are found in Congress. Again, the House Ways and Means Committee provides the important actors in the House, and the

[3] Pechman, p. 39.

Senate Finance Committee is important in the Senate. Additionally, there is a Joint Committee on Taxation consisting of members from both chambers. It is the Joint Committee that often must work out the details of legislation adopted with different language or different provisions in the separate houses. The Joint Committee has recently developed a substantial amount of staff expertise on taxation matters; as a result, it has played an expanded role in analyzing different provisions of tax legislation.

THE INNER WORKINGS OF THE REVENUE COMMITTEES IN CONGRESS

As we have noted, much of what gets enacted by Congress in the way of tax policy legislation is the product of the Ways and Means Committee in the House and the Finance Committee in the Senate, although most of the emphasis is usually placed on the function of the Ways and Means Committee. There are several important studies of these committees and how they have affected tax and revenue policy. Space does not permit a full review of these studies, but there are at least two important analyses that take somewhat different views of the revenue committees.

Perhaps one of the more thorough analyses of the House Ways and Means Committee is that by Manley.[4] His analysis traces the operations of the committee from about 1933 to the late 1960s. Manley describes a committee that experienced some fluctuations in the kinds of policies it developed (at least partly because of fluctuations in the nature of the House membership) yet one that attempted, usually with success, to internally resolve partisan, ideological disagreements. The chairman of the committee often worked toward achieving internal consensus over tax legislation through bargaining and compromise. As a result, when this committee recommended passage of specific tax bills by the entire House, such a recommendation was met with considerable success. In some ways, Manley suggests, achieving this consensus became the overriding concern of the committee.[5]

In a very critical analysis of the "revenue committees" of Congress, the Ralph Nader Congress Project argued that these committees are perhaps among the most closed in the entire institution.[6] This project studied the internal workings of the House Ways and Means and the Senate Finance committees, as well

[4] John F. Manley, *The Politics of Finance: The House Committee on Ways and Means* (Boston: Little, Brown, 1970). See also John F. Manley, "The House Committee on Ways and Means: Conflict Management in a Congressional Committee," *American Political Science Review*, Vol. 59, Dec. 1965, pp. 927–39; and John F. Manley, "Congressional Staff and Public Policy-Making: The Joint Committee in Internal Revenue Taxation," *Journal of Politics*, Vol. 30, Nov. 1968, pp. 1046–67.

[5] Manley, *The Politics of Finance*, Ch. 2.

[6] Richard Spohn and Charles McCollum, *The Revenue Committees: A Study of the House Ways and Means and Senate Finance Committees and the House and Senate Appropriations Committees* (New York: Grossman, 1975).

as the Joint Committee on Internal Revenue Taxation and the House and Senate Conference committees. In this report, it is argued that these revenue committees define rules and procedures that guarantee that their work will be conservatively biased and very incremental, i.e., resistant of change. For example, nearly all of the House Ways and Means Committee's bills go to the floor of the House for consideration with a closed rule, which means that they cannot be amended on the floor and have to be approved or defeated in the precise form they are voted out of committee.

The importance of this can be traced to the internal composition of the committees. The Nader report argues that the committees are composed of politically and fiscally conservative representatives. Although the committees maintain the appearance of being open to a variety of viewpoints by taking open testimony, few committee members attend. Instead, the committee members and staff often get their information for tax legislation decisions from business and industry.

THE FEDERAL TAX POLICY IMPLEMENTORS   The role of tax policy implementor is played by a single federal agency, the Internal Revenue Service (IRS). The IRS has responsibility for collecting revenues as required by the Federal Tax Code. It also performs a rulemaking function, where it interprets existing legislation and determines what individual taxpayers may or may not do in paying taxes. For example, it is the IRS, through its rulemaking function, that decides whether a college professor is permitted to deduct the cost of a home office from her income taxes as a legitimate professional business expense. And it is this agency that must put into practice changes made by Congress. For example, when Congress decides to add a deduction to the tax, the IRS must revise the tax forms and prepare new instructions for taxpayers.[7]

There have been many other actors involved in specific tax proposals. As we examine some of these proposals, you will see the roles attributed to these other actors, as well as to those discussed above. With this in mind, let's take a look at some studies of specific tax policy enactments to see what transpired.

THE POLITICS OF A TAX INCREASE: THE REVENUE AND EXPENDITURE ACT OF 1968   Late in his term of office, President Johnson became convinced that the growing deficit the country faced constituted what he called a clear and present danger to the nation's economic health. In order to begin to overcome this growing deficit, which was quite small by today's standard, he proposed a surcharge on the income tax. A surcharge is a flat-rate tax increase that is usually enacted as a temporary measure. In 1968, Congress adopted such a surcharge as the Revenue and Expenditure Act of 1968.

[7] Pechman, p. 51.

Perhaps the most comprehensive analysis of the process that occurred in the development of this surcharge is a study by Pierce.[8] This analysis traces the Johnson proposal from its formulation within the executive branch through consideration and adoption by Congress. This investigation reveals many of the patterns we have alluded to in general during our previous discussions.

Pierce describes the process of fiscal policy formulation during the Johnson administration as one that involved a troika of executive branch officials: the Council of Economic Advisors, the Bureau of the Budget, and the Treasury Department.[9] In particular, these actors played the roles of technical advisors, conducting economic projections of the effects of various fiscal policy alternatives. Although these participants had difficulty agreeing on the best course of action, eventually they argued that a tax increase was necessary in order to achieve the fiscal policy goal of keeping inflation in check. President Johnson and most members of Congress were reluctantly convinced that a tax increase was needed, at least partly because they apparently did not see inflation as a problem.[10] Ultimately, the idea of enacting a temporary surcharge emerged in Congress as a solution that promised to help check inflation while satisfying other congressional interests. As part of this compromise, the surcharge was levied against both personal and corporate incomes.

MAJOR TAX CHANGES: THE TAX REFORM ACT OF 1969 As early as 1969, policy makers began to anticipate the advent of the taxpayers' revolt. At least partly in response to this, Congress enacted the Tax Reform Act of 1969, which addressed a wide range of tax issues. For example, it reduced the tax rate paid by the highest income bracket from 70 percent to 50 percent, provided some business tax incentives, reduced the oil depletion allowance, and changed the status requirements for tax-exempt foundations.

According to Reese, however, the reforms made in this act represent some general patterns of tax reform. In the case of the attack on foundations, Reese suggests that this is representative of Congress's need to take symbolic action, which ends up directed toward politically weak or disorganized groups, especially groups that are widely perceived as abusing the tax system. Reese also argues that the fairly far-reaching targets of this tax reform act were the result of several conditions not commonly encountered in the federal tax policy making process. In particular, he suggests that because the Nixon administration had only been in office a short time, it had not yet gotten its policy agenda organized. At the same time, the House Ways and Means and Senate Finance committees found that they had virtually nothing else on their agendas. Con-

---

[8] Lawrence C. Pierce, *The Politics of Fiscal Policy Formation* (Pacific Palisades, Calif.: Goodyear, 1971).

[9] Pierce, Ch. 3 and 4.

[10] Pierce, Ch. 6.

sequently, both committees could devote an unusual amount of time and effort to this reform package.[11]

WHAT HAPPENED TO TAX REFORM? THE REVENUE ACT OF 1978   Early in the administration of Jimmy Carter, a set of proposals to change the federal income tax system was sent to Congress. Congress considered this set of proposals in 1978. Carter's proposals called for specific tax cuts amounting to $33.9 billion and increases of $9.4 billion in other areas, for a net reduction of $24.5 billion. The proposals focused on tax reform defined as closing loopholes on such extravagances as the "two-martini lunch" as a legitimate deduction. It also provided reduced tax rates for lower- and moderate-income taxpayers.

In his analysis of the process the Carter proposals invoked, Kenski describes how Congress proceeded to transform them into a final legislative package that looked quite different.[12] It was during this time that the idea of using federal tax cuts to stimulate economic growth began to gain ascendancy in the House of Representatives, as reflected in the initial proposals by Representatives Kemp and Roth to enact massive tax reductions. Kenski argues that House Republicans, fearing the inflationary effects of the Carter proposals, successfully built a coalition with conservative Democrats in support of the final bill.[13] This bill had virtually none of the provisions of the Carter proposals; in fact, it directed tax cuts to the upper- and middle-income taxpayers. The final bill also included cuts in the capital gains tax that President Carter threatened to veto.[14] Kenski's conclusion supports Reese's contention that by the Ninety-fifth Congress (1977–78), the conservative coalition in the House had become fairly well entrenched.[15]

Kantowicz offers an alternative explanation for the failure of the Carter administration to accomplish much in the way of true tax reform.[16] In his analysis, Kantowicz argues that the 1978 Revenue Act can be best understood as the third part of a three-part series. Carter's initial proposals, which eventually resulted in the Tax Reduction and Simplification Act of 1977, mixed the goals of achieving equity and stimulating the economy. But by the time Con-

---

[11] Thomas J. Reese, *The Politics of Taxation* (Westport, Conn.: Quorum Books, 1980), pp. 204–9.

[12] Henry C. Kenski, "Partisanship and Ideology in the Revenue Act of 1978," in Warren J. Samuels and Larry L. Wade, eds., *Taxing and Spending Policy* (Lexington, Mass.: Lexington Books, 1980), pp. 95–101.

[13] Kenski, pp. 98–100.

[14] Congressional Quarterly, *Taxes, Jobs, and Inflation* (Washington, D.C.: Congressional Quarterly, Inc., 1978), p. 21.

[15] Reese, pp. 130–35.

[16] Edward R. Kantowicz, "The Limits of Incrementalism: Carter's Efforts at Tax Reform," *Journal of Policy Analysis and Management,* Vol. 4, No. 2, Winter 1985, pp. 217–33.

gress began examining the proposals, the economy had improved to the point where Carter withdrew his support of two key provisions, a one-time $40 rebate to taxpayers and tax credits for businesses. This had the effect of opening the door to a variety of congressional changes. These changes watered down the Carter proposals until they were no longer very sweeping in their impact. Kantowicz lays the blame for this on the priority the Carter administration assigned to tax reform relative to other policy goals, especially energy.[17]

The Federal Corporation Income Tax

The federal corporation income tax was enacted in 1909, thus predating the personal income tax by four years. It, too, was legally challenged and finally upheld by the U.S. Supreme Court. Although the corporation income tax now raises a fairly small percentage of federal taxes, this was not always the case. According to Pechman, the corporation income tax produced more revenue than the personal income tax in 17 of the 28 years before 1941.[18] Even in recent years, the decline in the relative contributions from the corporation income tax is substantial. For example, in 1968, this tax accounted for about 19 percent of federal receipts; but by 1982, it had diminished to about 6 percent.[19]

Not all corporations are treated equally by the corporation income tax. Many types of companies benefit from special provisions, exemptions, or deductions not available to all corporations. Perhaps most notable among these is the oil depletion allowance, an exemption for companies involved in petroleum production. This allowance has been the source of substantial political debate, so we will examine some studies of the processes involved with making changes in this allowance.

Common wisdom would suggest that taxing corporations could substitute for taxing individuals. Yet in recent years, economists have been quick to point out that this is not really the case. Corporations merely shift some portion (even all) of this tax to individual consumers. Thus, consumers end up indirectly paying the tax anyway.

Despite this fact, corporations do not often act as though they are unaffected by such taxes. Indeed, various types of corporations within specific industries fight hard to obtain some special tax benefit. For example, as we discussed in Chapter 3, independent oil producers fought hard in 1981 to be exempted from the Windfall Profits Tax.[20] We will see this pattern emerge from several studies of specific tax policy changes.

[17] Kantowicz, pp. 229–30.

[18] Pechman, p. 129.

[19] Pechman, p. 129.

[20] Graham Wootton, *Interest Groups: Policy and Politics in America* (Englewood Cliffs, N.J.: Prentice-Hall, 1985), pp. 243–44.

BREAKS FOR BUSINESS: THE REVENUE ACT OF 1971   In 1971, the Nixon administration developed a tax proposal designed to help stimulate a depressed economy and to improve the international balance of payments. Although this proposal was formulated by Treasury Department staff, it was considered by many Treasury Department economists to constitute bad tax policy. One provision of this proposal would permit international corporations to set up domestic international sales corporations (DISCs), which would allow them to defer federal corporation income tax payments on part of their earnings until the earnings were returned to the United States. Reese suggests that this provision was thought to be so bad by many Treasury Department economists that they refused to work on it.[21] Despite this sentiment in some Treasury Department circles, Secretary of the Treasury John Connally supported the bill, and Congress enacted it with substantial bipartisan support as the Revenue Act of 1971.[22]

THE POLITICS OF THE OIL DEPLETION ALLOWANCE   We discussed some aspects of the oil depletion allowance in Chapter 3, where we examined energy policy. You may wish to refer to our discussion there to refresh your memory about the history of this policy. Just as the oil depletion allowance constitutes a significant element of energy policy, it represents an important part of our federal tax policy as well. The policy changes in this tax over the past 15 years demonstrate how controversial this tax benefit is.

We noted earlier that the oil depletion allowance, providing a major tax exemption to large oil companies, was being phased out after more than half a century. In 1975, Congress decided to gradually reduce the depletion allowance so that it would be only 15 percent by 1984. Beginning with the budget process of 1981, the first of the Reagan administration, the oil depletion allowance emerged once again as a point of debate.

In his analysis of the role of major interest groups, Wootton describes the process that oil interests used to wield their influence in Congress in order to recoup the benefits they lost in 1975.[23] He suggests that numerous interest groups worked to ensure that the "right people" served in important positions on the key congressional committees, the House Ways and Means and the Senate Finance committees.[24]

Wootton argues that congressional leadership and the rules and procedures it supported lent themselves to protection of the oil depletion allowance until the mid-1970s. Then, because of the reform zeal of the Democrats in both

[21] Thomas J. Reese, *The Politics of Taxation* (Westport, Conn.: Quorum Books, 1980), p. 55.

[22] Reese, p. 139.

[23] Wootton, pp. 233–58.

[24] Wootton, p. 243.

houses, some of the rules were changed (for example, the House Ways and Means Committee modified its procedures to permit its bills to be amended on the floor of the House), and the House Ways and Means Committee was expanded from 25 members to 37. As a result—at least for a short time—the House committee's membership was not as strongly supportive of oil interests or the oil depletion allowance. Thus, the time was ripe for a decision to phase out the allowance. But by 1981, oil interests had reestablished their connections with the key congressional committees, which resulted in the formulation and passage of the Economic Recovery Tax Act of 1981, a piece of legislation estimated to have provided perhaps as much as $11 billion in tax breaks for the oil industry.[25]

The Politics of State and Local Taxation

We have explained increases in federal taxes as being at least partly the result of the desire to achieve fiscal policy goals (e.g., reducing inflation) and political expediency. You might wonder how we can explain increases in state and local taxes, especially since analogous fiscal policy goals do not seem applicable in states or cities. In fact, we know much less about the policy making processes used in the states to raise taxes or to adopt new taxes.

Based on some important case studies, it seems that state and local policy makers begin with an assessment of how much revenue will be needed to finance desired levels of services. Once this is determined, they assess the revenue-raising capacity of different taxes and the political consequences associated with each. For example, in an analysis of the revenue decision process in Oakland, California, Meltsner explains this strategy,[26] stating that policy makers carefully weigh the use of different revenue instruments against the level of public acceptance. For example, given an assessed need for increased revenue, policy makers study the several different taxes or fees that would produce the needed revenue. Then they assess what they consider to be the political consequences of each tax or fee. In Meltsner's opinion, policy makers often end up settling for decisions that produce small amounts of revenue but that also produce the least public opposition.[27]

In the policy making process approach to state taxes, we often hold a view of political accountability that does not fully square with political reality. We often wonder, for example, how governors can support new or higher taxes, given the almost universal belief that such positions are politically unpopular. The answer is that it is extremely rare for voters to ever hold a governor, or by extension any other policy maker, accountable for his or her position on taxes.

Perhaps the most comprehensive study of this issue was conducted by

[25] Wootton, pp. 243–44.

[26] Arnold J. Meltsner, *The Politics of City Revenue* (Berkeley, Calif.: University of California Press, 1971).

[27] Meltsner, p. 101.

Pomper,[28] who analyzed the extent to which governors who have been responsible for large tax increases (measured in five different ways) were more likely to suffer electoral defeat. He examined election results and tax and revenue data for a 16-year period. His results indicate that "Governors who lead in increasing taxes do not suffer at the polls significantly."[29] He also suggests that governors who show fiscal restraint are not necessarily more likely to be rewarded by being returned to office. Although this analysis was conducted before the contemporary "tax revolt," there is little evidence to suggest that the nature of state politics has changed.

Analysis of Interest Groups in State Tax Policy Making

Our knowledge about the role played by interest groups in state tax policy making is quite limited. Perhaps the most systematic estimation of the strength and positions of different kinds of interest groups in the states was conducted by Bingham, Hawkins, and Hebert.[30] In this study, Bingham et al. sent a questionnaire to someone they identified as an "informant" in each state. They asked these informants questions about which interest groups were involved in different kinds of tax issues and what the political positions of those groups were. Focusing on the major state taxes, their findings reveal some clear patterns. For example, they found that such general business groups as the chambers of commerce and manufacturing associations were universally against tax increases. On the other hand, state education associations were generally in favor of tax increases, especially increases in personal and corporation income taxes. Organized groups of taxpayers basically opposed tax increases, although some apparently supported the increased use of sales taxes.[31]

Analyses of the State and Local Tax Revolt

In the contemporary era of state and local tax politics, common wisdom suggests that U.S. taxpayers have risen in opposition to the ever increasing taxes imposed on them. Although people have undoubtedly become discontented with the level of state and local taxes, many studies of the processes involved in the tax revolt bring out a slightly different picture. For example, we will see studies that show that the use of the tax initiative or ballot proposition (for example, Proposition 13 in California and Proposition 2½ in Massachusetts), tools of the tax revolt, possess significant biases in favor of certain interests.

[28] Gerald M. Pomper, *Elections in America: Control and Influence in Democratic Politics* (New York: Dodd, Mead, 1974), Ch. 6.

[29] Pomper, pp. 133–34.

[30] Richard D. Bingham, Brett W. Hawkins, and F. Ted Hebert, *The Politics of Raising State and Local Revenue* (New York: Praeger, 1978), Ch. 9.

[31] Bingham, Hawkins, and Hebert, pp. 201–6.

A related question—What do voters have in mind when they support tax limitation referenda?—will be deferred until we shift our focus to tax policy cause and consequence analyses, which indicate that voters generally are not voting to limit government per se, or even to limit the state or local tax in question. Rather, they often vote in favor of tax limitation out of frustration, as a symbolic act directed more at federal than state or local policy makers.

Analyses of Tax Initiatives

The findings of the studies of people's voting patterns on tax initiatives and referenda raise some important questions about the use of tax initiatives in the political system that deserve some discussion.

The initiative and referendum process is one that has been used repeatedly over the years for tax policy formulation. Initiatives and referenda are ballot questions that provide the general public with the opportunity to formulate public policies.[32] Some people make the distinction between initiatives and referenda, suggesting that the former produce an opportunity for the electorate to take part in policy formulation, while the latter is simply an opportunity for the electorate to ratify a decision already made by the legislature. Despite the notoriety that several of these ballot questions have received, only about 20 states permit this form of direct democracy, and very few of them have had tax limitation referenda or initiatives.

Perhaps more important, there seems to be a particular political bias in the use of the initiative process. A study by Gazey, for example, contends that initiatives and referenda are "often used by conservative groups against liberal legislation."[33] In a fairly comprehensive assessment of the use of initiatives, Graham suggests that this process has been commonly used to limit the tax powers of the state in about 20 states.

In this process, initiatives have been more commonly used to repeal or block progressive and broad-based taxes than for any other tax-related purpose.[34] Apparently, the reason why this conservative bias emerges so clearly is that the initiative or referendum process requires the mobilization of substantial financial resources. In theory, resources need be nothing more than people power: citizens volunteering to work on behalf of a cause they feel strongly about. In practice, however, it's more likely that organized groups with sub-

---

[32] Thomas Durbin and Rita Ann Reimer, *Initiative, Petition, and Recall: A Resume of State Provisions* (Washington, D.C.: Congressional Research Service, 1976, 1978); Charles M. Price, "The Initiative: A Comparative State Analysis and Reassessment of a Western Phenomenon," *Western Political Quarterly*, Vol. 28, No. 2, June 1975, pp. 243–62; Hugh A. Bone and Robert C. Benedict, "Perspectives on Direct Legislation: Washington State's Experience, 1914–1973," *Western Political Quarterly*, Vol. 28, No. 2, June 1975, pp. 330–51; and Penelope J. Gazey, "Direct Democracy—A Study of the American Referendum," *Parliamentary Affairs*, Vol. 24, No. 2, Spring 1971, pp. 123–39.

[33] Gazey (see Note 32).

[34] Virginia Graham, *A Compilation of Statewide Initiative Proposals Appearing on Ballots Through 1976* (Washington, D.C.: Congressional Research Service, 1976, 1978).

stantial financial resources are better able to take advantage of the initiative or referendum systems—and these groups often turn out to be conservative. For example, the driving force behind the Massachusetts ballot initiative to limit local property taxes was a group called Citizens for Limited Taxation. This group was organized and wholly financed by private industry.

CAUSE AND CONSEQUENCE RESEARCH
IN TAX AND REVENUE POLICY

Cause and consequence research on areas of public tax and revenue policy has provided us with a substantial understanding of some fundamental issues often raised in the political process. Perhaps most important among these is the issue of who pays our taxes. Obviously taxpayers pay taxes—but not all taxpayers are the same. Indeed, as we witnessed earlier, much of the debate in the policy making process revolves around who is going to pay how much of different taxes. So one of the major topics of cause and consequence research focuses on this question. We consider this type of analysis to constitute tax policy cause and consequence research in that these studies investigate the distributional impacts caused by various taxes.

On its face, this would seem like a fairly easy question to answer, but analyses by economists have shown us that it is quite difficult to estimate who really pays the various taxes. To economists, this type of policy research analyzes what is called tax incidence. Its main focus is on finding out how much relatively well-off people pay in taxes compared to people who are less well-off. In other words, the issue is whether specific taxes tend to be progressive, proportional, or regressive.

In a *progressive* tax, people with higher incomes pay higher proportions of their income in taxes than people with lower incomes. In a *proportional* tax, all taxpayers pay the same proportion of their incomes in taxes. And in a *regressive* tax, relatively poorer people pay a higher proportion of their incomes in taxes.

For the most part, the analyses of tax incidence do not make direct judgments about whether one type of tax is better than another. They simply try to find out for particular taxes and for the entire tax system who pays how much. Obviously, people do differ in their opinions about which type of tax incidence is fairer. People who consider themselves politically liberal are somewhat more likely than political conservatives to define a progressive tax as fair. Conservatives, on the other hand, are probably somewhat more likely to consider a proportional or regressive tax to be fairer.

Some economists have provided fuel for the political debate by conducting analyses illuminating some of the consequences of one type of tax compared to others. Some of them argue that steeply progressive taxes stifle economic growth because they prevent capital formation. Thus, if someone is an advocate of economic growth and adheres to these studies, it becomes quite easy to oppose progressive taxes.

The novice in tax policy analysis may believe that determining a tax's incidence is rather straightforward. We might be fooled into thinking that all we have to examine is the nature of the tax rate as set by law. This is often called the nominal tax rate. But this tax rate only tells a small part of the story. In order to look below the surface, one must examine effective tax rates, that is, the rates that people actually pay. In some instances and for some taxes, the nominal tax rate may be the same as the effective rate. But with other taxes, especially personal income taxes, there is a substantial difference between the two. The reason for this is that some people are better able to take advantage of the many tax breaks (exemptions, deductions, etc.) than others. So the real issue for this type of tax is how much do people really pay as a percentage of their incomes.

For corporation income taxes, there is another complication. Many people believe that because the corporation income tax has continued to decline over the past couple of decades as a revenue source that this is a sign that corporations are not pulling their weight. Indeed, many people in the political process advocate a reduction in personal income taxes, substituting increases in corporate income taxes. On its face, this may seem to be a good idea. We are often lured into believing that people can get something for nothing, in a sense, but economists' studies indicate that individual consumers end up paying corporate taxes anyway.

The reason for this is that corporations are usually able to shift a substantial portion of their taxes to the people who buy their products or services. In other words, corporations that have to pay a particular tax simply treat it as one of many costs incurred in their operation, a cost, like any other, that must be considered in their decisions about how much to charge consumers. If their taxes are increased, their costs also increase. When their costs increase, the prices they charge for their goods and services increase. And who ends up paying? The people who buy the goods and services.

Economic analysts tend to agree that such shifting of the tax burden does occur. They do not agree, however, on the extent to which it occurs. Some analysts believe that corporations are able to shift all or nearly all of their tax onto consumers, while others believe that only a portion of the taxes can be shifted and the remainder must be paid by the corporation through decreased profits. The real issue is not so much whether corporation income taxes are shifted but who pays when it *is* shifted. Here economists have found that if the corporation income tax is levied against all or nearly all corporations, then the result is that consumers who have relatively lower incomes end up paying more as a percentage of their incomes than people with relatively higher incomes. Thus, the net result of a corporation income tax may well be a regressive tax, something which many proponents of corporation income taxes seek to avoid.

The Incidence of Federal Taxes

Perhaps one of the better known studies of federal tax incidence is that by Pechman and Okner.[35] This study was one of the first major analyses attempting to estimate the distributional impacts of numerous taxes on a full range of taxpayers with different levels of income. What made this study somewhat more impressive than its predecessors is that it uses data that are clearly more appropriate for this type of analysis. In previous studies, it was very difficult to estimate what a particular family's income tax liability was. In the Pechman and Okner study, the data clearly measure the relevant income characteristics of some 72,000 families from the year 1966.

This study does not attempt to determine the extent of tax shifting that takes place. Rather, it estimates the distributional impacts of taxes under different sets of assumptions about shifting. Although the assumptions in this study are fairly complicated (there are actually nine different sets), they fall into three major categories.

In the first category, it is assumed that there is perfect competition in industry, payroll taxes on employers and employees are paid by employees in proportion to their taxed earnings, and the corporation income tax is paid by consumers in proportion to the amount of property income they have. In the second category, the corporation income tax is allocated to corporate stockholders in proportion to the dividends they receive, and the payroll tax is assumed to be paid either totally by employees or half by employees and half by consumers. And in the third category, half of the corporation income tax is assumed to be paid by stockholders, the rest paid in equal shares by consumers and corporate employees.

The results of this analysis tell us a great deal about our tax systems. Focusing only on the results for federal taxes (we will discuss state and local taxes later), Pechman and Okner find that the personal income tax is progressive. Specifically, they found that if you examine the percentage of families' income that is paid in taxes from the lowest- to the highest-income families, the percentage increases fairly consistently. And this tends to hold true under each set of assumptions. For example, under the third set of assumptions, it was found that families with incomes between $3000 and $5000 (in 1966) paid 2.8 percent of their income in income tax, on average. Families with incomes between $25,000 and $30,000 paid 9.1 percent of their income. Families with incomes between $500,000 and $1 million paid 17.7 percent of their income in personal income tax. For those families with incomes over $1 million, there was a slight decrease in the percentage.

These results can be contrasted with those for the corporation income tax. Under the third set of assumptions, the corporation income tax appears to be

---

[35] Joseph A. Pechman and Benjamin A. Okner, *Who Bears the Tax Burden?* (Washington, D.C.: Brookings Institution, 1974).

somewhat regressive. Families with incomes between $3000 and $5000 paid 5.3 percent of their income in corporate taxes (through their consumer purchases). Families with incomes between $25,000 and $30,000 paid only 4.3 percent of their income in corporation income taxes. Despite this, families with the highest incomes do pay more. Thus, for a good portion of the American taxpayers, the corporation income tax appears to be regressive.

The Incidence of State and Local Taxes

One of the more detailed studies of the distribution of tax burdens created by state and local taxes is that by Phares.[36] This analysis is very much like the one conducted by Pechman and Okner, with a specific focus on the taxes in various states. Because Phares analyzes numerous taxes, he incorporates a variety of assumptions into his analysis. In general, he tried to present estimates of tax incidence under three sets of assumptions: the "most progressive," the "most regressive," and "benchmark" (a middle ground) assumptions. Without going into detail about how each of these were defined, suffice it to say that the intent was to locate the range of incidence that could exist for each state and local tax.

Phares's analysis shows several clear patterns. First, personal income taxes in the states do not seem to be as progressive as the federal income tax.[37] In general, state personal income taxes, after accounting for different provisions in each state, tend to be slightly progressive or proportional, except in New Hampshire, where it is regressive.[38] California is shown to have the most progressive tax.

The state sales tax shows a different pattern. Largely because of the differences in the ways states choose to tax such articles as food and clothing, some states end up with much less equitable sales taxes. Phares's analysis indicates that all state sales taxes are regressive, but those of many of the Southern states are more so, the most regressive being in Alabama, Arkansas, Oklahoma, Tennessee, and Virginia.[39] The least regressive state sales taxes are found in New Jersey, Pennsylvania, Connecticut, Massachusetts, and Ohio.

The state corporation net income tax is a tax not relied upon by most states. In fact, according to Phares, only about 4.7 percent of all state-raised revenue comes from state corporation income taxes. Even so, Phares's analysis indicates that these taxes tend to be, on average, proportional.[40] Phares assesses the net impact of these taxes on individual taxpayers. In most instances, this

---

[36] Donald Phares, *Who Pays State and Local Taxes?* (Cambridge, Mass.: Oelgeschlager, Gunn, and Hain, 1980).

[37] Phares, p. 121.

[38] Phares, p. 122.

[39] Phares, pp. 118–19.

[40] Phares, pp. 105–6.

type of tax is regressive among the lowest income categories of taxpayers, but it becomes fairly progressive for the uppermost income categories of taxpayers.

Who Pays the Local Property Tax?

As we have already noted, local governments rely extremely heavily on the local real estate tax. Several important studies have examined the incidence of these property taxes. The studies of property tax incidence are of two varieties. The earlier studies argued that the property tax was extremely regressive, with low-income homeowners paying much greater proportions of their incomes in property taxes than higher-income homeowners. Then, several studies appeared that argued that these earlier studies were wrong, that for several reasons we will examine shortly, the property tax is not all that regressive.

Perhaps the most challenging study of property taxes was conducted by Aaron.[41] Aaron's analysis sought to challenge the common wisdom about local property taxes as being the most regressive of all broad-based taxes. Aaron argues that a substantial portion of the property tax is capitalized into the value of the home, that is, local property taxes paid on homes and land have an effect on the price that can be charged for the property when it is sold. Although the distributional effect of the property tax may be very different in the short run and the long run, eventually the effect is much less regressive than had previously been thought.[42]

The Economic Consequences of Federal Taxes

As we noted in our discussion of the federal tax policy making process, federal taxes are often used for the purpose of achieving specific results. For example, our tax policies have often been altered in an effort to stimulate the rate of economic growth, to reduce the rate of inflation, and so on. The idea that tax policy can be used for such purposes comes directly out of studies of the consequences of tax policy.

The body of research addressing these issues is quite vast, composed of more studies than we could ever hope to cover here. Much of this research has addressed the Keynesian theories prescribing the economic effects and uses of taxes. A good portion of this research has endeavored to establish the idea that federal taxes generally have a dampening effect on the private-sector economy. It is thought to produce this effect through several mechanisms. First, when

---

[41] Henry J. Aaron, *Who Pays the Property Tax?: A New View* (Washington, D.C.: Brookings Institution, 1975).

[42] For a modification of this finding, see Charles E. McClure, "The New View of the Property Tax: A Caveat," *National Tax Journal,* Vol. 30, No. 1, 1977, pp. 69–76; and Peter Mieszkowski, "The Property Tax: An Excise Tax or a Profit Tax?" *Journal of Public Economics,* Vol. 1, April 1972, pp. 73–96.

people's incomes are taxed, they are thought to lose their incentive to be productive. In this view, personal income is the product of personal investment in human capital (through education, job training, etc.). When the returns on the investment in human capital are taxed, people make smaller investments in their own human capital. The net result is a smaller return on investment and ultimately a reduction in the supply of labor.[43]

A second mechanism through which taxes are thought to dampen the economy is by reducing the supply of private capital and the demand for goods and services. When people have to pay taxes, their money is diverted away from productive uses. As taxes increase, private capital formation decreases, which ultimately reduces economic growth.[44]

In an analysis of these mechanisms, Thurow suggests that different federal taxes produce different economic effects.[45] Different taxes may also produce similar economic impacts at very different rates, with some taxes exhibiting major time lags before effects are actually felt. Thurow's analysis argues that reducing the level of taxation is not the only way to cause improvements in the performance of the national economy. Indeed, he suggests that manipulation of the personal income tax is at least 30 percent more effective than the corporation income tax in affecting unemployment through its effect on the demand for goods and services. The corporation income tax, although acting much more slowly, can be used to affect both the supply and demand of goods and services.[46]

The Economic Consequences
of State and Local Taxes

One of the common arguments heard from advocates of reduced state and local tax levels is that these taxes stifle economic growth and cause industries or businesses to locate elsewhere. The theory is that when tax levels rise, business and industry move to locations where tax levels are lower. When deciding on new locations, industry is thought to stay away from high-tax areas.

If a general conclusion can be drawn from these studies, it is that taxes are but one of many factors that influence industrial location decisions. Indeed, taxes do not seem to be among the most important influences. Unless a particular business is considering several different sites that are essentially identical in

---

[43] Gary S. Becker, *Human Capital* (New York: National Bureau of Economic Research, 1964).

[44] Marvin Kosters, "Effects of an Income Tax on Labor Supply," in Arnold C. Harberger and Martin J. Bailey, eds., *The Taxation of Income from Capital* (Washington, D.C.: Brookings Institution, 1969).

[45] Lester C. Thurow, *The Impact of Taxes on the American Economy* (New York: Praeger, 1971).

[46] Thurow, pp. 160–61.

their access to factors of production, such as labor, the particular market, and raw goods, taxes are not likely to be primary considerations.[47]

More recently, Grieson et al. studied the separate effects of property taxes on manufacturing and nonmanufacturing industries in New York City.[48] They found that there is a clear tendency for higher property taxes to discourage the location of manufacturing industries in the city. But this relation does not seem to hold for nonmanufacturing industries, such as finance, law, and communications. The conclusion reached by these researchers is that relatively more of the local tax burden should fall on nonmanufacturing industries.

This raises a related question for public policy. Much has been written about the need for economic incentives to stimulate industrial and economic development in the states. The implications of such prescriptions is that economic incentives cause businesses and industries to alter their location decisions, and perhaps provide increased opportunity for local capital investment. Although space does not permit us to review analyses of this issue, numerous studies have investigated the extent to which economic incentives can be said to have this impact. In general, there is only moderate evidence suggesting that financial incentives provided to industry by states have this effect.[49]

The Causes of Our State and Local Tax Systems

Much of the policy research we have examined so far focuses on describing some distributional or other impact of our tax systems. Many other studies have tried to determine why states and local governments develop their various tax policies. In these studies, we find that there are several different dependent variables: specific descriptive characteristics of the states' taxes. We often refer to these characteristics as different dimensions of state and local tax policies. They include *tax reliance,* or the extent to which states use one specific type of tax rather than others; *average tax burden,* which attempts to measure, either for specific taxes or for all taxes, how much of a bite taxes take out of personal income; and the *distribution of tax burdens,* the measure of tax incidence we discussed earlier.

One final set of state tax characteristics have been used as dependent variables. They focus on how innovative states have been in developing new revenue instruments. Space does not permit us to examine studies using all of these tax

---

[47] For a review of some of the earlier studies, see John Due, "Studies of State-Local Tax Influences on Location of Industry," *National Tax Journal,* Vol. 19, 1961, pp. 163–73.

[48] Ronald E. Grieson et al., "The Effect of Business Taxation on the Location of Industry," *Journal of Urban Economics,* Vol. 4, No. 1, Jan. 1977, pp. 170–85.

[49] For a review of some of this literature, see Roger J. Vaughn, *Taxation and Economic Development* (Washington, D.C.: Council of State Planning Agencies, 1979). See also William E. Morgan and Merlin M. Hackbart, "An Analysis of State and Local Industrial Tax Exemption Programs," *Southern Economic Journal,* Vol. 41, No. 2, 1976, pp. 200–5.

policy dependent variables, so we will focus on some of the studies explaining the dependent variables tax incidence and tax innovation. As we do this, we will find that the studies vary a great deal in the kinds of independent variables they identify as being hypothetical or actual causes of tax policy incidence and innovation.

THE CAUSES OF STATE TAX BURDEN DISTRIBUTIONS We have already examined some studies that analyzed differences in state tax incidence or tax burden distributions from state to state (these terms are usually used interchangeably). We saw that some states have developed much more progressive tax systems than other states. Recently, a study by Jacobs and Waldman attempted to determine why this pattern exists.[50] Using the Phares index of tax burden distribution we discussed earlier, Jacobs and Waldman correlated several social and political independent variables with the level of regressivity. They found that states in the South and states with lower percentages of black residents, with greater income inequality, and with lower percentages of small businesses tended to have the most regressive taxes. Jacobs and Waldman interpret these findings as providing some support for the idea that the states' tax systems are structured to be hostile to racial minorities and favorable to small businesses.

STUDIES OF STATE TAX INNOVATION In addition to the fiscal tax policy dependent variables, at least several analyses have tried to examine some qualitative characteristics of states' taxes. For example, Hansen analyzed why different states decided to enact various taxes from among the range of tax instruments they might have chosen.[51] Her analysis indicated that there is substantial correspondence between periods of political party "realignment" (where major changes occur in people's political party identifications) and tax innovation. This is especially true for adoptions of taxes not then in existence in the state.

Extending this type of analysis, Portney focused on the patterns of adoption that different states experienced.[52] His analysis showed that several distinctly different patterns of tax adoption over time could be discerned in the states. Many states went through a process where personal income taxes were enacted at the same time as the enactment of corporation income taxes. Other states enacted sales and income taxes at the same time. But rarely did a state enact a single broad-based tax by itself. The implication of this is that the enact-

[50] David Jacobs and Dan Waldman, "Toward a Fiscal Sociology: Determinants of Tax Progressivity in the American States," *Social Science Quarterly,* Vol. 64, No. 3, Sept. 1983, pp. 550–65.

[51] Susan Hansen, *The Politics of Taxation* (New York: Praeger, 1983).

[52] Kent E. Portney, "State Tax Preference Orderings and Partisan Control of Government," in Samuels and Wade (see Note 12), pp. 109–18.

ment of new taxes is the result of a legislative agreement to impose new burdens on several different groups of people rather than on a single group. The type of partisan control of the governorship and state legislature seemed to play a role in the decision about which pair of groups would be asked to bear increased tax burdens. In states where control was in the hands of a single political party, the same pattern emerged: a trade between personal income and corporation income taxes prevailed. Yet in states with divided party control, personal income taxes were avoided until other instruments had been used.

The Causes of the State and Local Tax Revolt

Earlier in this chapter we noted that the use of referenda and ballot questions generally tends to have a strong antitax, especially anti-income tax, bias. When we discussed this, we deferred discussion of a related question concerning why voters support such ballot propositions. Although most people assume that voters are making unambiguous statements about the level of taxes, numerous cause and consequence studies have cast some doubt on this conclusion.

In a study of electoral behavior and opinion in California, Citrin studied the causes of voting in support of the Jarvis-Gann proposition, commonly known as Proposition 13.[53] Citrin tried to determine what attitudinal factors accounted for the favorable support given to the property tax limitations called for in the proposition. He concluded that different groups of voters sought to achieve different ends. While most of the voters who favored the proposition believed they were making some sort of general statement on the need to reduce the size of government, they held no common set of beliefs on which, if any, particular government services should be cut.

In a similar analysis, Courant, Gramlich, and Rubinfeld studied voting on the 1978 Michigan ballot question that was designed to create a constitutional tax limit amendment.[54] The results of this study disagree with those in Citrin's analysis. In Michigan, voters who supported the Tisch or Headlee amendment propositions apparently did not desire to limit the size of government, and they

---

[53] Jack Citrin, "Do Voters Want Something for Nothing?" *National Tax Journal,* Vol. 32, No. 2, Supp., June 1979, pp. 113–29. See also David O. Sears and Jack Citrin, *Tax Revolt: Something for Nothing in California* (Cambridge, Mass.: Harvard University Press, 1982). For other studies of voting on Proposition 13, see F. Ted Hebert and Richard D. Bingham, "Public Opinion, the Taxpayers Revolt, and Local Government," in John Blair and David Nachmias, eds., *Fiscal Retrenchment and Urban Policy* (Beverly Hills, Calif.: Sage Publications, 1980); William J. Scott, Harold Grasmick, and Craig M. Eckert, "Dimensions of the Tax Revolt: Uncovering Strange Bedfellows," *American Politics Quarterly,* Vol. 9, 1980, pp. 71–87; and J. P. Magaddino, Eugenia Toma, and Mark Tom, "Proposition 13: A Public Choice Appraisal," *Public Finance Quarterly,* Vol. 8, 1980, pp. 223–35.

[54] Paul N. Courant, Edward M. Gramlich, and Daniel L. Rubinfeld, "Why Voters Support Tax Limitation Amendments: The Michigan Case," *National Tax Journal,* Vol. 33, No. 1, March 1980, pp. 1–20. See also Edward M. Gramlich, Daniel L. Rubinfeld, and Deborah Swift, "Why Voters Turn Out for Tax Limitation Votes," *National Tax Journal,* Vol. 34, No. 1, March 1981, pp. 115–24.

did not seem to want to punish public employees for being unproductive. In this case, voters simply seemed to perceive that their own taxes would be reduced without any reduction in the quality of government services. Obviously, the target was more the perceived need to achieve greater efficiency in providing services. However, in a reanalysis of these results, Freiman suggests that Michigan voters expressed a fairly clear preference for reducing the size of government.[55] And in an analysis of voting patterns in over 600 of the more than 1,500 municipalities in Michigan, Lowery found that there was a moderate tendency for voters in cities or towns with higher tax rates to vote in favor of the Tisch amendment.[56]

In several studies of voting for property tax limitations in Massachusetts, Ladd and Wilson expand the analysis of voters' motivations.[57] The results of the Massachusetts study indicate that passage of this limitation proposal was directed more toward achieving greater government efficiency and lower taxes (although not necessarily property taxes) than in cutting services.

While supporting the lack of clear evidence that voters really desired to reduce the size of government, Lowery and Sigelman entertain numerous other explanations.[58] Using attitudinal information from a nationwide survey, Lowery and Sigelman found very little evidence that voters favored tax limitations for any single reason. They suggest that perhaps the most that can be said about voters' opinions is that they reflect a high degree of symbolism, the specific focus of which varies from voter to voter.

These studies of voters' attitudes seems to point in a common direction. Voters are not necessarily demanding less government, at least not in the form of reduced governmental services. Rather, they wish to maintain services at their current levels and pay less for them. Thus, the tax revolt may be thought of as not a revolt against government per se, but rather against high taxes.

PRESCRIPTIVE ANALYSES OF TAX POLICIES

There is perhaps no area where prescriptive analyses have been better developed than in tax policy. Tax policy provides an almost ideal situation for prescriptive studies to be effective. The substantive issues involve easily quantifiable data,

[55] Marc P. Freiman, "Why Voters Support Tax Limitation Amendments: A Comment," *National Tax Journal,* Vol. 33, No. 4, Dec. 1980, pp. 497–99.

[56] David Lowery, "Explaining Michigan's Vote on the Tisch Amendment," in Samuels and Wade (see Note 12), pp. 133–48.

[57] Helen F. Ladd and Julie Boatright Wilson, "Why Voters Support Tax Limitation: Evidence from Massachusetts' Proposition 2½," *National Tax Journal,* Vol. 35, No. 2, June 1982, pp. 121–48; and Helen F. Ladd and Julie Boatright Wilson, "Who Supports Tax Limitation: Evidence from Massachusetts' Proposition 2½," *Journal of Policy Analysis and Management,* Vol. 2, No. 2, Winter 1983, pp. 256–79.

[58] David Lowery and Lee Sigelman, "Understanding the Tax Revolt: Eight Explanations," *American Political Science Review,* Vol. 75, No. 4, Dec. 1981, pp. 963–74.

and our policy makers have an urgent need to acquire information best derived from prescriptive studies. In their most basic form, prescriptive analysis of tax policy may simply consist of models to predict levels of revenue that will be derived in the future (often the next fiscal year) from various taxes. Thus, in the budget-making process, our policy makers often want to know what the revenue picture looks like before making decisions about expenditures. Much of the information on the revenue picture comes from prescriptive analyses.

Yet prescriptive analyses have transcended this basic projection capability. We will look at some studies that attempt to project the impact of various tax changes on such factors as the performance of the economy, the distribution of burdens on individual taxpayers, and so on. We will see that these models provide us with substantial information concerning the extent to which tax policy changes seem to be likely to produce the desired impact. This includes, for example, analysis of the extent to which tax cuts can be expected to cause a reduction in the federal deficit. With this in mind, we can turn to some of these prescriptive studies.

The "TAXSIM" Model

One of the earliest and best-developed tax policy prescription models is the TAXSIM program developed by the National Bureau of Economic Research (NBER).[59] The main motivation behind the development of this model was the need to incorporate estimates of behavioral responses into analyses of tax policy changes.[60] Up until that time, economists had developed numerous ways of understanding how a change in tax policy would affect revenues if taxpayers' behavior remained the same. But in fact, there is good reason to believe that taxpayers' behavior does not remain the same. For example, if Congress were to eliminate an existing tax shelter, we might be tempted to project an increase in federal revenues equal to the tax that would be paid on the previously sheltered capital. But, in fact, taxpayers would very likely seek other tax shelters so that tax revenues would not increase as much as we might otherwise project. The TAXSIM model tries to account for many of these changes in taxpayers' behavior.

The TAXSIM model contains data on a sample of well over 2000 tax returns filed in 1974 and aged (adjusted) over time through 1979. These data have been augmented with survey research data from the University of Michigan's Panel Study of Income Dynamics and other sources. It is largely these latter sources that permit projections based on behavioral relationships. The result is a basic model that can be—and has been—used for a wide range of prescriptive

---

[59] Martin Feldstein and Daniel Frisch, "Corporate Tax Integration—Estimated Effects on Capital Accumulation," *National Tax Journal,* Vol. 30, No. 1, Jan. 1977, pp. 37–51.

[60] Martin Feldstein, ed., *Behavioral Simulation Methods in Tax Policy Analysis* (Chicago: University of Chicago Press, 1983), pp. 1–2.

analyses. We can take a brief look at a couple of applications to problems of tax policy.

ANALYSIS OF THE KEMP-ROTH TAX CUT PROPOSALS   During the early 1980s, Representative Jack Kemp and Senator William Roth proposed substantial changes in the federal personal income tax. The main part of the proposal calls for substantial decreases in the tax rates paid by individual taxpayers. The principal rationale behind this proposal is that such tax cuts would create stimulation of the economy by encouraging increased work and earned income. The idea is that federal revenues would actually increase as a result of a tax cut because of growth in personal income. Although the tax rate would be lower, the income base being taxed would increase by so much that it would overcompensate for the loss of revenues from the tax cut. Ultimately, the size of the federal budget deficit would be reduced by tax cuts rather than tax increases.

Analysis by Hausman using the TAXSIM model focuses on this question.[61] By examining the relationship between the tax rate and labor supply characteristics, Hausman projected federal revenues after substantial tax cuts. He actually examined what would happen to the labor force under several different large reductions in personal income taxes as proposed by the Kemp-Roth reform. He analyzed a 10 percent and a 30 percent tax cut. The results of this analysis suggest that revenues would not increase after tax cuts. The 10 percent tax cut would eventually lead to a 3.8 percent loss of revenues, and a 30 percent tax cut would produce a 16.2 percent loss of revenue. In other words, while the tax cuts would stimulate the labor force, it would not do so enough to fully compensate for the loss of federal revenue.

ALTERNATIVE POLICIES FOR DEFINING "FAMILIES" IN INCOME TAXATION   As the federal individual income tax is currently structured, different taxpayers with identical incomes can be treated differently because of their family statuses. A married couple faces different tax treatment than two unrelated people who have identical taxable incomes. This different treatment results from the fact that the lower income earner in a two-income family actually pays income taxes based on a higher marginal tax rate dependent upon the income earned by the higher-income earner. Thus, the marginal tax rate paid by the lower-income earner in a two-income family pays a higher marginal rate than a person with the same amount of earned income filing by himself/herself. Some economists argue that this differential treatment introduces inefficiency into the economy because it discourages labor force participation of people who face the higher marginal tax rates.

---

[61] Jerry A. Hausman, "Stochastic Problems in the Simulation of Labor Supply," in Feldstein (see Note 60), pp. 47–69.

Feenberg and Rosen use the TAXSIM model, augmented by the results of the Panel Study of Income Dynamics, to creatively evaluate four alternatives to the existing system.[62] They studied proposals for providing an exemption from taxation of 25 percent of the first $10,000 earned by the lower-income earner; a tax credit of 10 percent for the first $10,000 of the secondary income earner; taxing each of the two income earners on half of their joint income; and giving income earners the choice between being taxed in the current way or being taxed on the amount he/she earned plus half of the family income not earned by that person.

The ultimate goal of this study is to assess the future impact of each proposal in terms of labor force effects and tax collections. Under the first plan (the 10-percent exemption), secondary workers would be projected to work more hours, perhaps as much as 35 more hours per year. The net result would be about a 5 percent loss of revenue from such couples. The second proposal (the 25-percent exemption) would lead to a greater increase in the number of hours worked, but an even greater loss of tax revenue. Under the third plan (taxing half of joint income), the number of hours worked would increase substantially over the existing system, and tax revenues would decrease by about $28 billion a year. When the pattern of impacts is examined by income level, the analysis shows that people in the lower income categories would actually decrease their labor force participation under the third proposal. And under the fourth proposal (the option plan), labor force participation would increase by an average of 80 hours per year, with an overall 10 percent loss of tax revenues. Again, people in the lowest income categories would experience the opposite effect from people in the middle and upper income categories. This analysis shows clearly that the loss of tax revenue can be balanced against increases in labor force participation.

Simulating Policies to Integrate Corporate and Personal Taxes

One of the problems with federal taxation is that corporate incomes are, in a sense, taxed twice. This double taxation occurs because corporate stockholders pay income taxes on dividends and capital gains and corporations pay taxes directly on the profits they make at their source. Ultimately, so the argument goes, this reduces capital accumulation and constrains economic growth.

In a study of four proposals to integrate the corporate and personal income taxes, Fullerton et al. develop a simulation model of the entire U.S. econ-

---

[62] Daniel R. Feenberg and Harvey S. Rosen, "Alternative Tax Treatments of the Family: Simulation Methodology and Results," in Feldstein (see Note 60), pp. 7–41.

omy using data from many different sources.[63] They attempt to project the effects of eliminating the corporate income tax altogether and modifying the personal income tax to include shareholders' earnings; allowing a dividend deduction in the personal income tax, but leaving the capital gains tax as it currently stands; allowing a dividend deduction from taxable corporate income, with no change in the capital gains tax on individuals; and providing a tax credit to stockholders based on the income tax paid by corporations, with the tax credit taxable as personal income.

Under the first plan (eliminating the corporate income tax), nearly total integration would be achieved, with some $6 billion in efficiency gains, or tax revenue lost. The second and third plans produce almost identical results, efficiency gains (revenue losses) of about half the amount obtained in the first proposal. And the fourth plan (providing a tax credit to stockholders) produces very little change in tax revenue or efficiency over the existing system. Thus, the implication is that if elimination of the corporate income tax is not feasible but tax integration is desirable, the second or third plan might be acceptable compromises.

Simulating Income Tax Policy Changes in the States

Recently, microsimulation models have been applied to state tax systems, which provide a somewhat different challenge to analysts because of their interaction with the federal tax system. For example, most state and local taxes paid by individuals are—at this writing—deductible from the federal personal income tax. Thus, people do not end up paying as much of a state or local tax increase as it might initially seem.

In a recent study, Reschovsky analyzed several proposals to decrease the tax burden on elderly taxpayers in Massachusetts.[64] Using the Massachusetts Income Tax Simulation (MITS) model (a submodel of the Transfer Income Model we discussed in Chapter 5), Reschovsky provided an assessment of the distributional effects of eliminating the higher personal income tax rate applied to unearned (interest or dividend) income or of allowing elderly taxpayers to deduct the first $700 of their unearned income. The results showed that the latter proposal would be more effective in targeting the elderly, especially the

---

[63] Dan Fullerton et al., "Corporate and Personal Tax Integration in the United States: Some Preliminary Findings," in Robert H. Haveman and Ken Hollenbeck, eds., *Microeconomic Simulation Models for Public Policy Analysis, Vol. 2, Sectoral, Regional, and General Equilibrium Models* (New York: Academic Press, 1980), pp. 97–124.

[64] Andrew Reschovsky, "The Use of Microsimulation Models to Analyze State Income Tax Incidence," *Policy Studies Journal*, Vol. 12, No. 1, Sept, 1983, pp. 154–65.

elderly with lower incomes. The former proposal would provide tax breaks for all people receiving unearned income, regardless of their overall economic status or age.

WHAT HAVE WE LEARNED
ABOUT TAX POLICY ANALYSIS?

Once again, we have covered a lot of ground. Before we address some of the bigger questions in the final chapter, we should review what we have learned about tax policy analysis. Clearly we have extracted different information from each of the three approaches to tax policy analysis.

Perhaps first and foremost, we found that the idea of tax reform is a very difficult one for our political system to comprehend. Even when our public officials are under substantial scrutiny in their tax actions, they often find it desirable to raise taxes. They do so when they believe that it serves to achieve some broad economic or fiscal policy goal. Comprehensive policy changes require support from within the Treasury Department, which is very unlikely unless the appropriate House and Senate committees have little else on their legislative agendas. And incremental tax policy changes are most likely to affect narrowly defined groups of people, often resulting in tax increases for relatively weak or unorganized groups and tax decreases for stronger or better-organized groups.

Tax policy cause and consequence studies showed us how complicated the tax system is to fully understand. For example, determining exactly who pays how much of various taxes requires more than intuition or superficial analysis. This was perhaps best illustrated in the studies of the distributional impact of local property taxes. According to much research, property taxes are not nearly as regressive as they were once thought to be. In addition, local and state tax policies do not seem to create major deterrents to industrial and business location, except perhaps for manufacturing industries.

We also found that the taxpayers' revolt does not really seem to carry the kind of mandate that we often hear attributed to it. It is true that people who vote in favor of tax limitations in the states seem to want lower taxes. But they also want more services. So it is difficult for policy makers to respond to the messages voters send.

Finally, we saw that several fairly complex models have been developed to help us assess what impacts would likely be produced if our policy makers decided to change specific aspects of existing tax law. For example, we found that tax cuts of the Kemp-Roth type proposed during the early 1980s are not likely to have the economic impact their supporters claim. We also found that the way our tax law defines the family as the filing unit for the federal personal income tax has an impact on capital accumulation. If our policy makers were to change this definition in a way that eliminated the different marginal tax rates faced by similar taxpayers, people would generally work more.

Microsimulation models also showed that there are at least two reasonably effective ways to achieve corporate and personal income tax integration short of eliminating the corporation income tax. And a microsimulation model provided us with a clear picture of how the state of Massachusetts might best provide tax relief to elderly taxpayers.

FURTHER READING

The Tax Policy Making Process

BINGHAM, RICHARD D., BRETT W. HAWKINS, and F. TED HEBERT. *The Politics of Raising State and Local Revenue.* New York: Praeger, 1978.
HANSEN, SUSAN B. *The Politics of Taxation.* New York: Praeger, 1983.
PIERCE, LAWRENCE C. *The Politics of Fiscal Policy Formation.* Pacific Palisades, Calif.: Goodyear, 1971.
REESE, THOMAS J. *The Politics of Taxation.* Westport, Conn.: Quorum Books, 1980.

Tax Policy Cause and Consequence Research

AARON, HENRY J. *Who Pays the Property Tax?: A New View.* Washington, D.C.: Brookings Institution, 1975.
PECHMAN, JOSEPH A., and BENJAMIN A. OKNER. *Who Bears the Tax Burden?* Washington, D.C.: Brookings Institution, 1974.
PHARES, DONALD. *Who Pays State and Local Taxes?* Cambridge, Mass.: Oelgeschlager, Gunn, and Hain, 1980.
THUROW, LESTER C. *The Impact of Taxes on the American Economy.* New York: Praeger, 1971.

Tax Policy Prescription Research

FELDSTEIN, MARTIN, ed. *Behavioral Simulation Methods in Tax Policy Analysis.* Chicago: University of Chicago Press, 1983.
HAVEMAN, ROBERT H., and KEVIN HOLLENBECK, eds. *Microeconomic Simulation Models for Public Policy Analysis,* Vol. 2: *Sectoral, Regional and General Equilibrium Models.* New York: Academic Press, 1980.

CHAPTER EIGHT

Approaching Public Policy Analysis, Reconsidered

We have discussed a large number of studies. These studies were organized according to substantive areas of public policy (e.g., environmental policy and energy policy). Within a substantive policy area, the studies were organized according to whether they were based on the policy making process, the policy cause and consequence, or the policy prescription approach. Within each policy area, we found that abundant research has been done based on each of these approaches. And we found that each approach made a distinctly different contribution to our understanding of the nature and detail of the selected substantive policy areas. At this point, it is important for us to review what we discovered about the three approaches in each policy area, to reconsider the arguments made in Chapter 1, and to offer some suggestions about where public policy analysis might go from here.

WHAT DID WE DISCOVER
FROM THE THREE APPROACHES?

Although it is impossible to cover all that we discussed in each of the substantive chapters, we can highlight some of the more important points. As we do this, you might refresh your memory about which analyses led us to our conclusions and which provided counterevidence.

Public Environmental Policy Analysis

As we suggested, public environmental policy addresses governmental efforts to improve the quality of our physical surroundings and public health problems that may arise from these surroundings. Each of our three policy analysis approaches attacks different types of questions and offers a very different perspective on similar questions.

THE ENVIRONMENTAL POLICY MAKING PROCESS ANALYSES   Studies based on the policy making process approach suggested that we really do not have much in the way of a comprehensive environmental policy. What we commonly think of as environmental policy is the result of historical conditions that led our policy makers to think in terms of natural resource development and management. It was not until the conditions created by such development and associated industrialization began to affect people's health that the idea of an environmental policy emerged.

When major environmental interest groups emerged during the late 1960s and the 1970s, the federal policy making process finally began to respond to these problems. The result was a series of legislative efforts, such as the National Environmental Policy Act, which created an outline of what our policy should be. In the 1980s, this outline has been used once again to re-emphasize the economic development aspects of environmental actions by government.

ENVIRONMENTAL CAUSES AND CONSEQUENCES ANALYSES The studies of environmental policy relying on a cause and consequence approach focused on the effectiveness of specific actions in cleaning up the environment and on understanding why some states have been more active than others in initiating efforts to improve the environment. Effluent-discharge regulation, for example, was shown to be an effective method of controlling water pollution in Lake Michigan. In states' environmental policies, cause and consequence studies revealed that the seriousness of the pollution problem, the amount of resources available, and the way state agencies are organized helped determine how effective states' responses have been.

ENVIRONMENTAL POLICY PRESCRIPTION ANALYSES Prescriptive studies attempt to determine whether there is a level of regulation or pollution at which the benefits to society are greater than the costs to society. By and large, these studies argue that the marginal costs of environmental regulation are likely to be much higher than the benefits accrued. Linear programming studies suggest that in a world where the health and other costs of pollution must be balanced against the health and life-style benefits from economic development, there may well be some "optimal" or acceptable level of pollution. Generally, these studies tend to agree that environmental regulation throughout the 1970s moved beyond this optimal level.

Public Energy Policy Analyses

We discussed studies of many of the efforts by our governments to regulate the energy industry, including studies of oil and gas deregulation and efforts by the United States to become energy independent.

THE ENERGY POLICY MAKING PROCESS STUDIES Much like environmental policy, studies of the energy policy making processes look to the historical tendency to define energy issues in terms of resource development. It was not until the oil crises of the 1970s that our policy makers began to think in terms of a unified energy policy. Energy policy making process studies suggested that much of the reason why the oil crises occurred had more to do with historical decisions made by the large multinational petroleum corporations than the specific decisions of OPEC. These industry decisions were reinforced through the development of fairly influential industry interest groups. And our nation's ability to respond to the energy crisis was hampered by decisions made by government on behalf of the coal industry and other resource industries.

The efforts of the Carter administration to establish a comprehensive national energy policy were apparently doomed to failure. Rather than consulting with energy interest groups when formulating the comprehensive proposals, the administration ignored them. This had the effect of shifting the point of attack for such interest groups to the adoption and implementation stages, where they were successful in preventing Carter's proposals from becoming energy policy. Policy making process studies suggested that this, among other events, ended up making the energy policy implementation process extremely political. For example, in the monitoring of energy reserves, the Department of Energy was captured by major industrial interests that influenced how the Department performed its functions. We also found that the policy prescription model used by the Energy Department had been co-opted by the Carter administration to support its energy policy proposals.

ENERGY POLICY CAUSE AND CONSEQUENCE ANALYSES Numerous studies have attempted to systematically examine how effective various aspects of our energy policies have been. Studies of the effectiveness of automobile regulations (weight, exhaust, and speed regulations) show that considerable conservation of energy resources has resulted. At the same time, these studies also show that some of our energy policies, especially the Crude Oil Windfall Profits Tax, reduce corporate profits and decrease economic growth. Most of the studies trying to explain variations in energy policies (such as adopting renewable energy policies, demonstration projects, and so on) seem to agree with one another. There does not seem to be an easy explanation, and none of the expectations about states with greater vulnerability to energy shortages held.

ENERGY POLICY PRESCRIPTION RESEARCH Energy policy prescription analyses have produced substantial support for the idea that decontrol of energy will be the most effective way of increasing energy supplies. Many of these studies suggest that conservation by itself cannot insulate the United States from energy vulnerability. Even so, there is evidence that conservation does not produce the kind of limit to economic growth often ascribed to it.

Public Foreign and Defense Policy Studies

Just as the three approaches to public policy analysis have been applied to domestic policy issues, they have also been directed toward foreign and defense policies.

FOREIGN AND DEFENSE POLICY MAKING PROCESS ANALYSES The studies of the foreign and defense policy making processes demonstrated some unique patterns. For example, the processes of setting foreign policy are dominated by a much smaller group of people and interests than is generally the case in domestic policy areas. And there is no area where the administrative agencies have more influence over policy than in foreign and defense policy. Congress tends to play a more restricted role in formulation and adoption of such policies.

In defense policy making, we discussed studies of the weapon development and procurement processes. These studies seemed to indicate fairly clearly that the decision to develop the technology of a new weapon system was tantamount to adopting the system as part of the nation's arsenal. This suggests that a decision to develop the technology necessary to establish the Strategic Defense Initiative, popularly dubbed "Star Wars," will ensure its deployment.

FOREIGN AND DEFENSE POLICY CAUSE AND CONSEQUENCE STUDIES We reviewed numerous studies that systematically explored the correlates of war. Although different studies come to different conclusions, it is difficult to find enough evidence to make any universal statement about what causes wars. Arms build-ups, disarmament, and aggressive military postures do not seem to necessarily lead to war. There is also some debate about exactly what influences our nation to spend or not spend public monies on national defense. Some studies argue that spending is driven by arms races; other studies argue that spending is motivated by defense agencies' need for stability and predictability rather than some objective need for defense capability. Again, however, there is evidence in both directions.

FOREIGN AND DEFENSE POLICY PRESCRIPTION RESEARCH Numerous policy prescription studies have focused on almost every aspect of foreign and defense policies. Prescription studies have been used to make the case in favor of building the B-1 bomber, cruise missiles, the MX missile system, and other weapon systems. Other, more broadly based, prescriptive defense policy studies provide conditional responses to various kinds of attacks on the United States by foreign nations. Nuclear-exchange analyses, for example, provide a programmed response to attacks dependent on the nature and source of the attack and the goals of a defensive response.

Global simulations provide an opportunity to anticipate problems in foreign policy and to understand the effectiveness of different foreign policy responses. Several attempts have been made to anticipate how various specific foreign leaders might respond to different foreign and defense policy actions by the United States. By and large, however, these studies are in their infancy.

Public Welfare and Antipoverty
Policy Studies

Our discussion of welfare and antipoverty policies focused on a number of federal and state programs. We looked at Social Security, Supplemental Security Income, Food Stamps, Aid to Families with Dependent Children, and job training.

THE WELFARE POLICY MAKING PROCESS STUDIES   The research based on the welfare policy making process approach uncovered some important patterns. We found that many of the federal programs we often think of as being part of the welfare system were established, at least in part, with other goals in mind. For example, the Food Stamps program was enacted partly to help hungry people, partly to help stabilize agricultural prices by regulating surpluses. We also found that much of the expansion of the welfare system occurred during the early 1970s (the tenure of the Nixon administration). And we discovered that the federal agencies that implement welfare policies have a significant influence over the form the policies take. This influence is exercised both in the legislative process and through the implementation process, especially in developing eligibility requirements.

THE WELFARE CAUSE AND CONSEQUENCE STUDIES   A remarkable amount of evidence points to the effectiveness of the various public welfare programs in improving the quality of health and life for their recipients. Studies of Food Stamps, AFDC, Project Head Start, and other programs indicate that the programs do help reduce poverty and improve living conditions. Studies disagree about the price that is paid to accomplish these goals. Research on AFDC found that recipients tended to lose their incentive to work because of the way the program's benefits were structured. Reforms consisting of work incentives seem to have gone a long way toward overcoming this problem.

We also looked at studies of guaranteed-income programs of a type never actually enacted. These studies attempted to ascertain whether welfare actually would decrease recipients' incentive to work. Nearly all of the studies indicated that there was little evidence to support this expectation. And people who received a guaranteed annual income did not seem to experience many other behavioral changes.

PRESCRIPTIVE WELFARE ANALYSES   Much of the prescriptive research related to welfare policy focuses on the Social Security system. Substantial effort has gone into assessing the funds that finance benefits to try to prescribe the best ways to keep the funds solvent in the years to come. Increases in the payroll tax seem inevitable, and in the case of the hospital insurance fund, financing out of general revenues seems to be a long-term prospect.

Welfare policy simulations provide us with a fairly clear idea of how the many welfare programs interact with one another to affect people's eligibility. For example, if Food Stamps eligibility were made stricter, many people who cannot qualify now for other programs might then be able to qualify. Thus, the federal government may not save as much as initially estimated because a good portion of the costs would simply be shifted to another program. Similarly, loosening eligibility requirements might not cost as much as it would seem because of changes in eligibility for other programs.

Public Physical and Mental Health
Policy Analyses

We focused on studies of Medicare and Medicaid in physical health policy, as well as studies of the "right to treatment" and deinstitutionalization in mental health policy. We discovered that these constitute the main pieces of our national health policies, although many other fragments exist.

THE HEALTH POLICY MAKING PROCESS RESEARCH The studies of the health policy making processes argued that decision making is very fragmented, with numerous groups of people able to exercise influence over some aspect of health policies. Principally because health professionals wish to retain the legitimate responsibility for deciding who receives which treatment, efforts to involve the federal government have been blocked. We also found that—unlike many other policy areas—health policy tends not to be motivated by crises. Rather, it is a response to the accumulation of problems over time. Events such as elections or the functioning of the economy, for instance, can have the effect of opening a "window of opportunity" for policy makers to act. But the window tends to stay open only a short time, for events can close it again suddenly.

HEALTH POLICY CAUSE AND CONSEQUENCE STUDIES Studies revealed clearly that policies affect access to health care for people who had been excluded from the private health care system. They also showed that public health policies do not seem to affect the quality of their health. First, federal health policies seem to improve access to health care for people who would not otherwise be able to obtain it, although such people are not necessarily more healthy as a result. At the same time, governmental spending for health care has mushroomed, apparently playing a major role in the rapidly increasing costs of medical care. Other factors, such as improvements in health care technology, have also played a part in this. But the evidence seems strong that health care policy itself helps contribute to these high costs.

In mental health policy, studies focused on the effectiveness of deinstitutionalization as a form of community-based mental health treatment. Studies disagreed as to how beneficial such treatment has been. But there is some evidence that deinstitutionalization has been motivated by policy makers' desire to cut mental health expenditures rather than to improve the quality of treatment. Even so, there is little clear evidence that public mental health care costs have declined very much.

HEALTH POLICY PRESCRIPTION STUDIES   Several microsimulation models have been developed to try to prescribe how public policy ought to respond in the future. For example, a model was developed to project health manpower needs to attempt to ensure that governmental resources are placed where they are most needed. Other microsimulation models prescribe policy mechanisms for delivering health care to people who need it without causing serious burdens on the overall economy.

Studies of Tax and Revenue Policies

We focused on studies of some of the major tax and revenue instruments used by our federal, state, and local governments. We examined research on many aspects of the federal personal income and corporation income taxes; state income, sales, and corporation income taxes; and local property taxes. These instruments constitute the major revenue raisers for our governments.

TAX AND REVENUE POLICY MAKING PROCESS STUDIES   We examined studies that tried to explain why our representative governments have found it desirable to enact new taxes and increase tax rates. We found that policy makers often perceive that tax policy is a legitimate tool for controlling aspects of the national economy. Tax increases are often made when control of inflation or stimulation of the economy will result.

We also discovered some reasons why tax reform is so difficult to achieve. First, not everyone agrees on what the goals of tax reform should be. Some believe that reform is synonymous with making taxes more progressive. Other people believe that it is, or should be, a means to achieve tax cuts, regardless of how progressive or regressive the taxes turn out to be. Second, the legislative committees are hesitant to open the can of tax-reform worms because they highly value internal consensus. Tackling tax reform can only work against maintenance of consensus. Yet, if the legislative committees are relatively free of other work, and if public perceptions of abuses of the tax system are strong enough, tax reform can emerge as part of the public agenda.

TAX POLICY CAUSE AND CONSEQUENCE ANALYSES Studies of tax policy causes and consequences revealed a great deal of important information. For example, studies of the distributional impact of our taxes (tax incidence) showed that the federal income tax is fairly progressive. Federal income tax expenditures (exemptions and deductions) seem to be so widespread that they provide some benefit to almost all but the poorest of taxpayers.

Studies of state tax incidence indicate that there is substantial variation around the country. Generally, state income taxes tend to be much less progressive than the federal personal income tax, but more progressive than state sales or corporation income taxes. And studies of the local property tax indicate that it is not nearly as regressive as it was once thought to be. In general, this type of tax turns out to approach being a proportional tax.

Studies attempting to explain why some states pursue certain types of taxes while others rely on different taxes have provided little insight. The economic base of the states does not seem to influence state policy makers to adopt particular types of taxes. There is a moderate amount of evidence that the nature of partisan control of the institutions of state government plays some role in determining the order in which specific broad-based taxes are adopted.

Research also revealed that state and local taxes do not seem to play a major role in affecting industrialization and economic development. Business and industry location decisions do not seem to be greatly influenced by taxes. Instead, such factors as the price of land, availability of labor, access to raw materials, and the like, seem to be more important considerations.

Finally, studies of the tax revolt in the states indicated that voters seem to want lower taxes, but not necessarily at the expense of decreases in any particular public service. But other studies indicate that different voters desire cuts in different services. As a general rule, it would seem impossible to infer anything from the results of tax referenda other than that people tend to want lower taxes.

TAX POLICY PRESCRIPTION RESEARCH Prescriptive tax policy studies provide some insight into how the tax system can be altered without producing serious or unacceptable consequences. A study revealed that tax cut measures such as the Kemp-Roth proposal will probably not be able to improve the federal revenue picture, and they would likely contribute to increased, rather than reduced, federal deficits. We also found that apparent inequities caused by the definition of the family as a filing unit for federal taxation can be reduced through several different forms of income exemptions. There is also some evidence that the double taxation of corporation incomes can be rectified in ways other than by eliminating the corporation income tax. Finally, a prescription model suggested that tax relief for relatively poor elderly people in Massachusetts can best be achieved by providing an income exemption for elderly persons rather than an across-the-board tax rate reduction.

APPROACHING PUBLIC POLICY ANALYSIS

Now that we have reviewed the policy areas and their respective approaches, we can take another look at the arguments found in Chapter 1. With only the benefit of rather abstract descriptions of the approaches to public policy analysis, we argued that some kind of synthesis among them is in order. Now that the approaches are somewhat less abstract, we can entertain this possibility anew. It should be clear to you that each of the three approaches, in each policy area we have examined, defines public policy in a different way. Each approach brings with it a particular set of biases and carries a different vision of the potential contribution that can be made to our understanding of governmental issues.

Part of the difference among these approaches can be attributed to differences in methodology. Part of it can be traced to differences in what researchers think is important and what they think other people need to know. For example, a researcher might decide to focus explicitly on a policy implementation rather than a policy impact process, believing implicitly that implementation is the key to why the policy produced a particular impact. Part of the difference can be traced to researchers' implicit beliefs about what constitute the most important aspects of governmental action, i.e., the definition of public policy itself.

Despite these differences, it is also clear that most of the public policy research from all three approaches has elements of the same ultimate goals: to improve the quality of future governmental decisions; and to work toward improving the quality of some aspect of human life. In light of this, it would seem desirable for public policy analysts to seek a synthesis of the three approaches, but it is difficult to predict what form such a synthesis might take. We can, however, speculate about how to achieve this result.

INTEGRATING APPROACHES

As we have described the three approaches, it should be clear that in substantive terms they are quite disparate. We have described them as differing markedly with respect to methodology, i.e., the way their researchers go about trying to discover answers to the questions they deem important. You might wonder what, if anything, can be done to achieve a synthesis of policy analysis. Our argument is that the methodological distinctions among the approaches need to be dissolved.

You should recognize that the studies using a single approach use similar methodologies across policy areas. For example, policy making process research normally relies on case study, participant observer, nonquantitative methodologies. These methodologies place less value on scientific rigor than on the pursuit of detail. Cause and consequence studies tend to provide more methodological rigor, often based on quantifiable data for many cases or units of analysis. And prescriptive analysis takes the methodological rigor a step further, often using fairly sophisticated statistical methods to obtain answers. It is possible to imagine a field of public policy analysis where the methodological differences do not exist. And there are some specific ways that these methodological differences can be assimilated.

Toward a More Unified Approach

To a very modest degree, recent public policy studies have actually begun to accomplish the goal of synthesis. They have done so, whether intentionally or not, by applying the methodologies of one approach to the issues of another.

Studies using the methodologies we have ascribed to the cause and consequence approach can begin to address issues of the policy making process approach by seeking ways of measuring variables reflective of the policy making process itself, rather than simply focusing on the results of government action. We have seen some movement toward this effort. For example, when a researcher adopts a cause and consequence methodology to analyze aspects of the policy implementation process, such an integration of approaches emerges.[1] Increasingly, we are finding that elements of the policy implementation process are quantifiable, and their analysis provides important information.

So we can begin asking questions about what would seem to be the most effective method of implementing a particular governmental program. Indeed, application of experimental or quasi-experimental designs to this type of question is an area where integration has already progressed. But systematic measurement of other policy making processes is also conceivable. For example, it would be possible, although not easy, to examine a large number of legislative adoptions within and among substantive policy areas and to quantify elements of this process. Then we can begin to more systematically test some of the ideas propounded by the case study analyses of the policy making processes.

[1] For example, see Nelson Rosenbaum, "Statutory Structure and Policy Implementation: The Case of Wetlands Regulation," *Policy Studies Journal*, Vol. 8, No. 4, Special Issue No. 2, 1980, pp. 575-96. See also Charles S. Bullock III and Charles M. Lamb, eds., *Implementation of Civil Rights Policy* (Monterey, Calif.: Brooks/Cole, 1984). For an article that clearly establishes an integrated framework, see Paul Sabatier and Daniel Mazmanian, "The Implementation of Public Policy: A Framework of Analysis," *Policy Studies Journal*, Vol. 8, No. 4, Special Issue No. 2, 1980, pp. 538-60.

Policy making process analysts might begin addressing questions concerning the conditions under which policy cause and consequence or policy prescription analyses actually influence policy makers. Much has been written about such influences, usually arguing that such studies have little or no effect. The question now becomes, Are there conditions under which cause and consequence or prescriptive studies seem to have greater influences? The results of this type of analysis would provide some specific information on the question of what policy analysts can do, if anything, to maximize the effectiveness of their studies. It is possible that nothing can be done, but this seems unlikely, even given existing studies of policy research utilization.[2] This type of question fits nicely within the policy making process framework. Indeed, the question posed within the stages of the policy making process is, What are the characteristics of policy evaluation studies that provide useful feedback to policy makers? Again, we have many opinions about the answer to this, but policy making process researchers have not addressed it as squarely as the other stages of the process.

Policy prescription analysts can incorporate information about the decision-making processes into their prescription models and techniques. Perhaps the area where this has been accomplished to the greatest degree is in the foreign policy prescription studies we discussed in Chapter 4. When such a model attempts to incorporate such elements as regime stability and perceptions of political leaders into their prescriptive models, they are in a sense attempting to achieve a degree of integration.[3] Clearly, in those studies that have tried this, the effort is molded by the results of policy making process research. As we begin to incorporate such factors as electoral outcomes, policy makers' values and perceptions, and related variables into policy prescription models, a fuller integration of policy research approaches will result.[4]

A second set of ideas about how this can be achieved can be proposed.

[2] Some excellent studies of this nature already exist. See, for example, Daniel A. Dreyfus, "The Limitations of Policy Research in Congressional Decision-Making," in Carol H. Weiss, ed., *Using Social Research in Public Policy-Making* (Lexington, Mass.: Lexington Books, 1977), pp. 99–107; and Marvin C. Alkin, Richard Daillak, and Peter White, *Using Evaluations: Does Evaluation Make a Difference?* (Beverly Hills, Calif.: Sage Publications, 1979).

[3] You might recall our description of Hayward R. Alker and P. G. Bock, "Propositions about International Relations: Contributions from the International Encyclopedia of the Social Sciences," in James A. Robinson, ed., *Political Science Annual*, Vol. 3, 1972; M. J. Driver, "Individual Differences As Determinants of Aggression in the Inter-Nation Simulation," in M. G. Hermann and T. Milburn, eds., *A Psychological Examination of Political Leaders* (New York: Macmillan, 1977), pp. 337–53; Harold Guetzkow and Joseph J. Valadez, "International Relations Theory: Contributions of Simulated International Processes," in Harold Guetzkow and Joseph J. Valadez, eds., *Simulated International Processes: Theories and Research in Global Modeling* (Beverly Hills, Calif.: Sage Publications, 1981), pp. 197–251.

[4] For an excellent review of these and other topics in public choice analysis, see Dennis C. Mueller, *Public Choice* (England: Cambridge University Press, 1979).

Analysts conducting research within a specific approach should begin to understand that the approaches are not really mutually exclusive. Rather, research from one approach often provides the foundation for research in the others. Most commonly, studies of policy causes and consequences rely on hypotheses and observations from policy making process studies. For example, policy making process studies derived the hypothesis that interparty political competition affects public welfare policy. This hypothesis, in turn, provided the foundation for much policy cause and consequence research. It is common for policy making process analysts to avoid framing their questions in forms that can be easily addressed by cause and consequence analysis. But in most cases, it is possible to do so.

The reliance of the three approaches on one another extends even further. For example, almost all prescriptive models rely on the results of cause and consequence studies to provide an understanding of the relationships that must be included in any particular model. We might even argue that policy prescription researchers may find it difficult to incorporate aspects of the policy making process into their models until policy making process research succeeds in producing the foundation for cause and consequence studies. Thus, policy prescription studies may be thought of as being partly dependent on policy making process research.

All of these recommendations are geared toward beginning the process of integrating the three public policy analysis approaches. They are based on the belief that this process is a logical step in the evolution of public policy analysis as a field of study. And when this process is well under way, the state of our knowledge about public policy will have achieved greater maturity.

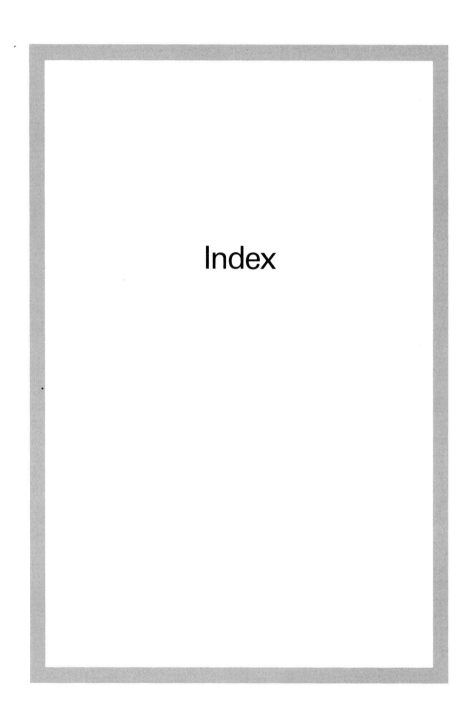

Index